A u s t r a

TOP
TOURIST
DESTINATIONS

Margaret McPhee

Gregory's

Published in Australia by Gregory's Publishing Company
(A division of Universal Press Pty Ltd)
ABN 83 000 087 132

Marketed and distributed by Universal Press Pty Ltd

New South Wales: 1 Waterloo Road,
Macquarie Park 2113
Ph: (02) 9857 3700 Fax (02) 9888 9850
Queensland: 1 Manning Street,
South Brisbane 4101
Ph: (07) 3844 1051 Fax: (07) 3844 4637

South Australia: Freecall: 1800 021 987
Victoria: 585 Burwood Road, Hawthorn 3122
Ph: (03) 9818 4455 Fax: (03) 9818 6123
Western Australia: 38a Walters Drive,
Osborne Park 6017
Ph: (08) 9244 2488 Fax: (08) 9244 2554

International: Ph: 61 (02) 9857 3700 Fax: 61 (02) 9888 9850

The Publisher would be pleased to receive additional or updated material, or suggestions for future editions. Please address these to the Publishing Manager at Universal Press Pty Ltd. If you would like to use any of the maps in this book, please contact the CMS Manager at Universal Press Pty Ltd.

Publishing Manager: David Jackson
Production Manager: Harold Yates
Internal Design by: *DiZign*
Cover Design by: Mike Moule
Layout: Bronwynne Davis

Project Editor: Scott Forbes
Photographic Research: Grant Nichol
Cartography: Universal Press Pty Ltd
Pre-press by: Jade Productions
Printed by: Jade Productions

Disclaimer

Mackenzie Falls,
Grampians NP, Victoria

Contents

Map Symbols

City

MOTORWAY	Dual Carriageway	🏛	Museum
HIGHWAY	Metroad	①	Metroad
HIGHWAY	Through Route	32	National Route Marker
MORT ST	Major Road	⟶	One - Way Street
LAWSON RD	Minor Road	🅿	Parking Area
LEURA ST	Other Road	🎪	Picnic Area
	Railway and Station	⑤	Place of Interest
	Walking Track	★	Point of Interest
	Ferry Route	○	Roundabout
	Ambulance	20	State Route Marker
	Boat Ramp	🚻	Toilets
	Camping Ground		Beach
	Caravan Park	▬ ■	Building
	Golf Course		National Park, Recreation Reserve
	Hospital		Mall
	Information Centre		School
	Lookout 360°, 180°		Other Areas

Suburban

FEDERAL HIGHWAY	Dual Carriageway	✈	Airport
BELCONNEN WAY	Metroad	✠	Aerodrome
BARTON HIGHWAY	Through Route	✚	Hospital
MAJURA ROAD	Main Road	★ Casino	Point of Interest
KURINGA DR	Other Road	+ Glebe Hill 135	Mountain, height in metres
	Railway and Station		
	Ferry Route	ϟ Gully Winds	Vineyard/Winery
①	Metroad Route Marker		National Park, Reserve, Recreation Area
23 A1 A1	National Route Marker		State Forest
20 C3	State Route Marker		
N.S.W. / A.C.T.	State Boundary		Educational Institution
CANBERRA	Major Centre		Other Areas
Gungahlin	Main Centre		Sand
Franklin	Suburb		

Key to Maps

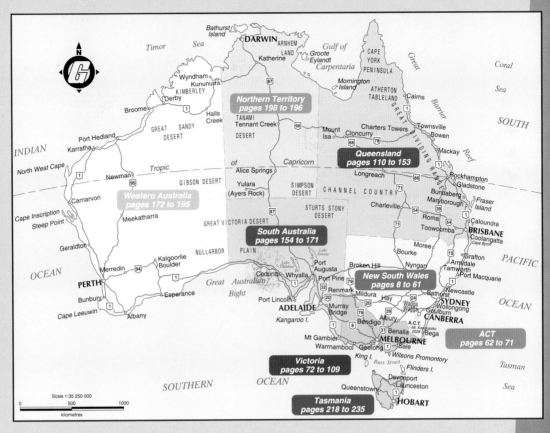

Regional

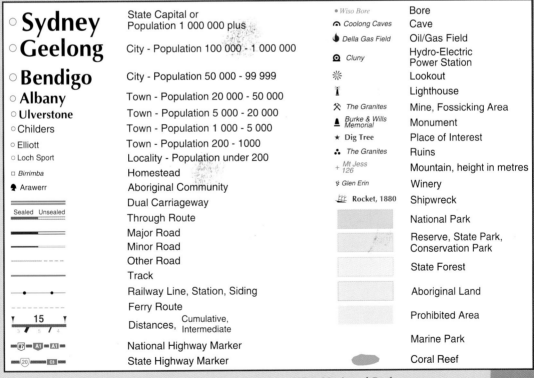

○ **Sydney**	State Capital or Population 1 000 000 plus	
○ **Geelong**	City - Population 100 000 - 1 000 000	
○ **Bendigo**	City - Population 50 000 - 99 999	
○ **Albany**	Town - Population 20 000 - 50 000	
○ Ulverstone	Town - Population 5 000 - 20 000	
○ Childers	Town - Population 1 000 - 5 000	
○ Elliott	Town - Population 200 - 1000	
○ Loch Sport	Locality - Population under 200	
□ Birrimba	Homestead	
♠ Arawerr	Aboriginal Community	

Dual Carriageway
Through Route
Major Road
Minor Road
Other Road
Track
Railway Line, Station, Siding
Ferry Route
Distances, Cumulative, Intermediate
National Highway Marker
State Highway Marker

• Wiso Bore	Bore
⌒ Coolong Caves	Cave
◗ Della Gas Field	Oil/Gas Field
◙ Cluny	Hydro-Electric Power Station
※	Lookout
☥	Lighthouse
⚒ The Granites	Mine, Fossicking Area
♠ Burke & Wills Memorial	Monument
★ Dig Tree	Place of Interest
∴ The Granites	Ruins
+ Mt Jess 126	Mountain, height in metres
⚱ Glen Erin	Winery
⌗ Rocket, 1880	Shipwreck
	National Park
	Reserve, State Park, Conservation Park
	State Forest
	Aboriginal Land
	Prohibited Area
	Marine Park
	Coral Reef

CP = Conservation Park; CR = Conservation Reserve; NP = National Park,
SF = State Forest; SP = State Park; SRA = State Recreation Area

Katoomba Falls,
Blue Mountains NP

New South Wales

New South Wales encompasses an astonishing diversity of tourist destinations. From its bustling and beautiful capital, Sydney, set on arguably the most magnificent harbour in the world, north to pristine subtropical beaches and rainforest-clad ranges, west to the red-sand deserts of the Outback, and south to the winter snowfields of the Southern Alps, it offers visitors a world of experiences. Sydney itself boasts not only its sparkling harbour and stunning ocean beaches, but also a host of fascinating urban attractions, such as the Sydney Opera House, the Sydney Harbour Bridge, the historic waterfront precinct of the Rocks, and Olympic Park, home of the 2000 Olympic Games. From the capital, surfing beaches, dramatic headlands, sheltered harbours and tranquil coastal lakes stretch north and south along almost 2000km of shoreline. A short distance inland, across the narrow coastal plain, the spine of the Great Dividing Range runs parallel to the sea, its rugged, forested slopes largely protected by a string of reserves, including the immense wilderness of the World Heritage-listed Blue Mountains, on Sydney's western fringes. Well-tended vineyards and welcoming wineries arc inland from the Hunter Valley, just north of Sydney, to Mudgee, in the Central West, a region that also encompasses picturesque goldrush towns. Further north, archetypal Australian wheat and sheep farmlands and highland wilderness characterise the New England 'Big Sky Country'.

Tourist Information

i **Tourism NSW**
Sydney Visitor Centre
106 George St
The Rocks
NSW 2000
Ph: 13 20 77
www.visitnsw.com.au

Top Tourist Destinations

Ⓐ Sydney
Ⓑ The Blue Mountains
Ⓒ Byron Bay
Ⓓ The Central Coast
Ⓔ The Central West
Ⓕ The Coffs Coast
Ⓖ The Hunter Valley
Ⓗ Illawarra and the Southern Highlands
Ⓘ Kempsey and the Macleay Valley
Ⓙ New England
Ⓚ Port Macquarie and the Manning Valley
Ⓛ Port Stephens and the Myall Lakes
Ⓜ Shoalhaven
Ⓝ The Snowy Mountains

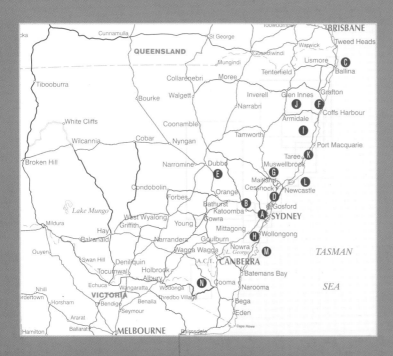

Sydney

Best time to visit: Year-round; summer for beaches, cultural offerings and free family entertainment, including spectacular New Year's Eve firework displays over the harbour

Average daily temperatures: Jan 17–26°C, Apr 13–22°C, Jul 6–17°C, Oct 12–22°C

Getting there: Direct flights from all state capitals; direct rail services from Brisbane (970km), Canberra (290km) and Melbourne (880km)

Festivals and events:

Jan: Sydney Festival, including events such as Opera in the Park, Symphony under the Stars; Sydney Fringe Festival, Bondi Pavilion; Australia Day celebrations, including Australia Day Harbour Parade with tall ships

Feb: Gay and Lesbian Mardi Gras

Feb–Mar (depending on lunar cycle): Chinese New Year, including dragon-boat racing at Darling Harbour

Mar–Apr: Royal Easter Show, Homebush

Apr: Heritage Week

Jun: Manly Food and Wine Festival; Feast of Sydney; Sydney Film Festival

Aug: City to Surf Fun Run

Sep: Manly Jazz Festival; Festival of the Winds kite festival, Bondi

Oct: Blessing of the Fleet, Darling Harbour

Nov: Sculpture by the Sea, Bondi to Bronte

Dec: Sydney–Hobart Yacht Race; New Year's Eve fireworks

Activities: Beach activities and watersports, sailing, arts and culture, wining and dining, parks and gardens, horseriding (Centennial Park), bushwalking

Highlights: The walk from Sydney Opera House around Farm Cove to Mrs Macquarie's Chair; picnicking in the Botanic Gardens; the ferry ride from Circular Quay to Manly; harbour cruises; Sydney Opera House; climbing the Harbour Bridge; the Rocks weekend markets; Yum Cha in Chinatown; Bondi Beach buzz; Bondi to Bronte coast walk; RiverCat trip to Parramatta

Tip: Take the red Sydney Explorer bus for a quick introduction to the main city sights. You can get off and rejoin at any of the 26 stops; the complete circuit takes less than 2hr; fee, Ph: 131 500. For one of the best, and free, views of the harbour, walk across the Sydney Harbour Bridge.

Kids' stuff: AMP Tower, Centrepoint; Powerhouse Museum; Sydney Aquarium; Taronga Zoo; Goat Island Ghastly Tales tour, Ph: (02) 9247 5033; Wonderland Sydney, entry fee includes rides, Ph: (02) 9830 9111; Fox Studios Australia's Bent St (eateries, specialty shops, interactive games, cinemas); Featherdale Wildlife Park, entry fee, Ph: (02) 9671 4140

Further information: Sydney Visitor Centre, 106 George St, Sydney, NSW 2000, Ph: (02) 9255 1788, www.sydneycity.nsw.gov.au; Darling Harbour Information Centre, Ph: (02) 9286 0111; City Info, Ph: (02) 9265 9007, darlingharbour.com.au

Sydney is superbly blessed with natural attributes, including a stunning setting on a sparkling harbour, golden beaches and spectacular coastal scenery, great bushland parks around its fringes, and a climate that permits the enjoyment of outdoor activities year-round. The oldest and largest city in Australia, it is vibrant, cosmopolitan and busy. Glass towers reach skyward in its commercial heart, while its past is on show in the colonial sandstone buildings of the Rocks and Macquarie St. The compact city centre makes for easy sightseeing, yet offers more than enough to occupy any visitor for several days—museums and galleries, harbourside parks with breathtaking views, exciting dining, great shopping (ranging from the elegant Queen Victoria Building to the hubbub of Paddy's Markets) and the twin icons of the Sydney Harbour Bridge and Sydney Opera House. In addition, a ring of inner sub-urbs—notably Paddington, Balmain and Glebe—offers charming heritage street-scapes and bustling weekend markets.

Places of Interest

- AMP Tower, Centrepoint (1)
- Art Gallery of New South Wales (2)
- Australian Museum (3)
- Australian National Maritime Museum (4)
- Cadman's Cottage (5)
- Chinese Garden of Friendship (6)
- Conservatorium of Music (7)
- Entertainment Centre (8)
- Government House (9)
- Great Synagogue (10)
- Hyde Park Barracks Museum (11)
- Museum of Contemporary Art (12)
- Museum of Sydney (13)
- National Trust Centre (14)
- Paddy's Markets (15)
- Powerhouse Museum (16)
- Queen Victoria Building (17)
- St Andrews Anglican Cathedral (18)
- St Marys Catholic Cathedral (19)
- Star City Casino (20)
- State Library of New South Wales (21)
- Sydney Aquarium (22)
- Sydney Harbour Bridge (23)
- Sydney Observatory (24)
- Sydney Opera House (25)
- Tumbalong Park (26)

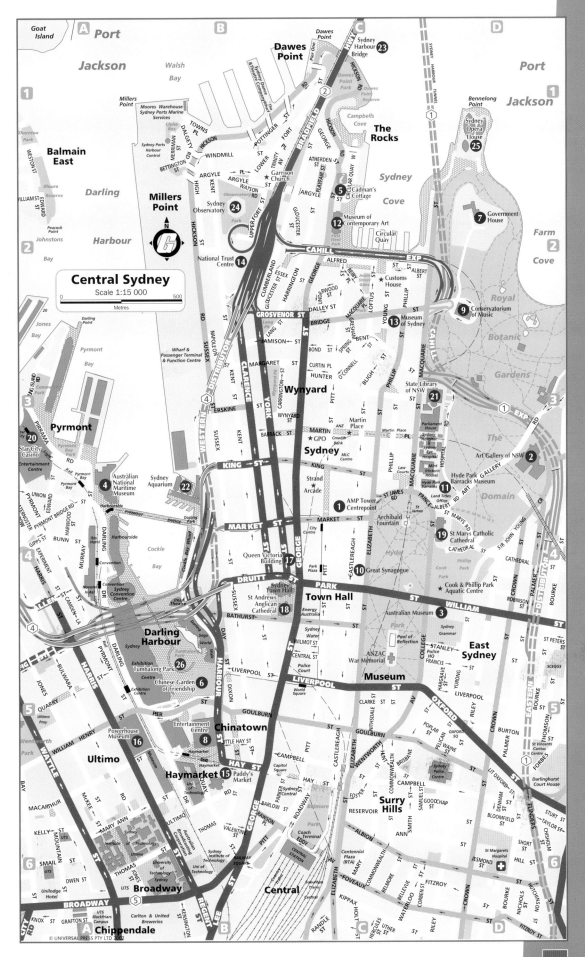

The CBD, Chinatown and Darling Harbour

AMP Tower, Centrepoint, is Sydney's tallest building; on a clear day, views from the observation deck extend north to the Central Coast, west to the Blue Mountains and south to Wollongong; entry fee (includes Skytour virtual reality overview of Australia's landscapes and most famous landmarks), Ph: (02) 9231 1000, www.centrepoint.com.au. The CBD's main shopping precinct spreads over several streets around the base of the tower and includes the **Queen Victoria Building** (QVB), an elaborately decorated and beautifully restored 1890s building on the site of the original Sydney markets.

A short walk south lies Haymarket and the clothing boutiques, restaurants and noodle bars of **Chinatown**. Bargain hunters should visit nearby **Paddy's Markets**, where more than 1000 stalls offer a wide range of goods including homewares, electrical equipment, CDs, clothing, jewellery, plants and fresh foodstuffs; open Thu–Sun and public holidays. The **Darling Harbour** entertainment and convention complex, which curves around **Cockle Bay**, has waterfront restaurants, a host of fast-food outlets, numerous Australiana shops, the Panasonic IMAX Theatre (with its gigantic movie screen) and a palm-filled park. It is a lively place, day or night, with free street entertainment, frequent musical events in **Tumbalong Park** and regular after-dark laser shows on water screens. The adjacent **Chinese Garden of Friendship** was a gift from the Chinese government. Its winding pathways, waterfalls and ponds are an oasis of tranquillity in the heart of the city; entry fee, Ph: (02) 9281 6863.

At the **Sydney Aquarium**, transparent underwater tunnels bring visitors face-to-face with sharks, eels and huge stingrays, and a viewing area with glass walls and floor allows you to watch seals swim beneath your feet; entry fee, Ph: (02) 9262 2300, www.sydneyaquarium.com.au.

The now pedestrian-only Pyrmont Bridge, built in 1902, crosses to the western shore of Cockle Bay, site of the **Australian National Maritime Museum**, with its fleet of historic craft (see p.14), and the **Star City Casino**, where you can have a flutter, catch a live show or dine at one of an array of restaurants.

The Metro Monorail links Darling Harbour with the city centre. The Metro Light Rail runs from Central Station to the inner-western suburb of Lilyfield, stopping on the way at Chinatown, the Powerhouse Museum (see p.14), Darling Harbour, the Australian National Maritime Museum, Star City Casino and the Sydney Fish Market (which incorporates a wide range of retail outlets and excellent waterfront eateries).

Sydney CBD viewed from Darling Harbour

The Rocks

The historic waterfront precinct of the Rocks has a long and colourful history. Its rocky shores were the site of the first European settlement in Australia and convicts quarried the cliffs here for many of Sydney's early buildings. In the 19th century, its inns and alleys were the haunt of hard-drinking seamen, water-side workers and larrikin gangs. In the 1920s, the building of the Sydney Harbour Bridge cut the district in 2, taking out whole streets to make way for the bridge's southern approach. Today the sandstone and weathered timber of the Rocks' beautifully restored buildings house shops and galleries selling quality Australian arts and crafts (including Aboriginal art, opals and other jewellery, ceramics and clothing), cafes, restaurants, boutique hotels and jazz pubs. A large market and street entertainment take place every weekend.

The Rocks weekend markets

The best way to see the Rocks is on foot; you can pick up a self-guided walking tour brochure from the Sydney Visitor Centre, Ph: (02) 9255 1788. You'll find a tangle of lanes and pathways, some ending at cliff faces, others linked by long flights of stone steps to streets on upper levels. Highlights include **Campbell's Storehouses**, now a row of waterfront restaurants with splendid harbour and Opera House views; the 1860s **Sydney Sailors' Home**, containing the Sydney Visitor Centre and displays relating to the area's rich history; **Cadman's Cottage** (see below); the **Argyle Centre**, a shopping arcade housed in an early-19th-century bond store; the massive walls of **Argyle Cut**, mostly hewn by convicts; charming **Argyle Pl**, where neat 1840s and 1850s cottages and the 1840s Garrison Church face a village green; and **Susannah Place**, a museum consisting of four historic terrace houses and a shop renovated in a range of period styles.

Excavated fortifications and 1850s cannons are on display at **Dawes Point Park**. For lively pubs, look in on the Hero of Waterloo and the Lord Nelson, both of which date from the 1840s. Climb to **Observatory Hill** for sweeping harbour views and maybe a picnic under the spreading Moreton Bay fig trees; the nearby **National Trust Centre**, originally built in 1815 as a military hospital, has information on historic houses open to the public; Ph: (02) 9258 0123.

Cadman's Cottage

Tiny Cadman's Cottage is the oldest surviving house in the city centre. It was built in 1816 as quarters for the coxswain of the government dockyard and for the next 30 years, when poor roads made the waterways the main form of transport, was the busy hub of the government fleet of 20 or so vessels.

At that time, cove waters lapped almost to the door; subsequent land-reclamation work and the construction of Circular Quay have left the building high and dry.

The cottage takes its name from ex-convict John Cadman, who as superintendent of boats from 1827 to 1845 lived on the upper level, now home to an information centre for Sydney Harbour NP. On the lower level, a free exhibition looks at the history of the cottage and life in early Sydney. Ph: (02) 9247 5033.

Galleries and Museums

The **Art Gallery of New South Wales** is home to some of the country's best-known Australian works and also includes the outstanding Yiribana Gallery, the world's largest permanent exhibition of Aboriginal art. Entry fee for special exhibitions, Ph: (02) 9225 1744, www.art gallery.nsw.gov.au.

Visitors to the **Australian Museum** are greeted by the skeleton of a enormous sperm whale, suspended from the ceiling, a foretaste of a whole gallery of skeletons which traces the development of life on Earth. The museum is also known for its cultural exhibitions: a large section deals with Aboriginal history and the impact of European settlement in Australia. The indigenous tribal cultures of Papua New Guinea are also well represented. Entry fee (and additional fee for special exhibitions), Ph: (02) 9320 6000, www.amonline.net.au.

The **Australian National Maritime Museum**, Darling Harbour, explores the history of Australia's mariners from the first local seafarers who arrived 60,000 years ago to the First Fleet and Matthew Flinders' circumnavigation of the continent. Exhibits include the 1974 *Spirit of Australia,* the world's fastest boat, and, in an outdoor section, a fleet of historic

Abelam spirit-house from Papua New Guinea, Australian Museum

craft, including a submarine and HMAS *Vampire*, the last of the Australian navy's big-gun destroyers. Entry fee, Ph: (02) 9298 3777, www.anmm.gov.au. The adjacent **Welcome Wall** pays tribute to the more than 6 million people who crossed the seas to settle in Australia.

Hyde Park Barracks Museum, on Macquarie St, occupies a splendid Georgian building designed by convict architect Francis Greenway and built in 1819. It originally housed male convicts and was later a home for Irish orphans and 'unprotected women'. Visitors can see how the convicts lived, where they slept, what they ate and how they were punished. There are also changing exhibitions of Australian history and culture. Entry fee, Ph: (02) 9223 8922.

Housed in the imposing Art-Deco building that was once home to the Maritime Services Board, the **Museum of Contemporary Art**, adjacent to **Circular Quay**, presents works by contemporary Australian and international artists in a wide range of media. Entry fee for temporary exhibitions, Ph: (02) 9252 4033.

The **Museum of Sydney** stands on the remains of Australia's first government house; the outline of the original building is depicted on the footpath and glass panels allow visitors to view the foundations and part of the excavated building. The museum contains a wealth of materials retrieved from the site and items removed from the house before its demolition in 1846, including governors' records and personal possessions, works of art and furniture; it also houses evocative exhibitions on the Aboriginal history of the area. Entry fee, Ph: (02) 9251 4611, www.hht.nsw.gov.au.

The **Powerhouse Museum** is housed in the soaring space of the 1890s electricity station that once powered Sydney's trams. Its many hands-on and interactive exhibits allow children and more mature visitors to have fun while finding out about science, technology and the decorative arts. Permanent displays include the oldest steam engines in the world, a piece of moon rock, vintage aircraft hanging from the ceiling and an operational model of the 600-year-old Strasburg clock; there are also regular exhibitions on particular themes. Entry fee, Ph: (02) 9217 0111, www.phm.gov.au.

Parks and Gardens

The **Royal Botanic Gardens** curve around Farm Cove (site of the country's first farm), immediately east of Sydney Opera House. Dating from 1816, the gardens incorporate a wide range of plants, all labelled and grouped in themed areas. 'Cadi Jama Ora: First Encounters' presents an indigenous perspective on the history of the site. Other areas include an oriental garden, rare and threatened plants garden, palm grove, herb garden and rose garden. Examples of the recently discovered Wollemi pine, a survivor from the age of the dinosaurs, are also on display here. Grassed and shaded areas, ponds, fountains and dazzling harbour views make this a top spot for a picnic. Entry fee to Tropical Centre glass pyramid, Ph: (02) 9231 8111, www.rbgsyd.gov.au.

The lush green swathe of the **Domain** runs SW from the scenic vantage point known as Mrs Macquarie's Chair, between the Royal Botanic Gardens and Woolloomooloo Bay, to St Marys Cathedral. Mrs Macquarie's Chair was named after Gov Lachlan Macquarie's wife Elizabeth, who regularly savoured the promontory's spectacular views from a rock bench carved by convicts. The bench is still there and the spot continues to delight; it is especially popular with tour buses and wedding photographers seeking the classic Sydney backdrop of harbour, Opera House sails and arching bridge. This is also a great place for a picnic, day or night. The southern section of the Domain, opposite the Art Gallery of NSW, is frequently used for open-air events in summer.

Hyde Park was the location of the nation's first cricket matches and horse races. With tree-lined walkways, formal gardens and elegant statuary, it is a popular lunchtime destination for Sydney's office workers. The granite, Art Deco-style Anzac War Memorial in Hyde Park South pays homage to the many Australian soldiers who died in WWI. In Hyde Park North, the flamboyant Archibald Fountain commemorates the association of Australia and France in the same conflict.

Centennial Parklands, SE of the city centre, encompasses 3 great recreation areas—Centennial, Moore and Queen's parks. The shaded avenues, playing fields, ponds and formal gardens are favoured by early-morning and lunchtime joggers and for weekend picnics. There are also cycleways and a horseriding circuit—bicycle and rollerblade hire is available from Centennial Park Cycles, Ph: (02) 9398 5027; riding tuition and horse hire from Moore Park Training Stables, Ph: (02) 9360 8747.

Wish statue, Royal Botanic Gardens

Sydney Harbour Bridge

One of the city's 2 great landmarks, **Sydney Harbour Bridge** crosses from the CBD to the north shore at the point where the harbour narrows just west of Circular Quay. It took 1400 workers 8 years to build and on its completion in 1932 was the longest single-span bridge in the world. First the 2 half arches were built outwards from each shore—being joined in 1930 amid much local celebration—then the decking was hung underneath. The massive, granite-faced, sandstone pylons were added for aesthetic effect only and play no structural role. The bridge is 1150m long (including the approach spans), with 49m of clearance for shipping, allowing most great liners and container ships to pass beneath it to the wharves of northern Darling Harbour.

To inspect the underside of the bridge from water level, take a ferry ride to Balmain or Woolwich or the RiverCat to Parramatta. To get onto the bridge, follow the pedestrian walkway that runs along its eastern side and offers spectacular views. Access is via steps from Cumberland St, above the Argyle Cut in the Rocks or, on the north side, from steps near Milsons Pt station. You can walk one way and make the return journey by train. Pylon Lookout, a demanding 200-step climb up the SE pylon, has panoramic harbour views as well as informative displays showing how the bridge was built; entry fee, Ph: (02) 9247 3408.

The Climb of Your Life

A 360° panorama of city and harbour is the breathtaking reward when you climb to the top of Sydney Harbour Bridge. From a vantage point on the crest of the arch, 134m above the water, the view stretches to the Heads and beyond, to the Blue Mountains, and across the sprawling city. Climbers use ladders and catwalks and all are attached to a safety line so that there is no possibility of an accident. You can climb day or night, but sunset is the prime time. Bookings are essential, and climbs go ahead come rain, shine or fog. Allow 3 hours, fee, Ph: (02) 8274 7777.

New Year's Eve fireworks display on Sydney Harbour Bridge

Sydney Opera House

Sydney's other major icon, **Sydney Opera House**, has been part of the harbour scenery since its completion in 1973. Danish architect Joern Utzon's dramatic design, which echoes the billowing sails of the harbour's weekend pleasure fleets, won an international competition in 1956. Construction, which began in 1959, was long and beset by regular budget blowouts and wrangles between Utzon and the State Government. In 1966, Utzon resigned and left the country; he has never returned to see the finished building. The stunning exterior remains close to his vision; the interior was extensively redesigned.

The Opera House is the major Sydney venue for theatre, ballet, opera and musical productions, but its location and distinctive architecture make it a major attraction in its own right. From the Forecourt, climb the Monumental Steps for a close-up view of the gleaming sails (which are covered by more than 1 million tiles), then stroll the surrounding broadwalks—ferries churn in and out of Circular Quay just metres away.

There are 3 restaurants at the Opera House itself, and many more eateries, including a waterside oyster bar, on the concourse leading to Circular Quay. For an in-depth exploration, the Opera House offers a range of guided tours as well as packages combining a tour, a show and a meal; Ph: (02) 9250 7250. There is also a special children's program, Kids @ the House. Bookings, Ph: (02) 9250 7777, www.soh.nsw.gov.au.

A harbour ferry passes Sydney Opera House

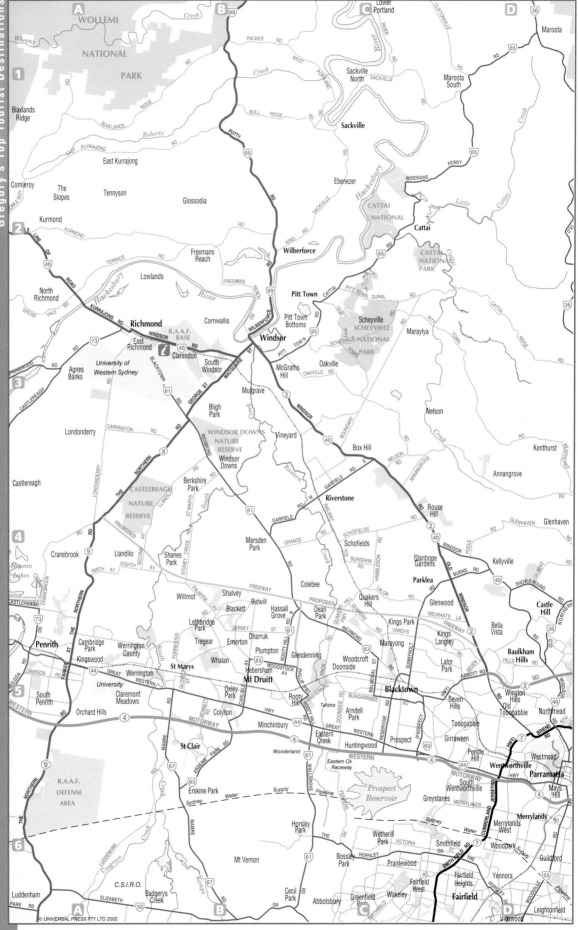

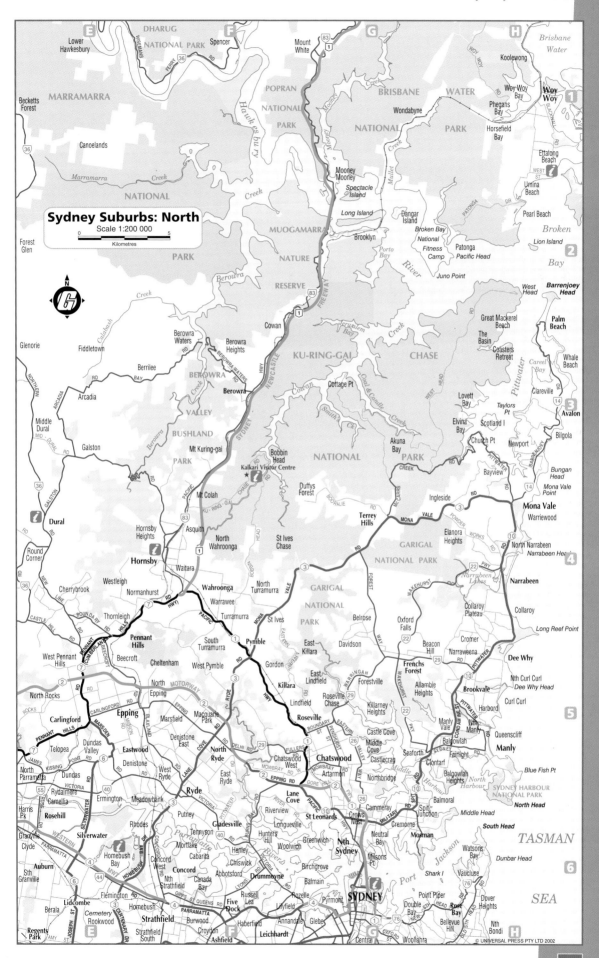

Sydney Suburbs: North

Scale 1:200 000

Kilometres

© UNIVERSAL PRESS PTY LTD 2002

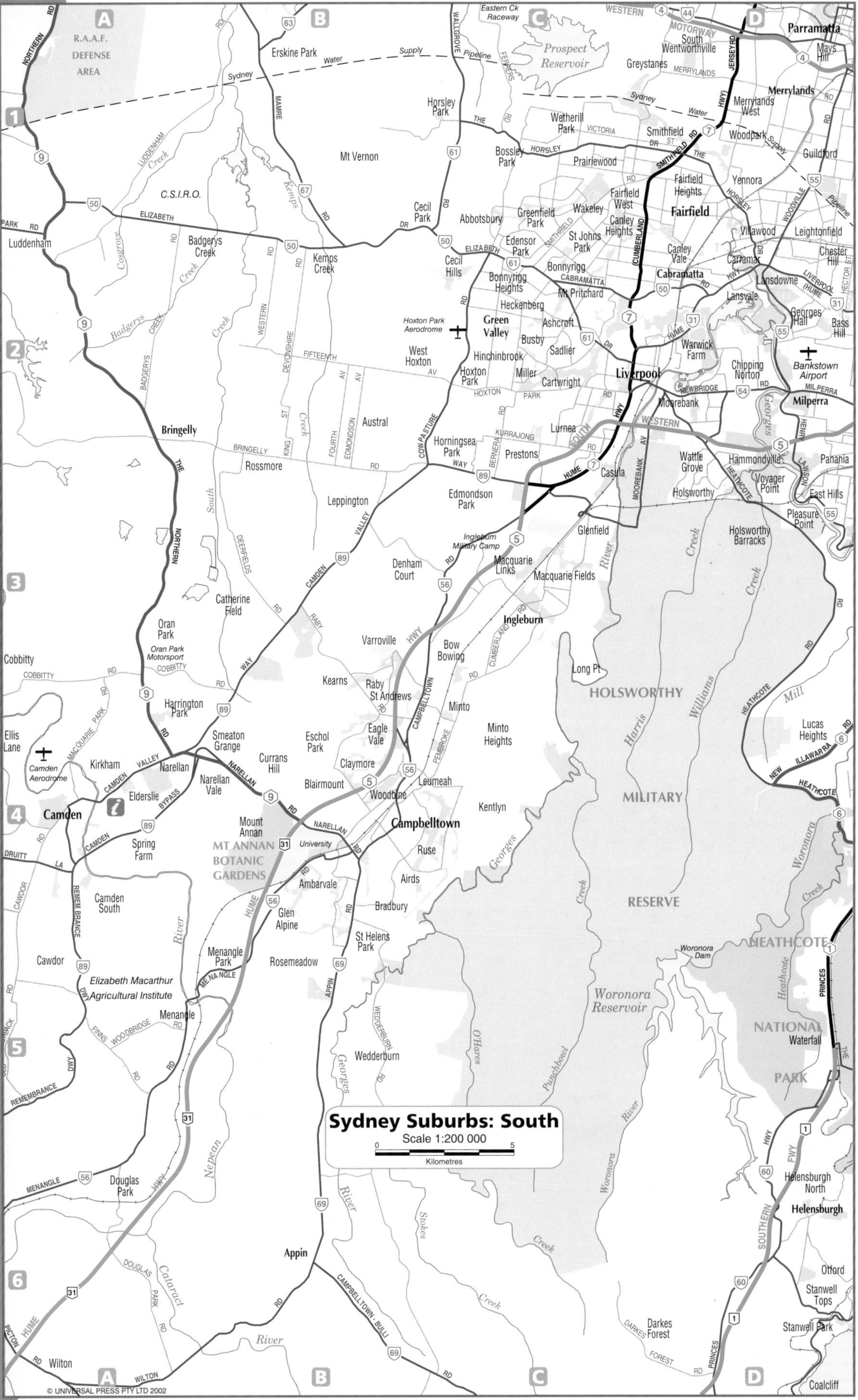

Sydney Suburbs: South

Scale 1:200 000

0 _____ 5

Kilometres

Map labels (north to south, west to east):

R.A.A.F. DEFENSE AREA

Erskine Park · Horsley Park · Mt Vernon · Bossley Park · Prairiewood · Wetherill Park · Victoria · Greystanes · South Wentworthville · WESTERN MOTORWAY · Parramatta · Mays Hill · Merrylands · Merrylands West · Woodpark · Guildford · Yennora · Smithfield · Fairfield Heights · Fairfield West · Wakeley · Canley Heights · Fairfield · Villawood · Leightonfield · Chester Hill · Carramar · Lansdowne · Georges Hall · Bass Hill

Luddenham · Badgerys Creek · C.S.I.R.O. · Kemps Creek · Cecil Park · Abbotsbury · Greenfield Park · Edensor Park · St Johns Park · Canley Vale · Cabramatta · Bonnyrigg · Mt Pritchard · Heckenberg · Busby · Cartwright · Sadleir · Ashcroft · Warwick Farm · Chipping Norton · Bankstown Airport · Milperra · Pahania

Bringelly · Rossmore · West Hoxton · Hoxton Park · Hoxton Park Aerodrome · Green Valley · Hinchinbrook · Miller · Cartwright · Liverpool · Moorebank · Lurnea · Prestons · Horningsea Park · Casula · Wattle Grove · Hammondville · Voyager Point · East Hills · Holsworthy · Pleasure Point

Leppington · Edmondson Park · Denham Court · Glenfield · Ingleburn Military Camp · Macquarie Links · Macquarie Fields · Holsworthy Barracks · HOLSWORTHY MILITARY RESERVE

Oran Park · Oran Park Motorsport · Catherine Field · Varroville · Kearns · Raby · St Andrews · Bow Bowing · Minto · Ingleburn · Long Pt · Lucas Heights

Cobbitty · Harrington Park · Smeaton Grange · Currans Hill · Eschol Park · Eagle Vale · Claymore · Minto Heights · Kirkham · Narellan · Narellan Vale · Blairmount · Woodbine · Leumeah · Kentlyn

Ellis Lane · Camden Aerodrome · Elderslie · Camden · Spring Farm · Mount Annan · MT ANNAN BOTANIC GARDENS · University · Campbelltown · Ruse · Airds · Ambarvale · Bradbury

Cawdor · Camden South · Elizabeth Macarthur Agricultural Institute · Menangle Park · Glen Alpine · Rosemeadow · St Helens Park

Menangle · Wedderburn · Woronora Dam · Woronora Reservoir · HEATHCOTE NATIONAL PARK · Waterfall

Douglas Park · Appin · Darkes Forest · Helensburgh North · Helensburgh · Otford · Stanwell Tops · Stanwell Park

Wilton · Coalcliff

Rivers / waterways: Nepean River · Georges River · Cataract River · Stokes Creek · O'Hares Creek · Punchbowl Creek · Woronora River · Williams Creek · Harris Creek · Heathcote Creek · Darkes Forest · Prospect Reservoir · Eastern Ck Raceway

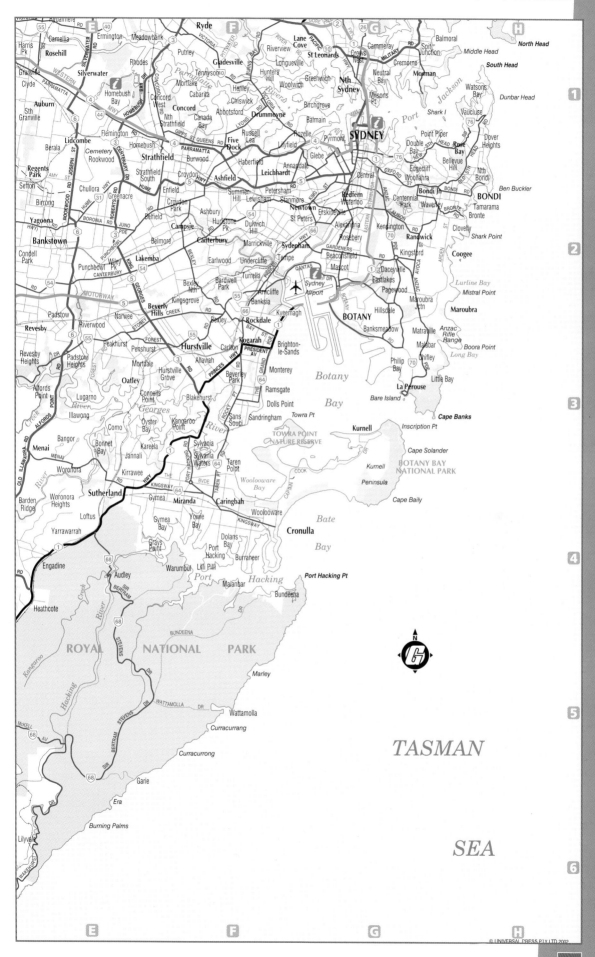

Sydney Harbour

Sydney Harbour is a deep drowned river valley, and its inlets and bays are the flooded valleys of ancient tributaries. Today, remaining areas of forested foreshore and several islands make up **Sydney Harbour NP** (see p.24).

One of Sydney's great experiences is the crossing from Circular Quay, past palatial harbourside homes and wooded **Middle Head**, to **Manly**, taking either the 10min JetCat or the more leisurely 30min ferry ride. Other attractions reached by ferry include **Taronga Zoo**, **Darling Harbour**, **Watsons Bay** and **Homebush Bay**. Sydney Ferries also offer day and after-dark sightseeing cruises with commentary; Ph: 131 500. Numerous other cruise options include Captain Cook Cruises, Ph: (02) 9206 1122; Sydney Showboats, Ph: (02) 9552 2722; a fully rigged replica of the *Bounty*, Ph: (02) 9247 1789; sailing with Eastsail, Ph: (02) 9327 1166, or Sydney by Sail, Ph: (02) 9280 1110; and kayaking tours with Sydney Harbour Kayaks, Ph: (02) 9960 4389. You can also hire a water taxi to take you to places not serviced by public transport or for personalised sightseeing.

East of the bridge, a string of sandy beaches and coves, many backed by bushland, offers fine swimming and stunning views. On the northern side, Clifton Gardens and **Clontarf** have large grassy areas and picnic spots. On the southern shores, **Nielsen Park's** wide sweep of sand, shaded and extensive grounds, and magnificent harbour vistas make it popular year-round.

Walking tracks wind along the foreshore on both sides of the harbour. A ferry ride to **Cremorne Point** accesses a magnificent 50min walk around the shores to **Mosman**. From Taronga Zoo, a 2hr walk takes in **Bradleys Head**, with its historic cannon and panoramic harbour views. Perhaps the most popular walk is the scenic 3–4hr Manly to the Spit Bridge track, which runs from Manly Wharf to the **Spit Bridge** on Middle Harbour; Ph: (02) 9247 5033. On the south side, the Hermitage Foreshore walking track links **Rose Bay** and **Nielsen Park**—walk west at dusk to see the sun set over the harbour. There are also magnificent walks on North Head and South Head (see p.24).

The harbour's many islands offer million-dollar views and secluded picnic spots. **Shark Island**, 1km off Rose Bay, is

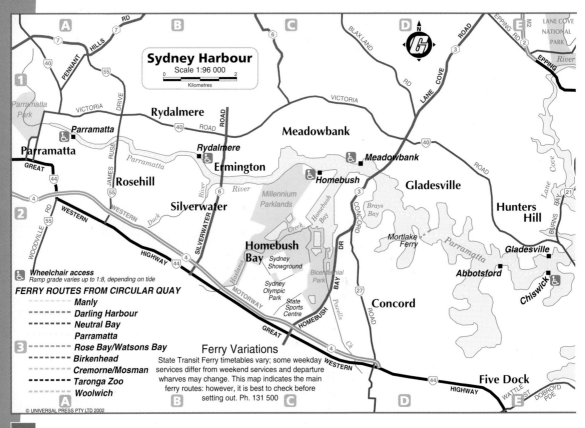

Zoo with a View

Surrounded by bushland, spectacularly sited Taronga Zoo spills down a hillside to the northern harbour foreshore, providing the animals here with one of the best views in Sydney. You can get close to a koala in a photo session, soar above the sights in the Sky Safari, join a behind-the-scenes tour, or even sleep in the zoo overnight. Entry fee, Ph: (02) 9969 2777. Taronga is a 12-minute ferry ride across the inner harbour from Circular Quay. Sydney Ferries' ZooPass includes the ferry trip, Sky Safari or bus to the main entrance, and the admission fee.

named for its shape, not its marine life, and has a grassy area, shade trees and large gazebo. Peaceful **Clark Island**, off Darling Point, was the site of one of Sydney's first vegetable gardens. **Rodd Island**, in Iron Cove, west of the Harbour Bridge, has a century-old, Colonial-style meeting hall. All of these islands have picnic tables, drinking water and toilets, and are reached by water taxi or private boat; visits must be booked through the National Parks and Wildlife Service (NPWS) as numbers are strictly limited; fee, Ph: (02) 9247 5033.

Fort Denison and **Goat Island** can only be visited on guided tours. In Sydney's first years, the sandstone out-crop now known as Fort Denison

became an open-air prison for unruly convicts; its distinctive Martello tower was constructed in the 1850s, when a Russian attack was feared. You can enjoy a breakfast here or take a sunset tour. Night tours of Goat Island delve into its convict past, whereas day tours take a peek at the set of *Water Rats*, a popular TV drama shot on the island; Ph: (02) 9247 5033.

Berry Island is linked by causeway to Wollstonecraft on the harbour's northern shore and is a place of deep significance to local Aborigines; numerous middens and carvings, including a depiction of a giant stingray, remain. The signposted Gadyan Track explores and explains the island's features and heritage.

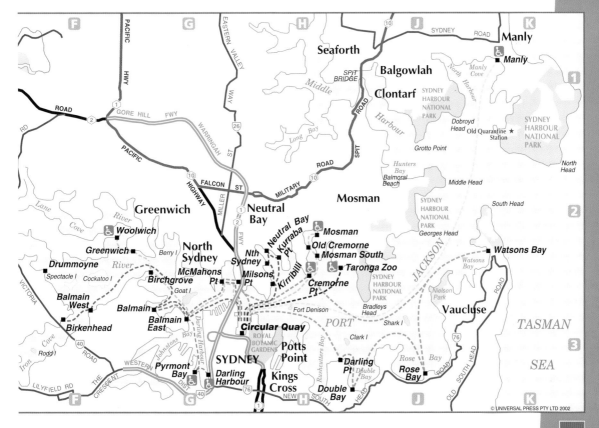

National Parks

Sydney is centred on 1 great national park—Sydney Harbour NP—and bordered to the north and south by 2 more—Ku-ring-gai Chase NP and Royal NP. Vehicle entry fees apply in all 3.

Sydney Harbour NP gathers 5 islands, discontinuous stretches of wooded harbour foreshore and headlands (mostly former Defence Department land) into a wonderful resource of bushland, beach and historic Aboriginal and European sites on the very edge of central Sydney. Easily accessible walks and scenic lookouts include **South Head**, with sweeping views and walking tracks leading past historic fortifications, and **North Head**, with sheer cliffs, equally magnificent views (this is a particularly good spot for watching the sunset), and extensive bushland. Ph: (02) 9247 5033. Visitors to the 19th-century **Quarantine Station** on North Head can take a 3hr night-time Ghost Walk; fee, Ph: (02) 9247 5033.

Ku-ring-gai Chase NP covers 15 000ha of rugged bushland fringing picturesque waterways. It is popular for sailing, kayaking, boating (including houseboats), fishing and bushwalking. There are marinas at **Bobbin Head** and **Akuna Bay**, and picnic areas throughout the park. Walking tracks lead to ridgetop vantage points, wooded valleys and

sheltered beaches. To view some of the park's extensive assemblage of rock art, follow the Aboriginal Heritage Walk, the Echidna Track or the Basin Track, all on **West Head**. Kangaroos and emus are frequently seen from the wheelchair-accessible walking track at Kalkari Visitor Centre, Ph: (02) 9457 9853.

Nearby **Garigal NP** includes wooded slopes, bushland shores and tranquil waters on upper Middle Harbour. There is easy road access from Warringah Rd to leafy Davidson picnic area, just 10km north of the CBD. Ph: (02) 9451 3479.

Royal NP, the oldest national park in the country, takes in Victorian-era riverside picnic grounds at **Audley**, noted for their pavilion, boating and fishing; **Wattamolla**, with its sandy lagoon and scenic waterfall; the surf beaches of **Garie**, **Burning Palms** and **Era**; and majestic clifftop walks offering expansive views over the ocean. Devastated by bushfire in 1994 and again in 2001, the park is an example of the remarkable ability of the Australian bush to regenerate after fire. Its diverse habitats include heath, woodlands and mangrove foreshore. **Lady Wakehurst Dr**, in the south of the park, winds through towering subtropical rainforest. **Bundeena**, an isolated township on the northern edge of the park, is reached by a pleasant ferry ride from Cronulla. Ph: (02) 9542 0648.

Wattamolla Falls, Royal NP

Bondi Beach, Bondi

Ocean Beaches

Sydney's famed ocean beaches, with their golden sand and rolling surf, stretch both north and south of the city centre. In the south, the beaches between Bondi and Maroubra are easily visited from the city by bus; Cronulla, the most southerly beach, can be accessed by train. In the north, ferries cross to Manly, but beaches further north are best reached by car. Lifesavers patrol most beaches during the summer months—pairs of red and yellow flags indicate that they are on duty; the area between the flags is the safest for swimming. Most beaches are also protected by offshore nets, so the risk of shark attack is extremely low.

Closest to the city is **Bondi Beach**, which is nearly 1km long, with wide sands and good surf. Summer crowds give it a carnival atmosphere; lively Campbell Pde, running parallel to the beach, has cafes, restaurants and beachwear boutiques. The northern end of the beach is favoured by families. The walk from the southern end to Coogee (6km, allow 2hr) takes in clifftop viewpoints and numerous swimming and eating spots. Each Nov, the section of the walk between Bondi and Tamarama is the venue for 'Sculpture by the Sea', a free open-air exhibition of up to 100 works. Further south, **Bronte** has fierce breakers, a safe sea pool, and shaded parkland (with playground); **Clovelly** offers a sheltered beach and a pool for children. Bustling **Coogee**, with its cafes, restaurants and backpacker accommodation, has reef-protected swimming, a grassy headland and children's playground.

The northside beaches are generally less crowded and more laid-back. In addition to great surf, wide sands, beachside eateries and souvenir shops, **Manly** offers a fascinating insight into marine life at Oceanworld Manly, a giant aquarium with easily observable sharks, seals, turtles and exotic fish; entry fee, Ph: (02) 9262 2300. It is also the location of the Manly Waterworks fun park, which features giant waterslides (summer only); entry fee, Ph: (02) 9949 2644.

Further north, **Dee Why** has excellent surfing and a large sea pool, while **Collaroy** and **Narrabeen** share a spacious, 3km-long stretch of sand, also with good surf; just inland, the coastal lagoon system of **Narrabeen Lakes** is popular for sailing, windsurfing and fishing. **Palm Beach**, holiday playground of the rich and famous, offers a fine surfing beach; calmer **Pittwater** is a short stroll away through pleasant parkland.

Sydney Olympic Park

A visit to the venues of the 2000 Sydney Olympics allows you to recapture the spirit of the Games while enjoying state-of-the-art sports facilities. Call in at the visitor centre, Ph: (02) 9714 7888, for maps and information, then hop on an Olympic Explorer bus (fee) for a guided tour of the major sites. There is a good range of restaurants and bars; alternatively, you can pack a picnic and relax in the **Overflow** alongside the water feature that incorporates the Olympic cauldron.

Guided tours of magnificent **Stadium Australia**, now a venue for major football games, follow in the footsteps of champions, provide spectacular views from the heights, and even take a peek at the athletes' change rooms; fee, Ph: (02) 8765 2300. You can also tour the **SuperDome**, Australia's largest indoor sports and entertainment venue; fee, Ph: (02) 8765 4321.

Sydney Showground is the venue for the Royal Easter Show, and has pavilions for livestock and produce displays. Visitors can enjoy a game of tennis on the Olympic courts of the **Tennis Centre** or take a dip at the popular **Sydney Aquatic Centre**, which boasts a competition pool, training pool, leisure pool (with slide, rapid river ride and spas), gymnasium and garden area. Tours of the centre feature audiovisual presentations on the 2000 Olympics; fee, Ph: (02) 9752 3666. The **Sydney Athletic Centre**, used as a training and warm-up venue during the Games, now hosts elite and amateur track-and-field events.

Bicentennial Park, has extensive cycling and walking trails (including a boardwalk through a mangrove wetland), a lookout tower with views to the city, playgrounds and picnic and BBQ facilities; Ph: (02) 9763 1844. A bird hide allows you to spy on the park's rich birdlife—more than 140 species have been recorded here, including migratory birds from the Northern Hemisphere. To the west, **Millennium Parklands** also offer cycling and walking tracks.

You can reach Olympic Park by rail, by RiverCat from Circular Quay to Homebush Bay wharf, or by bus from Parramatta, Strathfield or Lidcombe. Parking is available at the park; fee.

If you visit on the 4th Sun of the month, you can also enjoy the gourmet food and fresh produce markets held under the fig trees lining **Olympic Boulevard**.

Olympic cauldron water feature in the Overflow

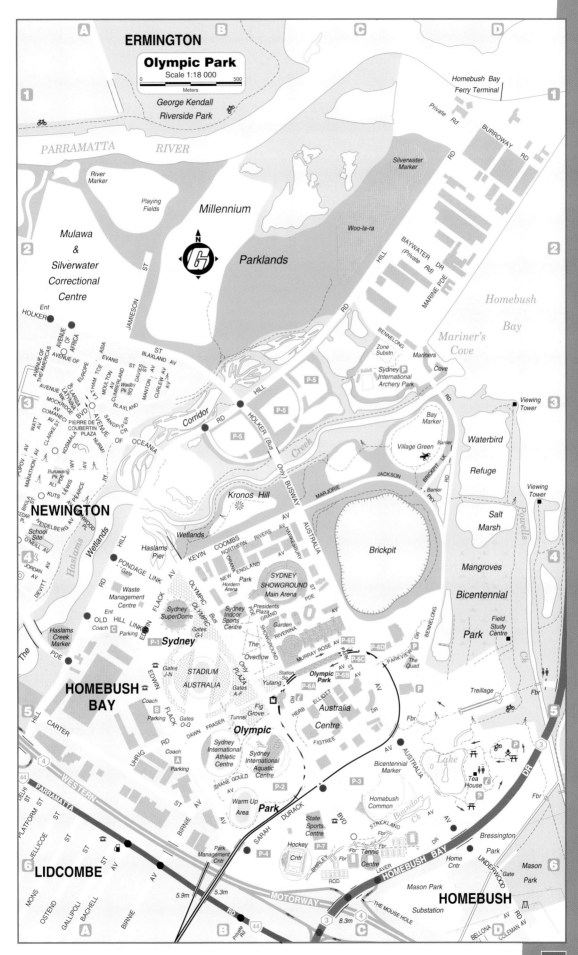

ERMINGTON

Olympic Park
Scale 1:18 000

0   500
Meters

George Kendall
Riverside Park

PARRAMATTA   RIVER

River Marker

Playing Fields

Millennium

Woo-la-ra

Homebush Bay Ferry Terminal

Private Rd

BURROWAY RD

Silverwater Marker

RD

BAYWATER DR (Private Rd)

MARINE PDE

Homebush Bay

Mariner's Cove

Mulawa & Silverwater Correctional Centre

HOLKER Ent

AVENUE OF AFRICA
AVENUE OF ASIA
AVENUE OF EUROPE
AVENUE OF THE AMERICAS
AVENUE OF OCEANIA

JAMIESON ST

Parklands

HILL ST

BLAXLAND AV

EVANS ST

DAVIES ST

CUMBERLAND AV

MANTON AV

CURLEW AV

MOULTON AV

LATHAM TCE

Wadby Pk SQ

ASIA

BLAXLAND

SANDPIPER CR

LARISA WY
MOCKRIDGE AV
COMANECI AV
KOSMALA AV
NURMI
CLARKE AV
PIERRE DE COUBERTIN PLAZA
AVENUE

WATT AV

POPOV AV
MARATHON AV
ALI
LEWIS WY
A PEARCE
KUTS

BIKILA
CEDAR PL
HEIDELBERG RD
O'NEILL AV
School Site
HASLAM WOOD RD

JORDAN AV
DEVITT AV

NEWINGTON

Haslams Wetlands

Haslams Pier

PONDAGE LINK
Gate

Waste Management Centre

Haslams Creek Marker

The

PDE

HOMEBUSH BAY

Coach Parking

HILL

CARTER

UHRIG RD

BIRNIE AV

PLATFORM ST
JELLICOE ST

JELHI ST

LIDCOMBE

MONS

OSTEND

GALLIPOLI

BACHELL

BIRNIE

Corridor

HILL RD

HILL RD

HOLKER (Bus Only) BUSWAY

Creek

Kronos Hill

Wetlands

COOMBS
OPORA RD
KEVIN
NORTHERN RIVERS
NEW ENGLAND
HAWKESBURY
AUSTRALIA AV
MARJORIE AV

New Hordern Arena
Park

SYDNEY SHOWGROUND Main Arena

ST PDE

Brickpit

P-5

BENNELONG RD

Zone Substn

Sydney International Archery Park

P-5

P-5

Bay Marker

Village Green

Barrier

BRICKPIT LK

JACKSON

Barrier PKY

Viewing Tower

Waterbird Refuge

Salt Marsh

Mangroves

Powells Ck

Viewing Tower

Bicentennial Park

Field Study Centre

Sydney SuperDome

Sydney Indoor Sports Centre

OLYMPIC BLVD

OLYMPIC BLVD

FLACK AV

EDWIN FLACK AV

OLD HILL
Ent
Coach C Parking

P-1
Sydney

Gates G-I

Gates J-N

STADIUM AUSTRALIA

Gates A-F

Gates O-Q

Presidents Plaza
GRAND

SHOWGROUND RD

Garden Riverina

The Overflow

Station Sq

Yulang

Fig Grove

Tunnel

DAWN FRASER AV

Olympic

Sydney International Athletic Centre

Sydney International Aquatic Centre

SHANE GOULD AV

Warm Up Area

Coach Parking

Coach B Parking

Park

MURRAY ROSE AV

P-6E

P-6D

P-6C

P-6B
Olympic Park

P-6A

HERB ELLIOTT AV

Australia Centre

FIGTREE AV

The Quad

PARKVIEW DR

BENNELONG DR

Treillage

Fbr

P

AUSTRALIA AV

AUSTRALIA DR

Bicentennial Marker

P-2

P-3

Homebush Common

STRICKLAND AV

Lake

Tea House

Fbr

HOMEBUSH BAY DR

Bressington Park

Home Cntr

Mason Park

SARAH DURACK AV

Park Management Cntr

P-4

State Sports Centre

Hockey Cntr

BVD

P-7

Fbr

SHIRLEY ROD

Tennis Centre

LAVER DR

Fbr

Substation

UNDERWOOD RD
Gate

Mason Park

BELLONA AV
COLEMAN AV

5.9m   5.3m

PARRAMATTA

WESTERN

44

MOTORWAY

RD

44

3   8.3m   4

THE MOUSE HOLE

HOMEBUSH

The Blue Mountains

Best time to visit: Spring for blooms; summer for sparkling days and cool nights; autumn for mists and leaf colour; winter for Yulefest activities

Average daily temperatures: Jan 13–23°C, Apr 9–16°C, Jul 3–9°C, Oct 8–17°C

Getting there: By road from Sydney via Great Western Hwy (M4, toll) to Glenbrook (75km) and Mt Victoria (140km) or via Bells Line of Road to Kurrajong (75km) and Mt Victoria (140km). By rail from Sydney's Central Station; usually limited stops to Penrith, then all stations to Katoomba, Mt Victoria or Lithgow (CityRail Info Line 13 1500)

Festivals and events:

Mar: Blue Mountains Festival of Folk, Roots and Blues, Katoomba

Jun: Winter Magic Festival (held throughout the mountains on the weekend closest to the winter solstice)

Jul: Yulefest

Oct–Nov: Spring gardens festivals, various locations

Nov: Blackheath Rhododendron Festival

Activities: Bushwalking, climbing, abseiling, golf, browsing galleries, bookshops and antique shops

Highlights: Norman Lindsay Gallery and Museum, Springwood, Ph: 02 4751 1067; Wentworth Falls lookouts and walks; Three Sisters, Katoomba; Scenic World, Katoomba; Govetts Leap, Blackheath; Hydro Majestic Hotel, Medlow Bath, Ph: (02) 4788 1002; Jenolan Caves

Tip: The weather can change suddenly and with little warning; be prepared with warm and waterproof clothes, especially if bushwalking.

Kids' stuff: Leuralla and NSW Toy and Railway Museum, entry fee, Ph: (02) 4784 1169; Zig Zag Railway, Lithgow, fee, Ph: (02) 6351 4826

Further information: Blue Mountains Visitor Information Centre, Great Western Hwy, Glenbrook, NSW 2773, Ph: 1300 653 408, and Echo Point Katoomba, NSW 2780, Ph: 1300 653 408, www.bluemountainstourism.org.au

A vast wilderness area encompassing 6 national parks, the Blue Mountains region is so valued for its natural grandeur and botanical diversity that it has been placed on the World Heritage list. Although certainly blue in appearance—the result of a haze of oil droplets dispersed by gum trees—these rugged heights are not mountains, but parts of an eroded sandstone plateau carved over millions of years by water and wind. Relics of prehistoric flora still grow in cliff-walled valleys here, and even today only 2 major roads wind over the plateau's stony ridgetops. The historic towns that line these routes, most notably Leura, Katoomba, Blackheath and Mt Victoria, have long been favoured as short-break destinations by Sydney-siders. In summer they offer relief from the city's humidity, in winter bracing bushwalks, crisp air and the possibility of snow. The Grand Circular Tourist Drive, which follows the Great Western Highway out of Sydney and returns via the Bells Line of Road, takes in all the main tourist sights and can be driven in a day.

The elegant eateries and galleries lining **Leura's** heritage mall make it a popular pit stop for Sydney daytrippers. Prince Henry Cliff Walk follows the clifftop from Gordon Falls to the Scenic Railway at Katoomba, passing the Leura Cascades and linking several lookouts with superb views over the Jamison Valley. Leura's numerous grand gardens include the Everglades, an outstanding, 5ha cool-climate garden designed in the 1930s by Paul Sorensen; entry fee, Ph: (02) 4784 1938. The town is also known for its magnificent golf course.

Katoomba's busy main street leads past bookshops and cafes, including the Paragon (famed for its confectionary and sumptuous, 1920s decor), to Echo Point, with its stupendous views of the **Three Sisters** (floodlit until 10pm) and the misty expanses of the **Jamison Valley**. Nearby, a well-stocked visitor centre

Sandstone cliffs, Blue Mountains

Yulefest: Christmas in July

The local celebration of Christmas in July dates from a snowy winter's evening in the late 1970s, when a guesthouse proprietor served traditional Christmas fare to a group of homesick Europeans. Now celebrated on winter weekends in hotels and resorts throughout the upper mountains, Yulefest is one of the region's biggest drawcards, promising bright, chilly days and brisk walks followed by cosy nights round log fires, roast turkey, carol singing and even a visit from Santa.

faces treetops where rosellas feed. The **Cliff Drive** links several dramatic lookouts and the **Scenic World** tourist attraction; entry fee, Ph: (02) 4782 2699, www.scenicworld.com.au. Here, the steepest incline railway in the world (formerly part of a coal-mining operation) offers a thrilling ride to the valley floor; the return trip can be made on the Sceniscender cablecar. Visitors can also cross the 300m-deep valley of Katoomba Falls Creek on the Scenic Skyway cable car.

Classy restaurants, woodland gardens and a village atmosphere characterise **Blackheath**, the highest town in the Blue Mountains. To the east, on the soaring rim of the **Grose Valley**, are 3 spectacular lookouts: **Evans Lookout**, **Govetts Leap** and **Perrys Lookdown**; these are also the starting and finishing points of a number of bushwalking tracks. Roads on the western side of Blackheath link the town with the rolling farmland and riding schools of the **Megalong Valley**.

After a steep and winding descent, the road to **Jenolan Caves** passes through the yawning mouth of the Grand Arch, a massive natural archway, to emerge in front of Swiss-chalet-style Caves House. Formations in the caves that honeycomb the surrounding slopes include shawls, columns and flowstones as well as the underground River Styx; 9 caves are open to the public; entry fee, Ph: (02) 6359 3311. Dating from 1884 and originally a bridle track, the **Six Foot Track** linking Jenolan Caves with Katoomba is a magnificent, though in places difficult, 3-day hike for serious walkers.

Mt Tomah Botanic Garden, a 28ha, cool-climate garden, sprawls across a hillside just off the **Bells Line of Road**. Plants are grouped according to geographical region, and range from African proteas to North American conifers; entry fee, Ph: (02) 4567 2154. A restaurant adjacent to the visitor centre offers panoramic views over valleys and bluffs.

Residence Garden, Mt Tomah Botanic Garden

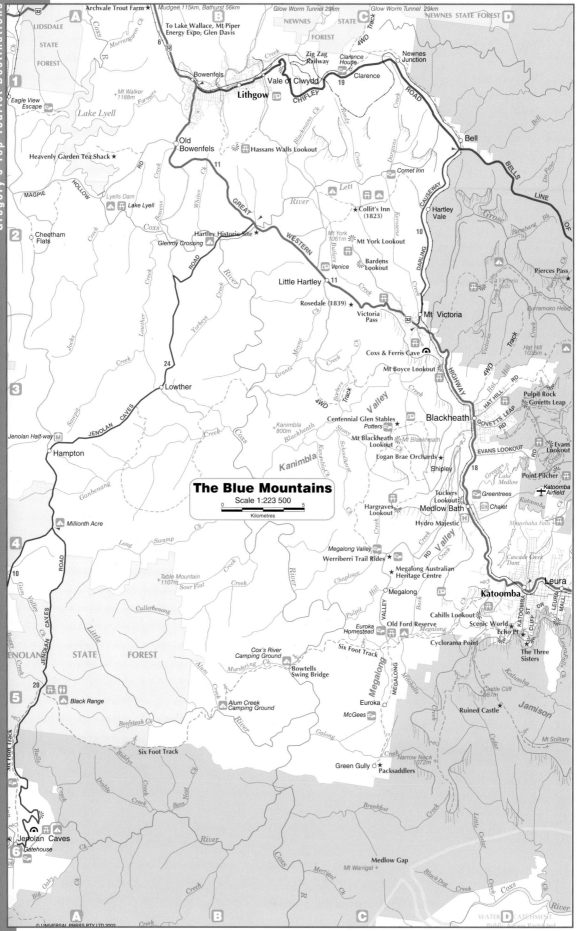

The Blue Mountains

Scale 1:223 500

© UNIVERSAL PRESS PTY LTD 2002

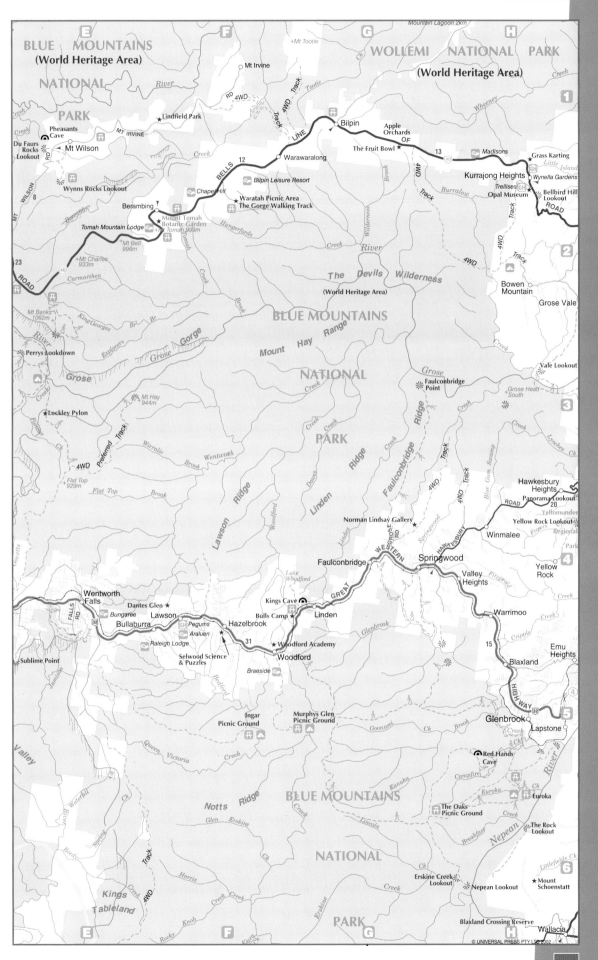

Byron Bay

Best time to visit: Summer for beachlife; winter for whalewatching

Average daily temperatures: Jan 21–28°C, Apr 17–26°C, Jul 12–19°C, Oct 16–23°C

Getting there: 175km south of Brisbane and 800km north of Sydney on the Pacific Hwy; by rail from Sydney only; by air to Coolangatta

Festivals and events:

Jan: Fish and Chips Festival and Brunswick Valley Woodchop Carnival, Brunswick Heads

Feb: Byron Bay Sailing Regatta

Easter: East Coast Blues and Roots Music Festival, Byron Bay

May: Nimbin Mardi Gras; Ocean Swim Classic, Byron Bay

Aug: Byron Bay Writers' Festival

Sep: A Taste of Byron Food Festival; Byron Bay Comedy Festival; Chincogan Fiesta, Mullumbimby

Oct: 'Buzz' Byron Bay Short Film Festival

Activities: Surfing, swimming, diving, fishing (beach and river), windsurfing, canoeing, whalewatching (in season), bushwalking, cycling, 4WD touring, browsing craft shops

Highlights: Pristine surfing beaches, relaxed lifestyle; Cape Byron lighthouse; views from Pat Moreton Lookout near Lennox Head; riverboat cruises, Ballina; hinterland rainforest

Tip: Visit the colourful weekend markets held alternately at Byron Bay and nearby towns (Ballina, Bangalow, Brunswick Heads, Lennox Heads, Mullumbimby, Nimbin and The Channon) for local produce, crafts and entertainment.

Kids' stuff: Macadamia Castle Animal Fun Park, Knockrow, entry fee, Ph: (02) 6687 8432; Summerland Surf School, Ballina, Lennox Head, fee, Ph: (02) 6682 4393

Further information: Ballina Visitor Information Centre, cnr River St and Las Balsas Plaza, Ballina, NSW 2478, Ph: (02) 6686 3484, www.ballina.tropicalnsw.com.au; Byron Bay Visitor Centre, 80 Jonson Street, Byron Bay, NSW 2481, Ph: (02) 6680 9271, www.byron-bay.com

Cape Byron Lighthouse

Basking in an exceptionally attractive location between sand-fringed ocean and rainforest-clad slopes, Byron Bay has grown from a quiet dairy town into a top holiday destination and a retreat favoured by artists and celebrities. It is known for its informal lifestyle and determined resistance to high-rise development (although this has not resulted in a lack of five-star luxury) as well as its quality dining and stylish boutiques.

Byron's swimming and surf beaches curve either side of **Cape Byron** (the most easterly point on the continent, dominated by a 1901 lighthouse) and include patrolled Main Beach, a short stroll from the centre of town and suitable for children, and quieter Wategos further east, which is regularly frequented by dolphins. In winter, passing humpback whales are easily spied from the cape's clifftop walking tracks; the headland is also a popular launch site for hanggliders. Tropical and temperate currents offshore result in an amazing diversity of marine life, especially around Julian Rocks, a site much visited by scuba divers and snorkellers.

Peaceful **Brunswick Heads**, at the mouth of the Brunswick River north of Byron Bay, is a fishing port that also offers excellent surfing, swimming and recreational fishing. To the south, the Point at **Lennox Head** is one of the east coast's top surfing spots; nearby, freshwater **Lake Ainsworth** is ideal for windsurfing.

Further south, a string of superb beaches leads to the riverfront fishing town of **Ballina**, which is surrounded by canefields and home to the fluoro-coloured Big Prawn tourist attraction. Also worth a visit are **Nimbin** and **Mullumbimby**, in the fertile hinterland, where traditional farming communities coexist with groups of alternative life-stylers who moved into the area in the early 1970s. Nearby, unsealed roads and walking tracks thread through rainforest to pristine waterfalls and secluded picnic spots in rugged **Nightcap NP**, on the edge of the Mt Warning caldera. Birdlife is especially prolific here.

Fishing boats, Brunswick Heads

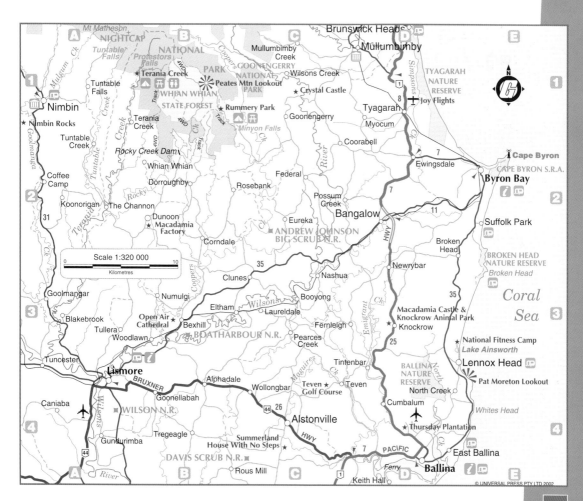

The Central Coast

Best time to visit: Summer for beach and watersports; autumn for bushwalking

Average daily temperatures: Jan 17–27°C, Apr 12–23°C, Jul 7–17°C, Oct 9–22°C

Getting there: By road from Sydney via F3 Fwy and Pacific Hwy to Gosford (80km), Wyong (95km); by rail from Sydney or Newcastle stopping at Woy Woy, Gosford, Tuggerah and Wyong (CityRail Info Line 13 1500)

Festivals and events:

Mar: Central Coast Festival of the Arts, Wyong Memorial Hall, Wyong

Jul: Terrigal Beach Food and Wine Festival

Aug: Gathering of the Clans, Toukley

Sep: Australian Springtime Flora Festival, Kariong; Central Coast Jazz Festival, Memorial Park, The Entrance

Nov: Tuggerah Lakes Mardi Gras Festival, The Entrance

Activities: Beach activities, windsurfing, sailing, canoeing, sea-kayaking, fishing, bushwalking, horseriding

Highlights: Relaxed mixture of beach and bushland; Hawkesbury Riverboat Postman ferry (departs Brooklyn wharf), Ph: (02) 9985 7566; Calga Springs Sanctuary, Calga (40ha wildlife sanctuary, walking tracks), Ph: (02) 4375 1100

Tip: Visit Captain Cook Lookout, off Del Monte Pl on First Point Headland between Copacabana and Avoca, for one of the best and most accessible views in the region.

Kids' stuff: Memorial Park at The Entrance has child-friendly fountains, a boardwalk and daily feeding of pelicans (3.30pm); Old Sydney Town, Somersby, Ph: (02) 4340 1104; Australian Reptile Park, Somersby, Ph: (02) 4340 1146

Further information: Gosford Visitor Centre, 200 Mann St, Gosford, NSW 2250, Ph: (02) 4385 4430; Lake Macquarie Visitor Centre, 72 Pacific Hwy, Swansea, NSW 2281, Ph: (02) 4972 1172; Terrigal Visitor Centre, Terrigal Dr, Terrigal, NSW 2260, Ph: (02) 4385 4430, www.cctourism.com.au; The Entrance Visitor Centre, Marine Pde, The Entrance, NSW 2261, Ph: (02) 4385 4430

Patrolled surf beaches, fish-rich coastal lakes, and the broad, island-studded Hawkesbury River—all less than 2hr drive from Sydney—make this spectacularly scenic region ideal for both summer family holidays and cosy winter weekends away. There is safe swimming in shark-free and relatively shallow **Tuggerah** and **Budgewoi** lakes. Along with larger **Lake Macquarie**, just to the north, these waterways are also popular for waterskiing, canoeing, sailing, rowing and windsurfing, as well as being favoured fishing and prawning waters. Cruises, charter boats and hire boats are available on all the lakes.

Ku-ring-gai, **Brisbane Water**, **Bouddi** and **Wyrrabalong** national parks preserve foreshores and heavily wooded ridges and ravines rich in wildflowers. Magnificent views reward those who hike to the sandstone tops and the keen-eyed may also spy some of the area's numerous Aboriginal rock engravings.

For all its wild grandeur, this region also includes the well-populated residential strip linking the major centres of Sydney and Newcastle. There is fine dining to be had in long-established and stylish oceanfront holiday villages such as **Avoca** and **Terrigal** and a wide range of accommodation is on offer.

Lake Macquarie

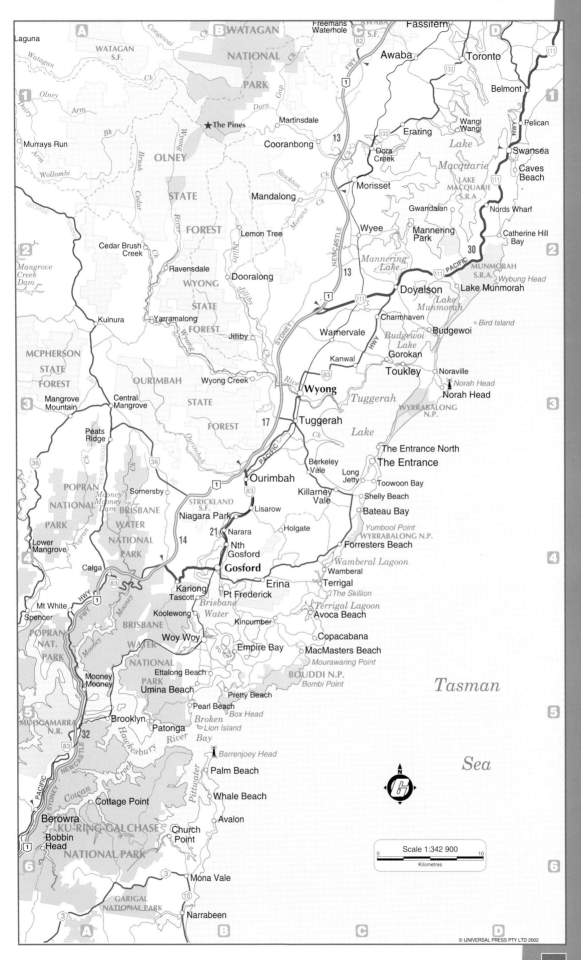

© UNIVERSAL PRESS PTY LTD 2002

The Central West

Best time to visit: Spring for blooms and seasonal produce; autumn for crisp, clear days and leaf colour in town parks

Average daily temperatures: Jan 16–31°C, Apr 11–24°C, Jul 4–16°C, Oct 10–24°C

Getting there: By road from Sydney via Great Western and Mitchell Hwys to Bathurst (200km), Orange (260km) and Dubbo (415km); via Great Western and Castlereagh Hwys to Mudgee (275km); via Dubbo and Newell Hwy to Coonabarabran (455km)

Festivals and events:

Mar: Bathurst Autumn Heritage Festival; Mudgee Show; Gulgong Show

Apr: Balloon Fiesta, Canowindra; F.O.O.D. (Food of Orange District) week; Royal Bathurst Show; Orana Easter Country Music Festival, Dubbo; International 24-Hour Kart Rally, Dubbo

May: Dubbo Annual Show

Jun: Henry Lawson Heritage Festival, Gulgong

Jul: Mudgee Small Farm Field Days

Sep: Mudgee Wine Celebration

Oct: Bathurst 1000, V8 Supercars; Orange Winefest; Australian National Field Days, Orange

Dec: Huntington Music Festival, Mudgee; Gulgong Folk Festival

Activities: Fishing, horseriding, bushwalking, cycling, canoeing, fossicking for gold, browsing antique shops, stargazing, 4WD touring, golf, scenic flights

Highlights: Mudgee wineries; historic Gulgong; Warrumbungle NP

Tip: Kangaroos are frequently encountered on rural roads at night, so keep your speed down when travelling after after dusk.

Kids' stuff: Gold panning, Hill End; Western Plains Zoo, Dubbo; Dubbo City Tourist Park (supermaze, mini-golf, military museum), entry fee, Ph: (02) 6884 5550; Siding Spring Observatory

Further information: Bathurst Visitors Centre, 28 William St, Bathurst, NSW 2795, Ph: (02) 6332 1444; Dubbo Visitors Centre, cnr Newell Hwy and Macquarie St, Dubbo, NSW 2830, Ph: (02) 6884 1422; Gulgong Visitor Information Centre, 109 Herbert St, Gulgong, NSW 2852, Ph: (02) 6374 1202; Mudgee Visitor Information Centre, 84 Market St, Mudgee, NSW 2850, Ph: (02) 6372 1020 or 1800 816 304; Orange Visitors Centre, Byng St, Orange, NSW 2800, Ph: (02) 6393 8226, www.orange.nsw.gov.au

The wide lands of the Central West hold a diversity of attractions—the stately city of Bathurst, goldrush ghost towns hidden in wild hills, the Orange and Mudgee food and wine country, trout-filled waterways, Dubbo's superb open-range zoo, and the dramatic volcanic spires of the Warrumbungles. A significant amount of driving between these attractions is required, mostly through open country interspersed with great islands of natural bush; kangaroos, wallabies and birdlife, especially galahs and cockatoos, are frequently seen. Peaceful byways invite exploration, picturesque picnic spots abound, and night skies dazzle with stars. A wide range of accommodation is on offer, including heritage guesthouses, farmstays, B&Bs, hotel-motels and self-catering bushland cottages.

Siding Spring Observatory, near Coonabarabran

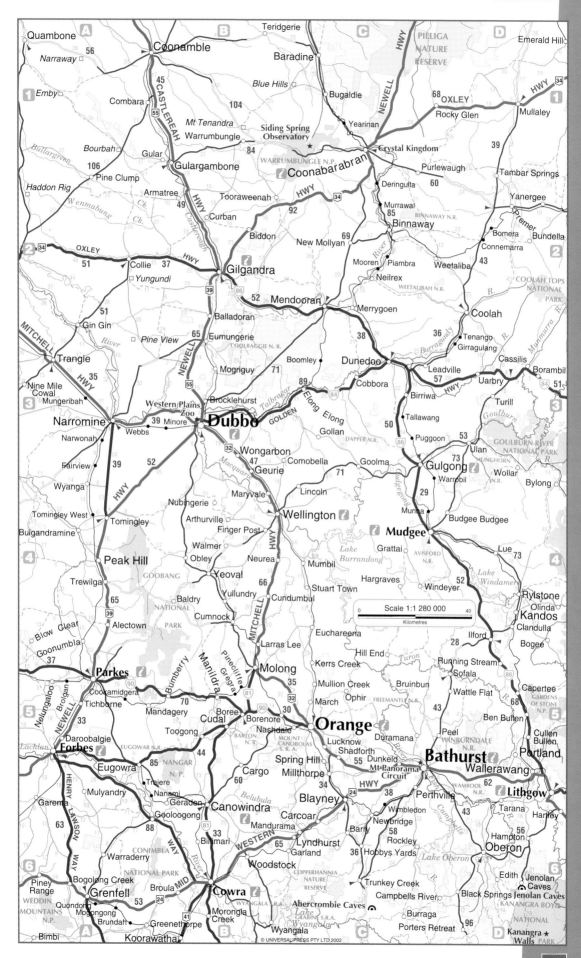

Goldrush Towns

Fast-growing **Bathurst**, with its elegant heritage architecture, dates from 1815 when it became the first European settlement west of the Blue Mountains. Maps of walking and driving tours of historical points of interest, including the imposing copper-domed 1880s courthouse and the home of Ben Chifley (the local engine driver who became prime minister), are available from the Bathurst Visitors Centre. Car-racing enthusiasts can drive Bathurst's famous **Mt Panorama Circuit** (originally constructed as a scenic drive) but must observe the comparatively sedate speed limit of 60kph.

Bathurst Courthouse

In April, the skies above **Canowindra** fill with colourful and fancifully shaped hot-air balloons as Australia's largest ballooning spectacular gets underway. This attractive town, with its well-preserved main street, is also the location of a major fossil site where thousands of fish perished when a lake dried up 360 million years ago. A slab of rock bearing their massed fossilised remains is on display at the Age of Fishes Museum; entry fee, Ph: (02) 6344 1008.

The 1851 discovery of gold at **Ophir**, near **Orange**, sparked a series of momentous goldrushes. From the 1850s to the 1870s, thousands of prospectors turned the rugged river gorges between Bathurst and Mudgee into a string of teeming tent towns. Today the almost deserted villages of **Sofala** and **Hill End** provide a tantalising glimpse of those frenzied years, and panning the creeks of the region for gold remains a popular pastime among both locals and tourists. Sofala's population peaked at more than 30 000 in the early 1850s, but by 1854 the rush had moved on. The historic 2-storey timber buildings lining the town's narrow main street have provided subject matter for artists including Russell Drysdale, Donald Friend and Brett Whiteley.

The discovery of a fabulously rich concentration of gold at Hill End sparked a second major rush in the 1870s, and for a short period the town was Australia's largest inland settlement. Many of the original buildings remain and the entire village is now preserved as a historic site. Car-based and caravan camping are available here (fees apply).

Old slab hut, Hill End

Bushwalkers on Crater Bluff, Warrumbungle NP

Wineries and Wilderness

The **Mudgee** district is home to approximately 25 wineries, all within an easy 10–30min drive of the town centre; at many, visitors are invited to cellar-door wine-tastings. The area is also famous for its flavoursome honeys and is becoming known for boutique food industries such as hazelnut, fruit and olive growing and rabbit farming. Settlement in the hill-encircled valley dates from the late 1830s. The town's grid was laid out by surveyor Robert Hoddle, who later designed Melbourne. Market St in particular has retained much of its elegant 19th-century architecture.

In contrast, **Gulgong's** narrow, twisting streets date from goldrush days (which peaked here in 1872) and follow tracks picked out between miners' huts. An illustration of the atmospheric main street, together with a portrait of Gulgong's most famous son, the poet Henry Lawson, graced Australia's first $10 bill.

Further west lies **Dubbo** and its top attraction, the **Western Plains Zoo**; entry fee, Ph: (02) 6882 5888. Here, visitors can drive, walk or cycle through natural bushland that is home to more than 1000 animals from 5 continental zones. The animals roam in tracts of land that are separated from other species— including humans—by concealed moats and ditches rather than visible fences.

The zoo also offers on-site accommodation packages at the Zoofari Lodge, where guests can participate in guided after-dark tours; Ph: 1300 720 018.

Viewed from the south, the jagged profile of the Warrumbungle Range rises abruptly from the inland plains and can be seen from more than 50km away. Now protected by **Warrumbungle NP**, it was a multivented volcano 13 million years ago and its present-day peaks and spires are the weathered remnants of solidified lava. Walking tracks lead to several vantage points with spectacular views. The 14.5km Grand High Tops walk takes in landmarks such as the Breadknife and Belougery Spire and is rated as one of Australia's finest scenic tracks; 2 short loops—the White Gum Lookout and Guianawa walks—are suitable for wheelchairs. The park lies 35km west of Coonabarabran. It has 10 camping areas, 5 of which are accessible by car; entry fee, Ph: (02) 6825 4364 for campsite bookings and general information.

The futuristic domes that gleam on the ridge near the park's eastern edge are part of **Siding Spring Observatory**. Here an international team of astrophysicists delves deep into the heavens using 9 optical telescopes, including the giant Anglo-Australian Telescope, which visitors can view from a gallery on the main observing floor. There is also a permanent interactive display, 'Exploring the Universe'; entry fee, Ph: (02) 6842 6211.

The Coffs Coast

Best time to visit: Summer for beachlife and whitewater rafting; winter for whalewatching
Average daily temperatures: Jan 19–27°C, Apr 15–24°C, Jul 7–19°C, Oct 14–23°C
Getting there: By rail from Brisbane and Sydney (Countrylink); 560km north of Sydney and 430km south of Brisbane by road via Pacific Hwy; by air to Coffs Harbour
Festivals and events:
Apr: Easter Fishing Classic, Coffs Harbour
May: Coffs Harbour Show
Aug: Bellingen Jazz Festival
Oct: Spring Festival, Dorrigo; Coffs Harbour Food and Wine Festival
Nov: Agricultural Shows, Dorrigo and Bellingen; Craft Carnival, Woolgoolga
Activities: Surfing, sea-kayaking, diving, whitewater rafting, fishing, whalewatching, bushwalking, browsing craft shops
Highlights: Skywalk lookout, Dorrigo Rainforest Centre, Dorrigo NP; view from Muttonbird Island, reached by breakwater from Coffs Harbour Marina; whalewatching Jun–Nov
Tip: Fresh, locally grown fruit and vegetables (avocados and bananas) are sold from roadside stalls and at weekend markets.
Kids' stuff: Big Banana, Coffs Harbour, fees for rides and tours, Ph: (02) 6652 4355
Further information: Coffs Coast Visitor Information Centre, cnr Pacific Hwy and Rose Ave, Coffs Harbour, NSW 2450, Ph: (02) 6652 1522, www.coffstourism.com; Bellingen Visitor Information Centre, Pacific Hwy, Urunga, NSW 2454, Ph: (02) 6655 5711, www.bellingen.com

This scenic coastal strip offers the appealing combination of pristine beaches and wild ranges cloaked with World Heritage-listed rainforest. In addition, its subtropical climate—sunny but not too humid—is claimed to be the best in Australia. A full range of accommodation and dining choices is available.

Coffs Harbour is a major centre for adventure sports, including whitewater rafting, abseiling, surfing, game-fishing, canoeing, hiking and hot-air ballooning. **Solitary Islands Marine Park**, which extends for 75km north from Coffs Harbour, is a meeting point for tropical and temperate currents, resulting in an extraordinary diversity of marine life. Among the activities on offer here are charter cruises (including whalewatching in season), sea-kayaking, and scuba diving in the clear waters.

The largest of the seaside towns north of Coffs Harbour is peaceful **Woolgoolga**. Its white-domed temple dates from 1970 and serves a sizable Indian population, descendants of Punjabi Sikhs who worked in the Queensland canefields in the 19th century. Just south of Coffs, **Sawtell's** figtree-shaded main street is known for its stylish sidewalk cafes; surf beaches and headland lookouts are nearby. **Urunga**, a fishing hotspot at the mouth of the Bellinger River, is linked by a delightful walkway over a lagoon to Hungry Head ocean beach.

In the lush hinterland, century-old commercial buildings give character to **Bellingen's** main street; the Old Butter Factory on the edge of town is an outlet for the works of local artists and craftspeople. The road inland to **Dorrigo** climbs through towering forest and past waterfalls. The Rainforest Centre Skywalk, on the edge of Dorrigo NP, juts out high above the tree canopy, providing stupendous views across the valley and ranges; Ph: (02) 6657 2309.

Pleasure-craft at Coffs Harbour marina

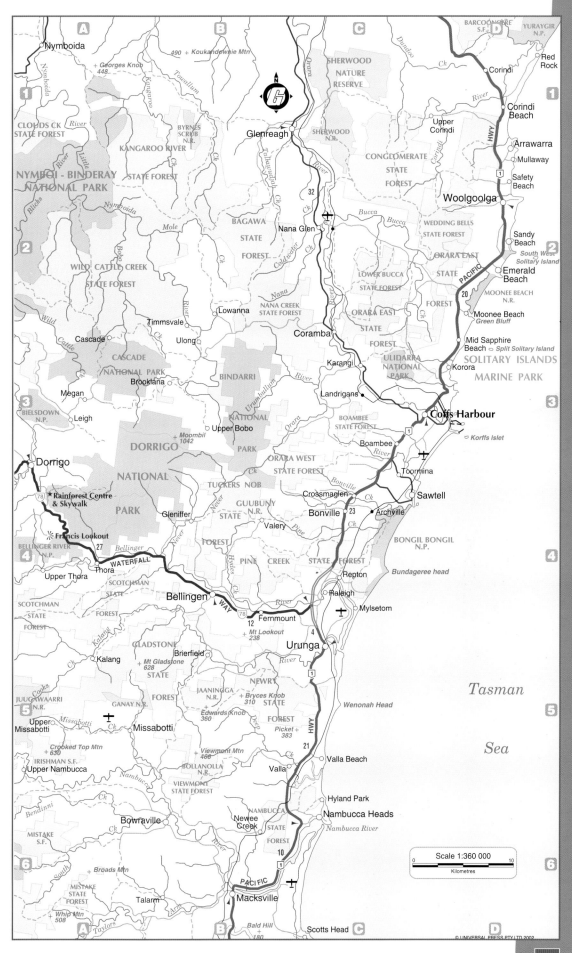

The Hunter Valley

The Lower Hunter, centred on the settlements of **Pokolbin**, **Lovedale** and **Rothbury**, is the heart of the famous Hunter Valley wine-growing district and home to some of the country's best-known wineries. It is a district that tempts indulgence. Rural and scenic, with picturesque rows of vines running to the foothills of the sheltering Brokenback Range, it has an extensive choice of eateries (many located at wineries), ranging from top-class restaurants to relaxed cafes, all serving high-quality local fare. Also scattered among the vineyards are numerous picnic and BBQ spots and children's playgrounds. A full range of accommodation is on offer and the district is also close enough to Sydney (90min by road) for daytrips.

Winemakers welcome visitors to sample their wares and are on hand to explain the wine-making process and discuss the finer points of their own products. Several wineries—including Rothbury Estate, Ph: (02) 4998 7363; McWilliams Mt Pleasant Estate, Ph: (02) 4998 7505; and Tyrrells, Ph: (02) 4993 7000—offer organised tours of their property. Wine-growing in the Lower Hunter dates from the 1860s, but it was not until the late 1960s, with the closure of local coal mines, that the wine industry began to boom. Today the region is renowned particularly for its semillon, chardonnay and shiraz varieties.

Cessnock, the regional centre, carries the name of a Scottish castle and developed from an 1850s crossroads inn catering to teamsters. Coalmining peaked here in the first half of the 20th century, with a string of mines named after coalmining districts of Wales and northern England, such as East Greta, Stanford Merthyr, Pelaw Main, Abermain, Aberdare and Hebburn.

Two often-overlooked local memorials commemorate nationally important incidents. The Rothbury Riot Memorial in North Rothbury records a 1929 protest, during which a striking miner was shot dead by troopers as a angry crowd charged locked mine gates. A memorial in Bellbird honours the 20 miners lost along with their horses in the 1923 Bellbird Colliery disaster. Today, coalmining continues around Cessnock, albeit unobtrusively.

Tyrrells winemaker sampling wares

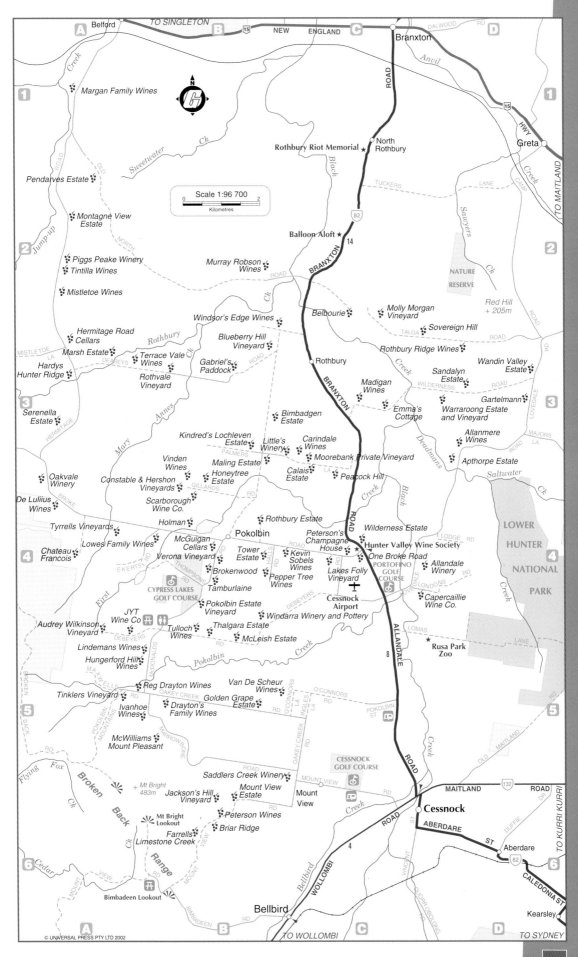

Scale 1:96 700

0 2
Kilometres

© UNIVERSAL PRESS PTY LTD 2002

Illawarra and the Southern Highlands

Kiama Blowhole

This diverse region encompasses the beaches, lakes and simple pleasures of the Illawarra coast and the mountainous wilderness, handsome country towns, leafy parks and formal gardens of the Southern Highlands. The wide variety of accommodation on offer includes secluded B&Bs, beach cottages, elegant guesthouses and stately hotels.

Stanwell Park, on the scenic coast road, is a favoured hang-gliding spot. To the south, a string of fashionably refurbished former mining villages perches on the cliff edge and offers sweeping views; to the west are the dramatically steep uplands of the Illawarra escarpment. **Wollongong**, the regional centre, is flanked by fine surf beaches and offers a wide range of accommodation. **Kiama** began life as a port for shipping cedar logs; the area's once heavily wooded foothills are now undulating dairy pasture. Caution should be exercised when visiting the town's famous blowhole; here, during a south-easterly swell, surging waves can spout up to 60m into the air. Inland, at **Minamurra Rainforest** in

Budderoo NP, an elevated timber board-walk suitable for wheelchairs meanders through rare remnant rainforest; entry fee, Ph: (02) 4236 0469.

Bowral, in the heart of the Southern Highlands, was the childhood home of legendary cricketer Sir Don Bradman; the Bradman Museum, adjacent to the picturesque Bradman Oval, houses a fascinating collection of cricketing mem-orabilia; entry fee, Ph: (02) 4862 1247. In spring, the town's Corbett Park is bright with multicoloured massed tulips.

Historic **Berrima** is dominated by its sandstone gaol and courthouse (the location of Australia's first trial by jury, and now a museum), both built in 1830, and the Surveyor-General Inn, built in 1835 and the longest continuously lic-ensed premises in the country.

Formerly a summer and weekend retreat for Sydney's wealthy, genteel **Moss Vale** is a horse and cattle stud centre. **Robertson** is known for its excep-tional potatoes and as the setting for the film *Babe*. The Fitzroy Falls Visitor Centre, Ph: (02) 4887 7270, on the edge

of wild **Morton NP**, is the starting point for easy walking tracks to **Fitzroy Falls**, where Yarrunga Creek drops 80m over the escarpment. The town of **Kangaroo Valley**, in the fertile valley of the same name, is the site of medieval-style Hampden Bridge, the country's oldest surviving suspension bridge.

Bradman Museum, Bowral

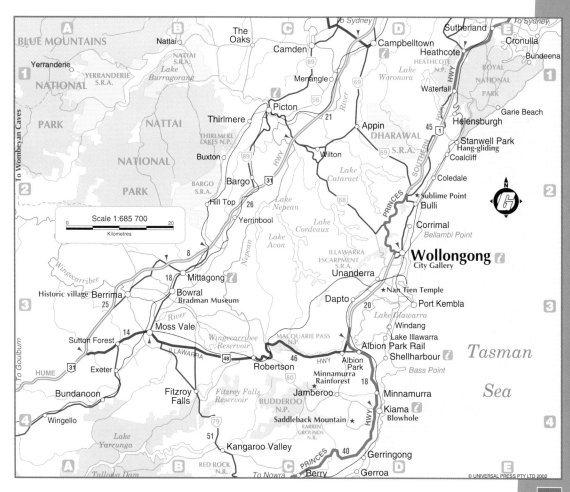

Kempsey and the Macleay Valley

Best time to visit: Summer for beachlife; winter for whalewatching

Average daily temperatures: Jan 18–27°C, Apr 14–24°C, Jul 6–19°C, Oct 12–23°C

Getting there: By road via Pacific Hwy from Sydney (430km) and Brisbane (540km); by rail from Brisbane and Sydney (Countrylink)

Festivals and events:

Jan: Great Australian Raft Race, Nambucca Heads; Australia Day Carnival, Nambucca Heads

Feb: Coastline Trial Bay Triathlon, South West Rocks

Apr: Kempsey Agricultural Show

May: South West Rocks Fishing Classic; 'Pub with No Beer' Annual Trek, Macksville; Malibu Surfing Classic, Crescent Head

Jun: Crescent Head Sky Show (kites, fireworks)

Jul: Kempsey Powerhouse Offroad Race

Sept: All Star Country Music Festival, Kempsey; Spring Flower Show, Kempsey; River Festival, Kempsey

Oct: Kempsey Truck Show; Australasian Bullriding Titles, Kempsey

Activities: Surfing, windsurfing, diving, fishing, boating, cycling, bushwalking, 4WD touring

Highlights: Top surfing spots of Crescent Head, Grassy Head and Scotts Head; Trial Bay Gaol

Tip: Drop into the Glen Murcutt-designed Kempsey Visitor Information Centre for leaflets on the area's many scenic walks and drives.

Kids' stuff: Tidal creeks at Crescent Head and Hat Head offer safe swimming

Further information: Kempsey Visitor Information Centre, South Kempsey Park, NSW 2440, Ph: 1800 642 480 or (02) 6563 1555, www.Kempsey.midcoast.com.au; Nambucca Valley Information Centre, 4 Pacific Hwy, Nambucca, NSW 2448, Ph: (02) 6568 6954; South West Rocks Visitor Information Centre, 1 Ocean Dr, South West Rocks, NSW 2431, Ph: (02) 6566 7099

With much of it protected in a patchwork of national parks and reserves, this unspoilt region has been aptly dubbed 'Nature's Retreat' and is especially appealing to holidaymakers looking for the natural attractions of surf, sand, spectacular scenery and peaceful bushland.

Sailboats at Arakoon State Recreation Area, South West Rocks

Here, the coastline has been spared major developments and its family-friendly beaches, dramatic headlands and fine fishing spots are reached on quiet back roads. Inland, rivers tumble down from the ranges and wind east through farmland. Although many activities are focused on the coast, the wooded slopes and picturesque villages of the hinterland also invite exploration. There is a wide selection of accommodation, ranging from luxury bushland retreats to waterfront camping areas, while dining choices include riverside restaurants specialising in local seafood and country cafes famous for generous servings.

Situated on the Macleay River and once a port for shipping cedar, **Kempsey** is now known as the home of the Akubra hat; the factory is not open to the public, but its products are on sale in local clothing stores. There are several good forest drives and 4WD routes around the town, and the level and scenic riverside roads make fine cycling routes.

Crescent Head ocean beach is popular with both board and body surfers; nearby, the clear waters and sheltered sandy mouth of Killick Creek offer safe swimming for children. **Limeburners Creek Nature Reserve**, to the south, is a wonderland of sparkling waters and pristine beaches backed by banksia forest and heathland that are home to kangaroos, echidnas and a myriad of small birds. Point Plomer, within the park, has facilities for car-based and caravan camping; Ph: (02) 6583 8805. Stretching north, the coast-hugging expanse of **Hat Head NP** contains uncrowded beaches, 2 camping areas and favoured fishing spots. The 360° views from the high bluff of Hat Head sweep inland to densely wooded slopes and north and south along shining seashore, with sightings of passing humpback whales a regular bonus for winter visitors.

South West Rocks, located at the mouth of the Macleay River and surrounded by a cluster of beaches, is the region's main sea-side resort; popular activities here include surfing, snorkelling, sailing, windsurfing, fishing, and scuba diving at Fish Rock Cave (renowned for its sponge gardens and variety of marine creatures). Visitors can also join river cruises or fishing charters. **Trial Bay Gaol**, sited spectacularly on a headland overlooking the crystal-clear waters of the bay, does not

date from convict days, as many suppose, but from the 1880s. It was abandoned in 1903, but during WWI it became an internment camp for German prisoners; entry fee, Ph: (02) 6566 6168.

Nambucca Heads is known for its extensive beaches and good fishing. In recent years, its 500m-long seawall has been transformed into a colourful 'graffiti' rock-art gallery; visitors are encouraged to add their own contributions.

The Pub with No Beer

The subject of the famous song is still open for business in Taylors Arm, an isolated hamlet about an hour's drive up the Nambucca Valley from Kempsey. Built in 1903 and formerly called the Cosmopolitan, the hotel has adopted the name of 'The Pub with No Beer' despite now having a reliable supply on tap. Things were different in 1950, however, when Taylors Arm, the sole watering hole for local timbercutters, was cut off by floods and ran out of beer for a few days. These events and the song they inspired are celebrated each May in the 'Pub with No Beer' Annual Trek, a 26km ('20 flaming miles') walk, run or horseride from Macksville. Ph: (02) 6564 2100.

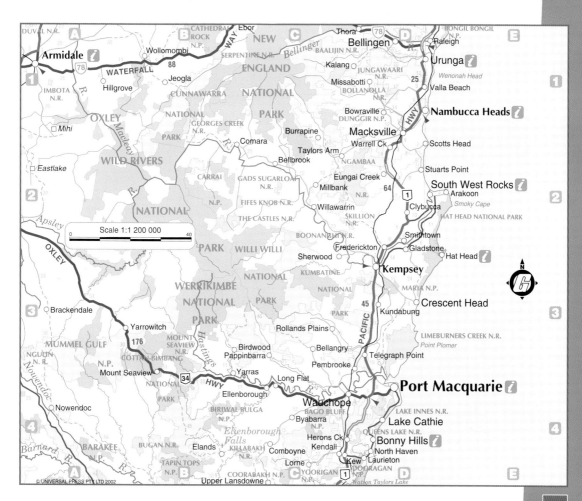

New England

Best time to visit: Spring for jacaranda display in Grafton, waratahs in Gibraltar Range NP; spring and summer for whitewater rafting on the Gwydir River; summer for country music in Tamworth; autumn for leaf colour; winter in the highlands can be very cold

Average daily temperatures: Jan 13–27°C, Apr 8–21°C, Jul 0–12°C; Oct 7–21°C

Getting there: By road from Sydney via F3 Fwy and New England Hwy to Tamworth (415km), Armidale (525km) and Glen Innes (625km). Tamworth, Armidale and Glen Innes are also linked by daily Countrylink rail services from Sydney.

Festivals and events:

Jan: Australasian Country Music Festival, Tamworth

Mar: Armidale Show and Autumn Festival

May: Australasian Celtic Festival, Glen Innes

Oct: Sapphire City Flora Festival, Inverell; Horsefest, Tamworth

Nov: St Peters Spring Gardens, Armidale

Activities: Bushwalking, 4WD touring, birdwatching, horseriding, dam and river fishing, fly-fishing, sailing, water-skiing, powerboating, canoeing, whitewater rafting, gem fossicking, river cruises

Highlights: Jacaranda display in Grafton; Country Music Festival, Tamworth; autumn colour in Armidale; whitewater rafting, Wildwater Adventures, Ph: (02) 6653 3500; wilderness parks

Tip: Drive the Gwydir Hwy between Grafton and Glen Innes; it passes through World Heritage-listed Gibraltar Range NP and leads to picnic areas, walking tracks, and roadside lookouts offering panoramic views over granite outcrops and rugged, rainforest-covered slopes.

Kids' stuff: Gem fossicking; Inverell Pioneer Village

Further information: Armidale Visitor Information Centre, 82 Marsh St, Armidale, NSW 2350, Ph: 1800 627 736; Inverell Tourist Information Centre, Water Tower Complex, Campbell St, Inverell, NSW 2360, Ph: (02) 6728 8161; Tamworth Visitors' Information Centre, cnr Peel and Murray Sts, Tamworth, NSW 2340, Ph: (02) 6755 4300, www.tamworth.nsw.gov.au

Known as 'Big Sky Country' for its expansive highlands and far horizons, this region offers both tranquil rural escapes and ecotourist adventures in World Heritage-listed wilderness parks. From Oct–Mar, water released from the mighty Copeton Dam into the Gwydir River (to supply downstream cotton crops) provides excellent whitewater-rafting opportunities. The dam, which is more than twice the size of Sydney Harbour, is popular for fishing (licence required) and watersports. The regional art galleries in Armidale, Grafton and Tamworth hold fine collections of Australian and European paintings. Gems, particularly sapphires, attract fossickers. Fine restaurants and superior cafes offer specialist local produce, including grain-fed lamb, smoked trout and fresh berries. As well as a range of hotels and motels, accommodation options include farmstays on working properties (where guests get an insider's view of life on the land), heritage guesthouses in handsome country towns, and comfortable B&Bs.

Whitewater rafting on the Gwydir River

'Booloomindah', University of New England campus, Armidale

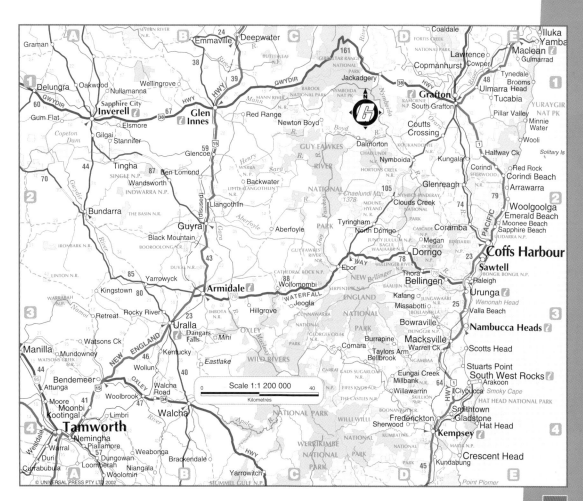

Tableland Towns

In Jan, **Tamworth** is host to the annual Country Music Festival, when the streets and shopping malls fill with buskers and line-dancers and the pubs and performance spaces are packed with singers and fans. The climax of the 2-week festival is the Golden Guitar Awards for country music artists and songwriters. On the city's southern outskirts, a 12m-high replica of the award stands at the entrance to the Golden Guitar and Gallery of Stars Wax Museum, Ph: (02) 6765 2688. Even the town's Visitors' Information Centre is guitar-shaped.

The university city of **Armidale**, the regional centre, is graced by elegant cathedrals, stately homes and other historic buildings. The influence of pioneer Scottish settlers remains strong in **Glen Innes**, where the Australian Standing Stones (a circle of granite megaliths) pay homage to the nation's Celtic settlers. The history, art, crafts and cuisine of the district's indigenous Ngoorabul people are highlighted at Glen Innes' Cooramah Aboriginal Cultural Centre.

At **Inverell**, heart of Australia's blue sapphire industry, you can buy direct from gem merchants and also try your luck in designated fossicking areas. Inverell Pioneer Village is a collection of more than 20 restored heritage buildings (including a school, church, hotel, blacksmith's shop, hall and homestead) that

Golden Guitar replica, Tamworth

were relocated here from the surrounding district; entry fee, Ph: (02) 6722 1717.

The former river port of **Grafton** lies within easy driving distance of both the pristine beaches of the coast and the upland wilderness parks. The town spreads along the banks of the mighty Clarence River and is famed for the colourful springtime displays of its thousands of well-established jacaranda trees. Also of note are its many elegant heritage buildings. Watersports—especially sailing, powerboating and water-skiing—are popular here.

Jacarandas in bloom, Grafton

Point Lookout, New England NP

New England's Wild Places

On the high New England tablelands, a chain of national parks protects precious and diverse habitats that are very different from those of the coast and the wide western plains. Within the parks lie some of the region's most spectacular features, including plummeting waterfalls such as Wollomombi, Apsley and Dangars, all of which are easily accessed via short walking tracks in Oxley Wild Rivers NP.

Three parks—Gibraltar Range, Oxley Wild Rivers and New England—form part of the sprawling Central Eastern Rainforests of Australia World Heritage Area. All the parks except Nymboida have facilities for both day visitors and campers. Unlike many parts of Australia, the high tablelands enjoy 4 distinct seasons; summers are cool and winter can bring occasional snowfalls.

Cathedral Rock NP is known for its sculpture-like formations of stacked granite boulders. Frequently sighted wildlife includes wedge-tailed eagles, grey kangaroos and cockatoos. The park is 65km east of Armidale off the Waterfall Way (Hwy 78); Ph: (02) 6657 2309.

Gibraltar Range NP is an immense wilderness of deep gorges, towering granite outcrops and lush temperate rainforest. Bushwalks, ranging from short strolls to a 5-day, 100km wilderness trek, lead through woodland, heathland and rainforest, and past creeks and waterfalls. Waratahs bloom in profusion between Oct and Nov. The park lies 80km east of Glen Innes and 100km west of Grafton and is easily accessed via the Gwydir Hwy; Ph: (02) 6732 5133.

Guy Fawkes River NP's dramatic wilderness attracts serious bushwalkers keen to attempt long, intensive hikes into its wild and remote interior. Day visitors can picnic beside 2-tier **Ebor Falls**, in a southern strip of the park 80km east of Armidale off the Waterfall Way (Hwy 78). This is trout-fishing country, though you need to obtain a licence before casting a line. At the L.P. Dutton Trout Hatchery, Ebor, you can hand-feed trout and tour the aquarium housing endangered freshwater fish; entry fee, Ph: (02) 6775 9139. The more remote north end of the park can be accessed via the Chaelundi Rd, which runs from the old Glen Innes–Grafton Rd. Ph: (02) 6657 2309 (Dorrigo) or (02) 6732 5133 (Glen Innes).

New England NP offers panoramic wilderness views, magnificent scenery and a range of walks. **Point Lookout**, on the edge of the escarpment, combines a delightful picnic spot with sweeping vistas; on a clear day you can see the ocean. The park is 85km east of Armidale off the Waterfall Way (Hwy 78).

Nymboida NP is famed for its challenging whitewater rafting. There are no marked walking tracks and no visitor facilities; access is by 4WD or canoe, or on foot. The park lies 45km west of Grafton on the Gwydir Hwy.

Oxley Wild Rivers NP protects extensive dry rainforest, deep gorges, dramatic waterfalls, wild rivers and abundant wildlife. At Wollomombi Gorge there are picnic facilities and an easy walk from the lookout over the falls; the gorge is easily accessed from the Waterfall Way (Hwy 78), 40km east of Armidale. The park can also be reached via the Oxley Hwy, 65km SE of Armidale.

Port Macquarie and the Manning Valley

Best time to visit: Summer for beach activities; winter for whalewatching; early spring for wildflowers

Average daily temperatures: Jan 18–27°C, Apr 14–24°C, Jul 6–19°C, Oct 14–23°C

Getting there: By road from Sydney via Pacific Hwy to Taree (320km), Port Macquarie (410km); by rail from Sydney

Festivals and events:

Jan: Manning River Sailing Marathon

Mar: Wingham Show; Camden Haven Music Festival

Mar–Apr: Wauchope Easter Show

Apr: Taree Aquatic Festival

Jun: Taree City Festival

Jul: Manning River Orchid Society Winter Show

Sep: Wingham Spring Fair; Nabiac Food and Wine Festival

Oct: Port Macquarie Food and Wine Festival; Cassegrain Discovery Concert; Taree Show; Oyster Festival, Forster-Tuncurry

Nov: Wingham Rodeo; Four Points Sheraton Golden Lure Fishing Tournament, Blue Water Aquatic Festival, Fighters over Port Airshow, all Port Macquarie

Activities: Surfing, windsurfing, sailing, sea-kayaking, fishing (beach and river), canoe safaris, diving, yachting, parasailing, hang-gliding, cycling, bushwalking, 4WD touring, browsing craft shops and galleries, wine-tasting, golf

Highlights: Pristine surf beaches; superb fishing; excellent oysters; river cruises (with dolphin sightings); urban koala population; Sea Acres Rainforest Centre, with boardwalk, Port Macquarie, Ph: (02) 6582 3355; view from North Brother Lookout, near Laurieton; and for 'Big' fans, the Big Oyster outside Taree and the Big Bull at Wauchope

Tip: Cattle may be encountered meandering along hinterland back roads.

Kids' stuff: Peppermint Park fun centre, Port Macquarie, Ph: (02) 6583 6111; feeding time at the Koala Hospital, Port Macquarie (8.00am, 3.00pm), Ph: (02) 6584 1522; lagoon at Saltwater, near Taree, ideal for toddlers; swimming in Lake Cathie

Further information: Port Macquarie Visitor Information Centre, cnr Clarence and Hay Sts, Port Macquarie, NSW 2444, Ph: (02) 6581 8000 or 1300 303 155, www.portmacquarieinfo.com.au; Manning Valley Visitor Information Centre, Manning River Drive, Taree North, NSW 2430, Ph: (02) 6552 1900 or 1800 801 522, www.retreat-to-nature.com

This peaceful holiday region is dominated by water—long ocean shores, wide lazy rivers, tranquil lakes, spectacular cascades and bubbling mountain streams. Its friendly seaside towns promise relaxed days of sun, sand and surf, and its inland waterways—the Hastings and Manning rivers, and a string of coastal lakes—offer boating, fishing and swimming. Accommodation includes resorts, caravan parks, B&Bs, holiday homes and country retreats.

Inland, tracks in **Coorabakh NP** lead through rainforest wilderness to lookouts providing dramatic views over volcanic formations and the Manning Valley.

Port Macquarie, at the Hastings River entrance, is the regional centre and a bustling holiday destination with great beaches and fishing, historic buildings, scenic coastal walks and a variety of children's amusement parks. The road west passes several wineries on the way to **Wauchope**, where you can visit Timbertown Heritage Theme Park, a working replica of an 1880s timber town; fee for rides, Ph: (02) 6585 2322.

Charming **Wingham**, where heritage buildings surround a central village green, is an excellent base for river and wilderness activities; nearby Wingham Brush protects tropical-floodplain rainforest with massive Moreton Bay fig trees. **Tinonee**, near **Taree**, is a local arts and crafts centre, with a number of galleries and craft shops. The twin towns of **Forster** and **Tuncurry**, on the edge of Wallis Lake, are a combination of holiday resort and commercial fishing port.

Tourist train at Timbertown, Wauchope

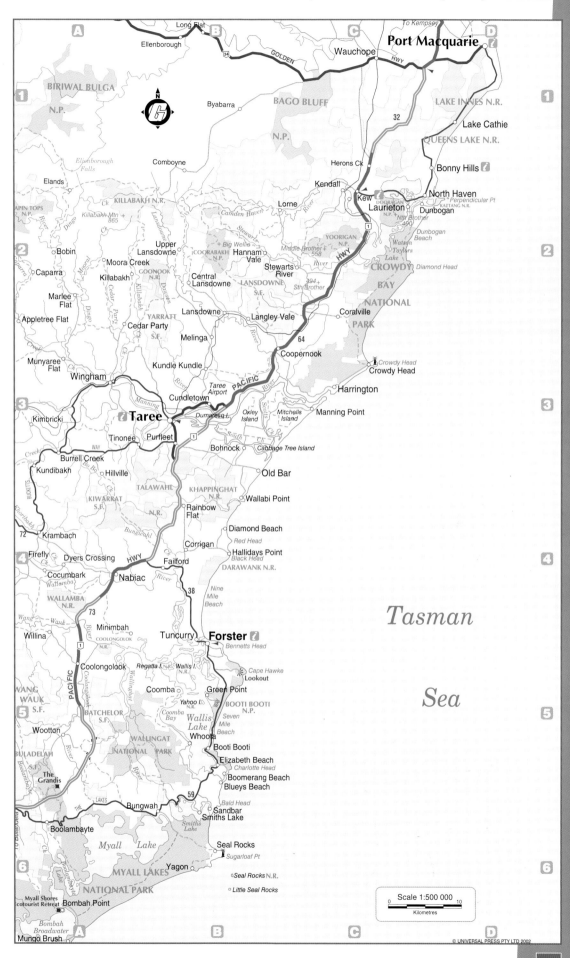

Port Stephens and the Myall Lakes

Best time to visit: Summer for busy beach buzz; winter for whalewatching

Average daily temperatures: Jan 17–27°C, Apr 16–23°C, Jul 8–16°C, Oct 12–20°C

Getting there: By road from Sydney via F3 Fwy and Pacific Hwy to Nelson Bay (225km)

Festivals and events:

Jan: Blessing of the Fleet, Nelson Bay

Feb–Mar: Game fishing competition, Port Stephens

Apr: Port Stephens Outrigger Regatta

Oct: Bass Bash fishing festival, Bulahdelah

Nov: Bulahdelah Show and Rodeo

Activities: Watersports, houseboating, fishing, whalewatching, bushwalking, 4WD touring

Highlights: Dolphin-watching cruises; houseboats on the Myall Lakes; coastal dunes; koalas; local oysters

Tip: Houseboats are slow and steady; you'll need at least a week to reach and enjoy the tranquil coves of the upper lakes.

Kids' stuff: Sliding down the sand dunes at the southern end of Hawks Nest Beach; Toboggan Hill Park, Nelson Bay, featuring toboggan run, minigolf, maze; entry fee, Ph: (02) 4984 1022

Further information: Bulahdelah Visitor Information Centre, cnr Crawford St and Pacific Hwy, Bulahdelah, NSW 2423, Ph: 02 4997 4981, www.greatlakes.org.au; Port Stephens Visitor Information Centre, Victoria Pde, Nelson Bay, NSW 2315, Ph: 1800 808 900 or 02 4981 1579, www.portstephens.org.au; Tea Gardens Visitor Information Centre, Myall Street, Tea Gardens, NSW 2324, Ph: 02 4997 0111

Surf beaches, national parks, coastal lakes and ease of access from Sydney make this region quietly popular year-round. More than twice the size of Sydney Harbour, the sparkling waterways of **Port Stephens** are edged by bushland, sandy bays and a scatter of former fishing villages where quaint weekenders are gradually giving way to holiday resorts and smart residential developments. More than 160 bottlenose dolphins live permanently in these waters, providing a daily spectacle as they ride the bow waves of cruise launches. To the north, a string of lakes—**Myall**, **Smiths** and Wallis—stretches all the way to Forster. Known as the Great Lakes, and separated from the ocean by a narrow band of sand dunes and scrublands, they are the largest natural fresh-brackish water

system on the New South Wales coast and are popular for both boating and camping. From May–Nov, migrating whales can be spotted off the coast, most notably from vantage points on Tomaree Heads, at the southern entrance to Port Stephens, and from **Sugarloaf Point**, at **Seal Rocks**. The region offers an extensive range of accommodation.

Sheltered by the bulk of the Tomaree Peninsula, **Nelson Bay** is home to a fishing fleet and marina, and is the largest town on Port Stephens. It is the departure point for dolphin-watching, whale-watching (in season) and deep-sea cruises, game-fishing charters, dive boats and the thrice-daily ferry to Tea Gardens (bookings can be made through the visitor centre). Houseboats, catamarans, runabouts, kayaks and powerboats, as

Yachts on Port Stephens seen from Nelson Head, Nelson Bay

well as equipment for parasailing, jet-skiing and water-skiing can also be hired here. Facilities at the 160-berth marina include restaurants and shops. In summer, the sandy waterfront is crowded with sunbathers and swimmers; in winter, walkers take to foreshore trails.

Riverfront **Tea Gardens** and surfside **Hawks Nest** are linked by the 'Singing Bridge', named for the whistling sound produced by its railings in a strong south-westerly wind. Koalas can often be seen in the reserve fronting Kingfisher Ave on the Hawks Nest side of the Myall River, while dolphins frequently catch waves with body surfers or weave beside vessels heading downriver to Port Stephens. The attractive surf beach at Hawks Nest is patrolled in summer. Dolphin-watch cruises and fine river and estuary fishing can be arranged locally. Houseboats can also be hired and there is water access to the Myall Lakes.

During summer holidays, the popular lakeside camping area at **Mungo Brush**, 19km by sealed road from Hawks Nest, becomes a tent city and a fleet of house-

boats and other small craft is anchored in the sandy bay nearby. A 30min rainforest loop walk leaves from the northern edge of the campsite; birdlife here is prolific.

Bulahdelah has a deep-water boat ramp on the banks of the Myall River, and is the closest point to the lakes for houseboat hire; cruisers and runabouts are also available. Walking trails wind through nearby state forests, and the 1886 Bulahdelah Courthouse, now an interesting museum chronicles the district's timber-harvesting past, open Sat or by appt; Ph: 02 4997 4838.

Tall Timbers

The Grandis, a massive 84m spotted gum growing north of Bulahdelah, is believed to be the tallest tree in New South Wales. A walking track leads from Stoney Creek Road (accessed from the Pacific Hwy and with care suitable for conventional vehicles) through a moist gully to a viewing platform and boardwalk. There are picnic and BBQ facilities, and toilets.

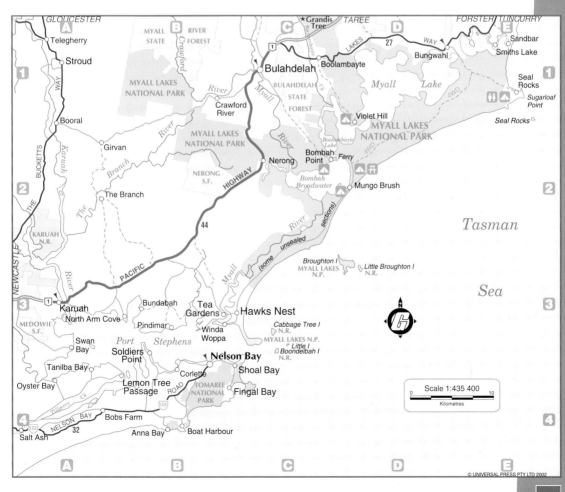

Shoalhaven

Best time to visit: Winter for whalewatching, seal and penguin sightings and best visibility for diving; spring for bright cottage gardens; summer for beachlife

Average daily temperatures: Jan 15–27°C, Apr 12–23°C, Jul 7–17°C, Oct 11–23°C

Getting there: By road from Sydney via F6 Fwy and Princes Hwy to Nowra (165km); by rail from Sydney to Bomaderry (just north of Nowra and terminus for the South Coast Line)

Festivals and events:

Feb: Nowra Show

Mar–Apr (Easter): White Sands Festival, Huskisson; Fishing Carnival, Greenwell Point

Jun: Music by the Water, Lady Denman Heritage Complex, Huskisson

Oct: Berry Garden Festival

Activities: Surfing, swimming, diving, snorkelling, sea-kayaking, sailing, fishing, windsurfing, whalewatching (in season), horseriding, bushwalking, birdwatching, 4WD touring, golf, browsing markets, craft shops and galleries

Highlights: Stunning Seven Mile, Callala, Vincentia and Hyams beaches; cycling along shady beachside tracks; dolphin and whalewatching cruises; diving in Jervis Bay Marine Park; walking tracks on Beecroft Head, Abrahams Bosom Reserve; Coolangatta Estate with restaurant, historic village and vineyard, Ph: (02) 4448 7131

Tip: Should you tire of sea and sand, take the winding road through rainforest pockets to Cambewarra Lookout and its tearooms for sweeping views of the Shoalhaven Valley and coast.

Kids' stuff: Lady Denman Heritage Centre, Huskisson; Nowra Animal Park, Ph: (02) 4421 3949; Marayong Park Emu Farm, Ph: (02) 4447 8505; dolphin cruises

Further information: Shoalhaven Visitors Centre, Princes Hwy, Nowra, NSW 2541, Ph: (02) 4421 0778, www.shoalhaven.com.au

The delights of incomparable white-sand beaches, scenic lakes, tranquil river country, lush dairy pastures, dramatic ranges and superb seafood combine to make Shoalhaven a perennially popular holiday destination. The region also offers an extensive range of dining and accommodation options.

Overlooking the sparkling waters of Jervis Bay, the former shipbuilding town of **Huskisson** is home to the Lady Denman Heritage Centre, a maritime museum centred on a retired Sydney ferry that was originally built here in 1910; Ph: (02) 4441 5675. The centre is also the departure point for year-round dolphin cruises—the bay is home to a sizable pod of bottlenose dolphins and in winter you can also expect sightings of fairy penguins and humpback whales. Sheltered Green Patch, in **Booderee NP**, is so popular with families that peak-season campsite bookings must be determined by ballot; Ph: (02) 4443 0977. Prolific birdlife here includes brilliantly coloured rosellas, king parrots and noisy black cockatoos. Nearby are the unspoilt parklands and safe waters of **St Georges Basin**. To the north, the **Australian Museum of Flight**, at HMAS *Albatross*, just south of **Nowra**, houses a collection of vintage naval aircraft.

The leafy township of **Berry**, known for its craft and antique shops and fashionable coffee houses, sits below the blue-smudged slopes of the Cambewarra Range. It has numerous buildings that are classified by the National Trust.

Slipway at Huskisson

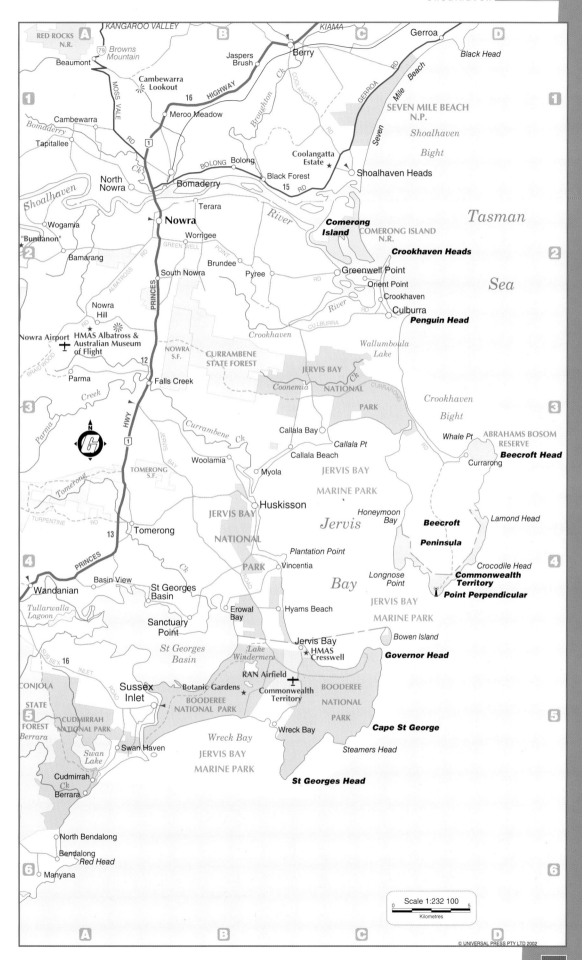

The Snowy Mountains

Best time to visit: Jan for fields of alpine wildflowers; spring, summer and autumn for bushwalking; winter (Jun–Oct) for skiing

Average daily temperatures: Jan 7–20°C, Apr 2–14°C, Jul –4–5°C, Oct 1–13°C

Getting there: By road from Sydney (460km) via Hume, Federal and Monaro Hwys, by road from Canberra (170km) via Monaro Hwy; by air to Cooma

Festivals and events:

Jan: Kosciuszko NP Discovery Program; Thredbo Art Exhibition; Man from Snowy River Mountain Muster, Lake Jillamtong; Blues Festival, Thredbo

Mar: Global Music Festival, Thredbo

Apr: Man from Snowy River Festival, Cooma

May: Legends of Jazz Music Festival, Thredbo

Jun: Opening of snow season

Aug: Wild Winter Weekend, Perisher Valley

Sep: Planet X Winter Games, Perisher Valley

Oct: Opening of fishing season

Nov: Opening of the walking season; Snowy Mountains Trout Festival, Cooma

Dec: Man from Snowy River Rodeo, Jindabyne; Kosciuszko NP Discovery Program

Activities: Bushwalking, climbing, downhill and cross-country skiing, snowboarding, mountain biking, horseriding, whitewater rafting, fly-fishing, sailing and watersports, lake cruising

Highlights: Winter sports; summer chairlift ride up Mt Crackenback and walk to Mt Kosciuszko summit; thermal swimming pool, Yarrangobilly Caves; Alpine Way scenic drive; crisp mountain air

Tip: Wear sunscreen, as well as a hat, even on cloudy days as UV radiation increases with altitude. 2WD vehicles must carry chains beyond Sawpit Creek and between Thredbo and Khancoban from Jun–Oct.

Kids' stuff: Bobsled, Thredbo, fee, Ph 1800 020 589; Murray 1 Power Station Interactive Centre, Khancoban, fee, Ph: (02) 6076 5115 or 1800 623 776

Further information: Cooma Visitor Centre, 119 Sharp St, Cooma, NSW 2630, Ph: 1800 636 525; Snowy Region Visitor Information Centre, Kosciuszko Rd, Jindabyne, NSW 2627, Ph (02) 6450 5600; Thredbo Information Centre, Friday Flat Dr, Thredbo, NSW 2625, Ph: 1800 020 589; Khancoban Information Centre, cnr Scott and Mitchell Aves, Khancoban, NSW 2642, Ph: (02) 6076 9373

The wild and beautiful Snowy Mountains include Australia's highest peak, Mt Kosciuszko, and its largest snowfields. Most of the region is protected by the state's largest national park, Kosciuszko NP. It is also the site of the Snowy Mountains Hydro-Electric Scheme, whose great dams, tunnels and power stations were built in the 1950s to harness upland waters for electricity generation.

This is a year-round destination: in winter, skiers flock to the snow-covered slopes; from spring to autumn the tops are the domain of walkers and riders, and the mountain streams and the waters of **Lake Jindabyne** and **Lake Eucumbene** (both storage dams) provide excellent fishing, especially for trout. The regional centre of **Jindabyne** is the start of the **Alpine Way**, a scenic drive which winds through the high country, past **Thredbo** and the **Murray 1 Power Station**, to the former dam construction base of **Khancoban**. Accommodation options include resorts, ski lodges, cabins and bushland camping areas.

Khancoban Dam in autumn

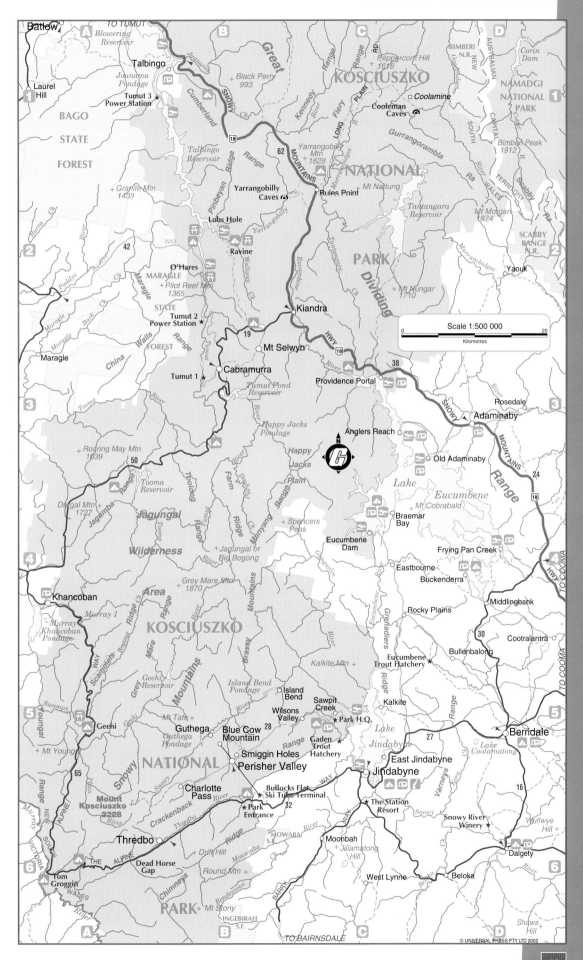

The Skifields

The official ski season runs from Jun–Oct. All the resorts lie within the borders of Kosciuszko NP, and most are on the eastern flank of Mt Kosciuszko, where linked pistes form a magnificent network of downhill routes. Accommodation is available at Perisher Valley, Smiggin Holes and Guthega. To avoid driving on icy mountain roads, skiers can leave their cars below the snowline at **Bullocks Flat Skitube**, Ph: (02) 6456 2010, 20km from Jindabyne, and take the Skitube railway which runs through one of the country's longest tunnels to the skifields at Perisher and Blue Cow.

Thredbo's chalets, restaurants, narrow winding streets and village atmosphere make it popular year-round. A snowsports school and beginners' area operate in winter. The Kosciuszko Express chairlift rises 600m from the valley floor, revealing a spectacular alpine panorama as it climbs the **Crackenback Range**. In winter, it carries skiers to snow-covered pistes; in summer, it takes walkers to high-country tracks. At the top, a raised metal walkway (built to protect delicate alpine vegetation) leads to the stony summit of **Mt Kosciuszko**, with its views over the Victorian Alps—allow 4–6 hr for the 13km return hike; guided walks are available. Access is via the Alpine Way; Ph: (02) 6459 4100 or 1800 020 589.

Perisher Blue Ski Resort encompasses Perisher Valley, Mt Blue Cow, Guthega and Smiggin Holes. A network of downhill runs, including some of the highest in the country, links these resorts and is served by 50 lifts; there are also cross-country ski trails and a snowsports school. The breathtaking view from Mt Blue Cow lookout takes in 5 of the highest peaks in Australia. Access is via the Skitube or Kosciuszko Rd; Perisher Blue Ski Resort, Ph: 1300 655 822.

Charlotte Pass, the highest and coldest alpine village, is the only ski resort in Australia that is snowbound in winter, giving it a secluded and intimate atmosphere. Kosciuszko Chalet has operated here since 1930. A number of walking trails, popular from spring to autumn, start at the pass, including a 9km trek to the top of Mt Kosciuszko along the Summit Rd (closed to vehicles). A snowsports school operates in winter. Summer access is via Kosciuszko Rd; winter access is via the Skitube to Perisher, then snowcat; Ph: (02) 6457 5247.

Mount Selwyn is in the northern section of Kosciuszko NP. It is an ideal family ski destination, with the region's gentlest slopes, a snowsports school and a 'New Chum Hill' beginners' area, as well as more challenging alpine and cross-country routes for the experienced. Access is by road, via Kiandra; Selwyn Snowfields, Ph: 1800 641 064.

Skiing at Thredbo

Thredbo River, Kosciuszko NP

Kosciuszko National Park

The vast and varied wilderness of **Kosciuszko NP** encompasses some of the most spectacular scenery in Australia and protects a remarkable array of plant and animal life, some of it unique to the area. Birdlife is especially prolific: soaring wedge-tailed eagles are frequently seen, as are emus, cockatoos and magpies. Grey kangaroos, wallabies, possums and wombats are also common. Forests of towering mountain ash cover the lower slopes; in summer, delicate wildflowers colour high meadows. Alpine walks can be enjoyed in the summer months, lower-altitude walks throughout the year; bush camping is permitted in most parts of the park and there are also some car-based campsites. Several old huts, originally built by cattle drovers, are dotted across the tops but can be used for emergency shelter only. Mountain bikers can follow management trails and there are also designated horse trails with camping areas where horses may be kept. Entry fee, Ph: (02) 6450 5600.

At **Yarrangobilly Caves**, you can take a self-guided tour of the Glory Hole Cave, or a guided tour of 3 other caves, including the wheelchair-accessible and highly decorated Jillabenan Cave; entry fee, Ph: (02) 6454 9597. A thermal spring here feeds a swimming pool with water that remains at a steady 27°C year-round; nearby are short bushwalks as well as picnic and BBQ facilities.

The Man from Snowy River

Banjo Paterson's stirring poem 'The Man from Snowy River' is believed to have been inspired by Irish-born high-country stockman Jack Riley, who worked on Tom Groggin Station, 'up by Kosciusko's side', and met Paterson in 1890. Riley, like the poem's hero, is said to have made a daring ride to recapture a thoroughbred colt that had escaped and 'joined the wild bush horses'. Several local events celebrate the ride as well as skills such as stockhandling and whipcracking, and bush poetry.

Australian Capital Territory

The Australian Capital Territory occupies 2500km² of mountainous country on the edge of the Australian Alps in south-eastern New South Wales. It was chosen as the site of the future national capital in 1908, after much bickering between the two rival contenders, Melbourne and Sydney. Today, the federal capital, Canberra, centred on the park-fringed waters of Lake Burley Griffin, spreads over most of the northern third of the Territory. It is the centre of government and home to the nation's major cultural and historical institutions, including the National Gallery of Australia and the Australian War Memorial. The rest of the Australian Capital Territory is bush-covered hills, grazing country and the slopes of the Brindabella and Bimberi ranges; the Murrumbidgee River cuts across the Territory on a south-easterly course. A 20min drive from the monuments, museums and galleries of Canberra is all that's required to reach rural landscapes, thick pine plantations or untouched wilderness. Visitors can follow walking tracks through forests, fish alpine streams, go whitewater rafting or step back in time at a stately homestead.

Tourist Information

i Canberra Visitors' Centre
Northbourne Ave
Dickson
ACT 2602
Ph: (02) 6205 0044
www.canberratourism.com.au

Top Tourist Destinations

A Canberra
B Regional ACT

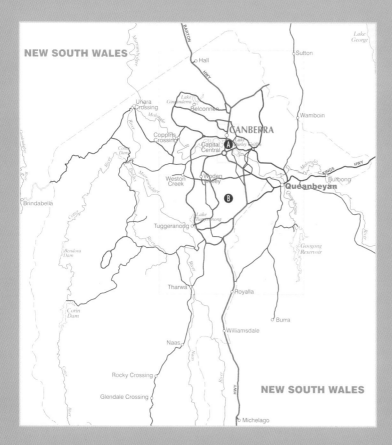

Canberra

Best time to visit: Autumn for leaf colour and crisp clear days; spring for blooms

Average daily temperatures: Jan 13–27°C, Apr 7–20°C, Jul 0–11°C, Oct 6–19°C

Getting there: By car via Hume Hwy from Sydney (305km) or via Hume Hwy from Melbourne (655km); by rail from Sydney; by air from all Australian capital cities

Festivals and events:

Jan: Summernats Car Festival; Canberra International (women's tennis tournament)

Feb: National Multicultural Festival

Mar: National Folk Festival

Apr: Anzac Parade Open Day

May: Subaru Rally of Canberra

Jun: Canberra 400 (V8 Supercar street-circuit car races)

Aug: Australian Science Festival

Sept–Oct: Floriade, Commonwealth Park

Activities: Visiting national monuments, cycling, watersports, fishing, golf, horseriding, bushwalking, hot-air balloon flights, 4WD touring

Highlights: Parliament House, Australian War Memorial, National Gallery of Australia, National Museum of Australia, Old Parliament House, view from Telstra Tower on Black Mountain

Tip: Plan your trip to coincide with Parliament sitting, then book a ticket to the public gallery to witness the prime minister's question time; Ph: (02) 6277 4889, Serjeant-at-Arms

Kids' stuff: Questacon—The National Science and Technology Centre and the National Museum both have 'hands-on' interactive exhibits; Cockington Green; National Zoo and Aquarium, Yarralumla, Ph: (02) 6287 11211; National Dinosaur Museum

Further information: Canberra Visitors' Centre, Northbourne Avenue, Dickson, ACT 2602, Ph: (02) 6205 0044, www.canberratourism.com.au

Elegant, orderly Canberra is the seat of the Australian Federal Government and a centre of culture, science and learning. Its scenic site, encircled by mountains, bush and farmland—a place where a city would not otherwise have grown—was selected in 1908. An international competition held in 1912 to select a design for the new national capital was won by American architect Walter Burley Griffin, and building began in 1913.

Canberra's major political buildings are set in a triangle (known as the Parliamentary Triangle), with Capital Hill at the apex and the twin bridges of Kings and Commonwealth Avenues, which stretch north and east across Lake Burley Griffin, forming the sides. The nation's major cultural institutions are also grouped here. The city's many diplomatic embassies, each designed in an architectural style that reflects its occupants' native culture, are concentrated in the leafy district of Yarralumla. Magnificent parklands fringe the lake.

Australian War Memorial

Places of Interest

Australian National Botanic Gardens (1)

Australian War Memorial (2)

Blundells' Cottage (3)

Captain Cook Memorial Jet (4)

High Court of Australia (5)

National Archives of Australia (6)

National Capital Exhibition (7)

National Carillon (8)

National Gallery of Australia (9)

National Library of Australia (10)

National Museum of Australia (11)

Old Parliament House (12)

Parliament House (13)

Prime Minister's Lodge (14)

Questacon—The National Science and Technology Centre (15)

ScreenSound Australia—The National Screen and Sound Archive (16)

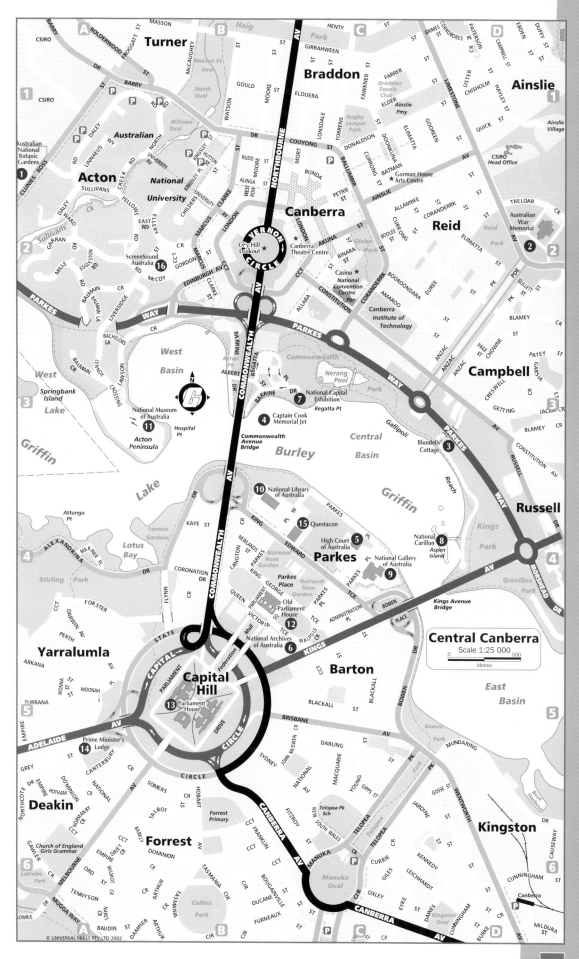

The National Capital

The **Australian National Botanic Gardens,** on the lower slopes of Black Mountain, contain the nation's largest collection of living native flora. About 90 000 plants grow here, grouped according to families and habitats. Marked walking trails help visitors explore environments as diverse as a rainforest gully (nourished by an automatic mister), desert and alpine rockeries, and mallee shrublands; free guided tours are also available. The eucalypt lawn is an ideal spot for picnics. Parking fee, Ph: (02) 6250 9540, www.anbg.gov.au.

The **Australian War Memorial** is a shrine, a museum, an archive and a research centre. The commemorative areas include the Roll of Honour, which lists more than 102 000 Australian war dead; the Pool of Reflection; and the Tomb of the Unknown Australian Soldier in the Hall of Memory. The memorial also houses an extensive collection of art, relics and photographs, ranging from battered signs retrieved from WWI trenches in France to the wedding dress of a war bride. In Anzac Hall, visitors can inspect a Japanese midget submarine and watch a multimedia presentation, 'Sydney under Attack', that relives the night the submarine entered Sydney Harbour. Broad **Anzac Parade,** lined with military memorials, links the War Memorial with Parliament House, on the opposite side of Lake Burley Griffin. Ph: (02) 62 43 4211, www.awm.gov.au.

Floriade

Now Canberra's biggest seasonal drawcard, Floriade grew out of a one-off floral display held in 1988 to celebrate the nation's

bicentenary and the 75th anniversary of the commencement of the construction of Canberra. More than a million bulbs and annuals are planted in Commonwealth Park and carefully nurtured to provide a colourful spring tapestry for the 30 days of the festival. The design of the flowerbeds follows a different theme each year.

At the **High Court of Australia**, visitors can admire the public hall (with its impressive 28m-high ceiling) and murals depicting the development of the nation and its constitution. The 3 courtrooms are also open to the public, and free guided tours are available. Ph: (02) 6270 6811, www.hcourt.gov.au.

The **National Archives of Australia**, housed in the city's former GPO building, preserve Commonwealth Government records. The Treasures Gallery displays an everchanging selection of its enormous store of documents, files and images; its most precious treasures, including Queen Victoria's *Royal Commission of Assent* (the document that established the Australian Commonwealth), are on permanent exhibition in the Federation Gallery. Ph: (02) 6212 3600, www.naa.gov.au.

The **National Gallery of Australia**'s outstanding collection of Australian art ranges from traditional Aboriginal works (including a permanent display of 200 painted hollow-log coffins from Arnhem Land and batiks and dot paintings from Central Australia) to paintings by Tom Roberts, Sidney Nolan and Arthur Boyd. Art from other parts of the world includes ancient Asian sculpture and the abstract painting *Blue Poles* by 20th-century US painter Jackson Pollock. The 3ha Sculpture Gardens stretch from the gallery to the lake; 24 works by Australian and international artists are on display here. Entry fee to major exhibitions, Ph: (02) 6240 6502, www.nga.gov.au.

The **National Library of Australia**, the largest library in the land, is custodian of the nation's recorded history. Housed in an imposing, marble-clad building, its enormous collection ranges from James Cook's *Endeavour* journal and the diaries of explorers Robert O'Hara Burke and William Wills to paintings, music scores, theatre programs, and posters from the Sydney Olympics. The library receives a copy of every book published in Australia. Exhibitions are held here regularly. Ph: (02) 6262 1111, www.nla.gov.au.

The **National Museum of Australia** uses modern technology and interactive exhibitions to help weave together the many stories that make up the past and present of Australia, its land and people. Visitors can touch time-worn Aboriginal

National Museum of Australia, Acton Peninsula, Lake Burley Griffin

grinding stones, view convict leg irons, listen to a story in a boab tree, and create a city of the future using virtual-reality software. Entry fee to major exhibitions, Ph: (02) 6208 5000, www.nma.gov.au.

Old Parliament House, designed by John Smith Murdoch and home of the Australian Parliament from 1927 to 1988, was originally intended as a temporary building. Guided tours highlight the many momentous events that took place here. The National Portrait Gallery, housed in the building, displays portraits of significant figures from a wide range of fields, including politics, sport, entertainment and science, and hosts special exhibitions. Entry fee, Ph: (02) 6270 8222, www.dcita. gov.au/oph. Visitors can also stroll through the adjoining historic rose gardens.

Parliament House nestles into Capital Hill, and sloping lawns carpet its sides and roof. Towering overhead is an 81m steel flagpole, a landmark visible from most parts of the city. Directly below, in the heart of the building's interior, is the lofty Members Hall, where one of only 4 surviving copies of the Magna Carta dating from 1297 is on permanent display. The forecourt mosaic at the ground-level entrance derives from Central Desert dot-style painting, while the foyer features marble columns, majestic stairways and expansive marquetry floors; in the Great Hall hangs one of the largest tapestries in the world, based on an Arthur

Boyd painting of a eucalypt forest. Public galleries overlook both the House of Representatives and Senate chambers. Ph: (02) 6277 5399, www.aph.gov.au.

The **Prime Minister's Lodge**, situated on Adelaide Ave to the SW of Parliament House, has been the official residence of Australian prime ministers since 1927; it is not open to the public, but there are open days throughout the year.

Questacon—The National Science and Technology Centre challenges visitors with more than 200 exciting exhibits, most of them interactive. Permanent exhibitions include Cybercity (which looks at future technologies), Awesome Earth (where visitors can experience a simulated earthquake) and Australian Innovations. Entry fee, Ph: (02) 6270 2800, www.questacon.edu.au.

The **Royal Australian Mint**, in Deakin, opened in 1965. It offers excellent presentations on the minting process and fascinating exhibitions tracing the history of Australian coins and coin design. You can even mint your own $1 coin. Ph: (02) 6202 6819, www.ramint.gov.au.

ScreenSound Australia, the National Screen and Sound Archive, is home to Australia's national collection of historic film, television and radio recordings. There are regular film, television screenings, interactive exhibitions and displays of movie props and costumes. Ph: (02) 6248 2000, www.screensound.gov.au.

Lakefront and Lookouts

Anzac Parade and Australian War Memorial viewed from Mt Ainslie

Lake Burley Griffin, created by the damming of the Molonglo River, is the venue for a range of watersports, including sailing, windsurfing, kayaking, sculling and fishing. Cycle and walking tracks follow the foreshores and sightseeing launches ply the waters. The International Flags Display, consisting of the national flags of 80 nations with diplomatic representation in Canberra, is a permanent feature of the lakefront between the High Court and Questacon. Across the waters, on Aspen Island, stands the pale tower of the **National Carillon**, a huge musical instrument consisting of 53 bronze bells; recitals are performed regularly.

Blundells' Cottage dates from the early 1860s, when it was built on the banks of the Molonglo River to house workers on the Campbell family's Duntroon property. In 1913, Duntroon was acquired by the government to form part of the Federal Capital Territory, but sheep remained in the surrounding paddocks until the 1940s and the cottage continued to be occupied until 1958. It is now a museum, with period furnishings and equipment. Entry fee; Ph: (02) 6273 2667.

Each spring, **Commonwealth Park** is the site for the massed blooms of Floriade (see p.66). At the **National Capital Exhibition**, Regatta Point, interactive displays and a high-tech laser model of the city tell the story of Canberra, including topics such as the region's Aboriginal history, its selection as the site for the national capital, Walter Burley Griffin's prize-winning design and its growth to gracious city. Nearby, the **Captain Cook Memorial Jet** sends a tower of lake water 145m skyward—up to 6t of water are in the air at any one time. The jet operates daily from 10am to noon and 2–4pm, as well as 7–9pm during daylight saving. Together with the lakeside globe, it was installed in 1970 to commemorate the bicentenary of Cook's voyage to the east coast of Australia.

Lookouts in Canberra include **Mt Ainslie**, which provides magnificent views south over the gleaming copper dome of the Australian War Memorial and along Anzac Parade to the Parliamentary Triangle; the **Telstra Tower**, which rises 195m above the summit of **Black Mountain** and offers a stunning, 360° panorama of the region from an enclosed viewing platform and two open (and frequently very breezy) platforms; and **Red Hill**, which has sweeping vistas to the north across Parliament House and Lake Burley Griffin.

Just Add Water

Although it is difficult to imagine Canberra without Lake Burley Griffin, this unifying feature did not exist until 1964 when the Scrivener Dam was completed. Hilltops then became islands as waters rose to lap at prepared beaches, jetty sites and undulating landscaped foreshore planted with thousands of ornamental trees; the rising lake also drowned the old Canberra golf course and its clubhouse, a renovated farmhouse.

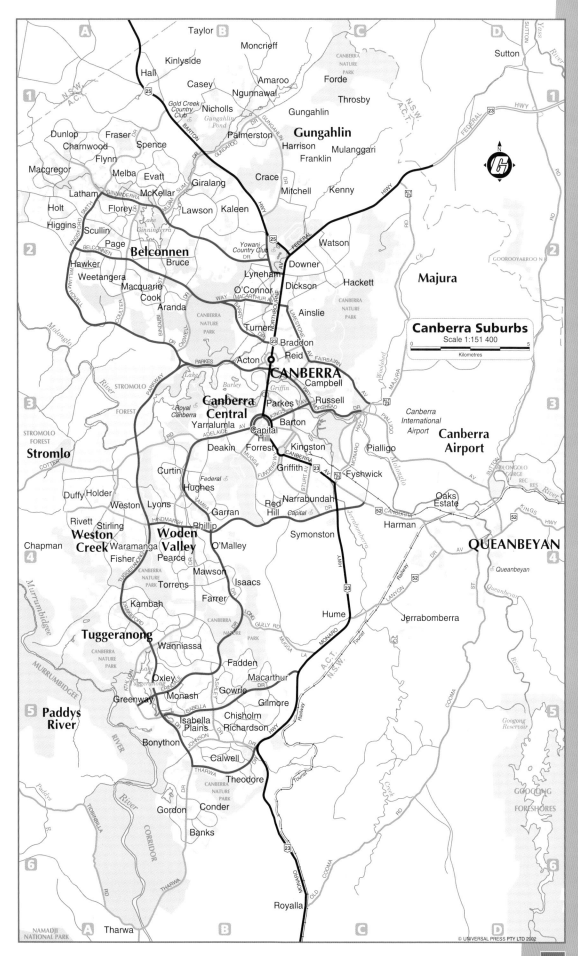

Canberra Suburbs
Scale 1:151 400
Kilometres

Regional ACT

A cluster of attractions NW of the city centre includes **Cockington Green**, which features highly detailed miniature representations of buildings from Britain and other parts of the world set in landscaped gardens; entry fee, Ph: (02) 6230 2273, www.cockington-green.com.au. At the nearby **Australian Reptile Centre**, visitors can cuddle a python; entry fee, Ph: (02) 6253 8533. The **National Dinosaur Museum** has 10 full-size dinosaur models, all cast from original fossils; entry fee, Ph: (02) 6230 2655, www.nationaldinosaurmuseum.com.au.

To the west are 2 important space facilities. At **Mt Stromlo Observatory**, off the Cotter Rd, 20min drive from Canberra, scientists research the very big picture—the origin of the universe. Guided tours take in the 3 working telescopes and allow visitors to ask astronomers questions; entry fee, Ph: (02) 6125 0232, www.anu.edu.au/msovc.

The **Canberra Deep Space Communication Complex**, off Paddy's River Rd, Tidbinbilla, about 50min drive from Canberra, is one of 3 such facilities that together form NASA's Deep Space Network. The huge dish-shaped radio antennas here (the largest is 70m across) track interplanetary spacecraft through the solar system. Exhibits in the information centre include a piece of moon rock and interactive displays chronicling space exploration. Outside there is a grassy picnic area with BBQs; Ph: (02) 6201 7880, www.cdscc.nasa.gov/.

An elite athlete will guide you around the world-class sports facilities of the **Australian Institute of Sport**; its interactive Sportex exhibit allows you to try virtual rowing, test your golf swing and measure yourself against sporting champions; Ph: (02) 6214 1010, www.ais.org.au.

Visitors to **Lanyon**, a working sheep property located on the Murrumbidgee River off Tharwa Dr, 30km south of Canberra, can view a range of exhibits covering thousands of years of human history; they include ancient Aboriginal campsites and trees whose bark was cut to make canoes, farm buildings dating from the convict era, the restored 1859 homestead, and 20th-century buildings and paddocks; entry fee, Ph: (02) 6237 5136. The nearby Nolan Gallery displays a superb collection of works by Sir Sidney Nolan, including his first Ned Kelly painting; entry fee, Ph: (02) 6237 5192.

The alpine wilderness of **Namadgi National Park** stretches across the south and west of the Territory, accounts for nearly half its area and includes **Mt Bimberi**, its highest point (1911m). From Canberra, it is an easy daytrip to **Mt Franklin** in the Brindabella Range, which offers high-country views and walks; the mountains are usually snow-covered in winter. In the adjoining **Tidbinbilla Nature Reserve**, walking trails wind through enclosures where koalas, kangaroos and emus can be seen in their natural habitat. The reserve has BBQs and picnic grounds; Ph: (02) 6205 1233.

Gibraltar Rocks, Tidbinbilla Nature Reserve

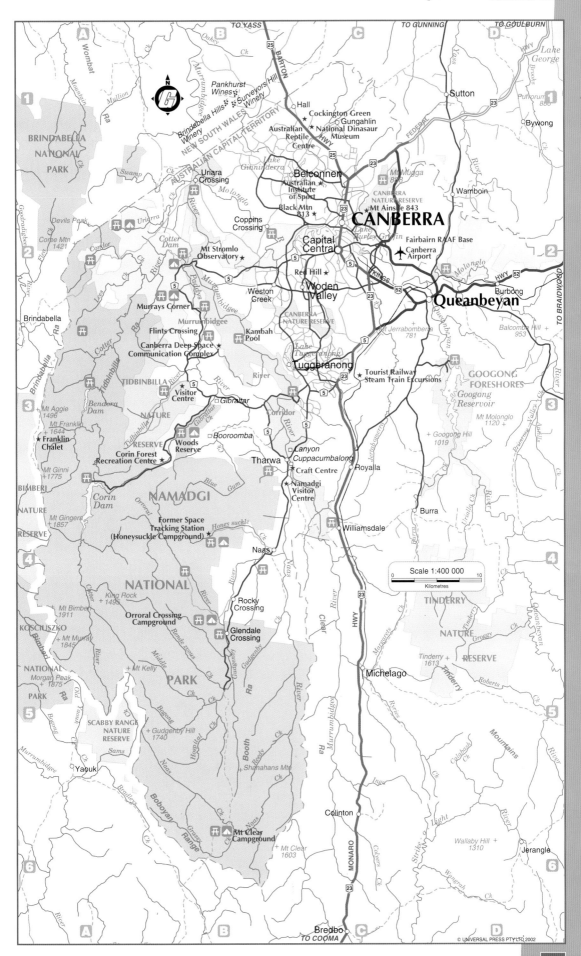

12 Apostles, Port
Campbell NP

Victoria

Victoria stretches from the wide waters of the Murray River, where old river ports are now tourist centres, south to the wild, sea-carved coastline of the Southern Ocean. Much is packed into this compact state, and most of the major tourist destinations lie within a few hours' drive of the capital, Melbourne. Some, such as the leafy Dandenongs, the holiday playgrounds of the Bellarine and Mornington peninsulas, Phillip Island (with its celebrated penguin parade), and the magnificent coastal scenery of Wilsons Promontory, are an easy daytrip. Further afield, gourmet trails wind NE to the wine and dairy lands of Milawa; beyond are the peaks, high plains, snowfields and vibrant ski resorts of the Victorian Alps. The east coast offers extensive, unspoilt beaches and the tranquil waterways of the Gippsland Lakes. To the west is the historic port of Geelong, with its colourful waterfront precinct, and the famed Great Ocean Road, which follows the twisting shoreline along clifftops and through picturesque seaside villages, passing dramatic rock formations such as the 12 Apostles. Tall timbers cloak the nearby Otway Ranges; to the north, the towns of Ballarat and Bendigo are rich in goldrush heritage. Further west, the rocky ramparts of the Grampians, the tail end of the Great Dividing Range, protect a rich heritage of rock art and abundant wildlife. Sophisticated Melbourne is known for its cultural attractions, cosmopolitan charm, fine restaurants and great shopping.

Tourist Information

ℹ️ **Melbourne Visitor Centre**
Federation Square
cnr Swanston and
  Flinders Sts
Melbourne
Vic 3000
Ph: (03) 9758 9658
www.visitvictoria.com

Top Tourist Destinations

- Ⓐ Melbourne
- Ⓑ The Bellarine Peninsula
- Ⓒ The Dandenongs
- Ⓓ The Gippsland Lakes
- Ⓔ The Goldfields
- Ⓕ The Grampians
- Ⓖ The Great Ocean Road
- Ⓗ The Mornington Peninsula
- Ⓘ The Murray River
- Ⓙ The Northern Wine Country
- Ⓚ Phillip Island
- Ⓛ The Victorian Alps
- Ⓜ Wilsons Promontory

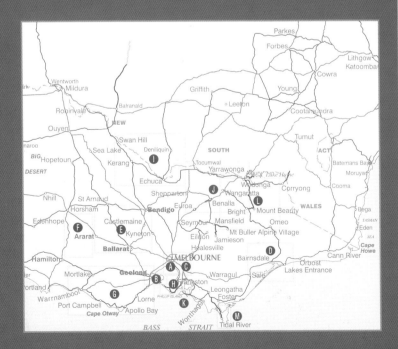

Melbourne

Best time to visit: Year-round
Average daily temperatures: Jan 14–26°C, Apr 10–20°C, Jul 5–13°C, Oct 9–19°C
Getting there: By road from Sydney (880km), Canberra (655km) and Adelaide (735km); direct flights from all state capitals; direct rail services from Sydney, Canberra and Adelaide
Festivals and events:
Jan: Australian Open (tennis)
Feb–Mar: Australian Grand Prix, Albert Park; Chinese New Year Festival (procession, fireworks)
Mar: Moomba (street parade, outdoor carnival)
Mar–Apr: Antipodes Festival (celebrates Melbourne's Greek heritage); Melbourne Food and Wine Festival
Apr: Melbourne International Comedy Festival; Melbourne Autumn Music Festival; Melbourne International Flower and Garden Show
Sep: Royal Melbourne Show; Melbourne Spring Fashion Week
Sep–Oct: Melbourne Fringe Festival (comedy, music and cabaret)
Oct: Melbourne Festival (visual and performing arts); Lygon St Festa
Nov: Melbourne Cup Day (first Tue); Chapel St Festival, Prahran
Dec–Jan: Sidney Myer free concerts, Sidney Myer Music Bowl

Activities: Arts and culture, wining and dining, visiting parks and gardens, shopping, river cruises, cycling, sailing, golf, hot-air ballooning
Highlights: Melbourne City Art Galleries Walk and Tram Tour, fee, Ph: (03) 9897 3174; shopping in the central retail district; Southbank's lively riverside cafes, bars and boutiques; buzz and restaurants of Lygon St and Brunswick St; St Kilda's foreshore and Acland St eateries; Royal Botanic Gardens; Yarra River cruise
Tip: A free city loop tram service runs every 10min to attractions such as the Old Treasury Building, Parliament House and the Princess Theatre, and to shops, restaurants and city parks. The service operates 7 days a week, 10am–6pm, and can be boarded at any of the special burgundy-coloured stops along the route; Ph: 131 638.
Kids' stuff: Melbourne Observation Deck; Polly Woodside Melbourne Maritime Museum; Dolphin Fountain, Fitzroy Gardens; Flagstaff Gardens children's playground; Kids' Tours Melbourne, fee, Ph: 0416 110 899; Royal Melbourne Zoo, entry fee, Ph: (03) 9285 9300; canoeing on the Yarra
Further information: Victorian Visitor Information Centre, Melbourne Town Hall, cnr Swanston and Little Collins Sts, Melbourne, Vic 3000, Ph: 13 28 42, www.visitmelbourne.com

The Melbourne skyline's harmonious blend of attractive Victorian architecture and late-20th-century skyscrapers reflects the city's impressive mix of elegance and commercial prosperity. The 1880s nickname 'Marvellous Melbourne' still applies today. The city is exceptionally well endowed with historical institutions, theatre, music and art experiences, and sufficient multicultural food outlets to satisfy all palates. Its renowned shopping outlets provide bargains aplenty for those on a budget, while encompassing upmarket boutiques and department stores of an international standard. Broad swathes of gracious, well-tended parkland extend along the Yarra River and around the edges of the CBD, and pleasant beaches fringe Port Phillip Bay. In addition, Melbourne's busy sporting calendar includes major events such as the Melbourne Cup, Australian Open tennis tournament and Australian Grand Prix. The city centre's compact grid layout makes it easy for all visitors to get their bearings; walking and cycling tours and accessible recreational facilities cater for the more active.

Places of Interest
Albert Park (1)
Chinatown (2)
Crown Entertainment Complex (3)
Exhibition Building (4)
Federation Square (5)
Fitzroy Gardens (6)
Flagstaff Gardens (7)
Flinders St Station (8)
Ian Potter Centre: NGV Australian Art (9)
Melbourne Central Shopping Centre (10)
Melbourne Cricket Ground (11)
Melbourne Observation Deck (12)
National Gallery of Victoria (NGV; closed until 2003) (13)
National Gallery of Victoria on Russell (14)
Old Melbourne Gaol (15)
Old Treasury Building and Gardens (16)
Parliament House (17)
Polly Woodside Melbourne Maritime Museum (18)
Queen Victoria Gardens (19)
Queen Victoria Market (20)
Royal Botanic Gardens (21)
Sidney Myer Music Bowl (22)
St Patricks Catholic Cathedral (23)
St Pauls Anglican Cathedral (24)
Town Hall (25)

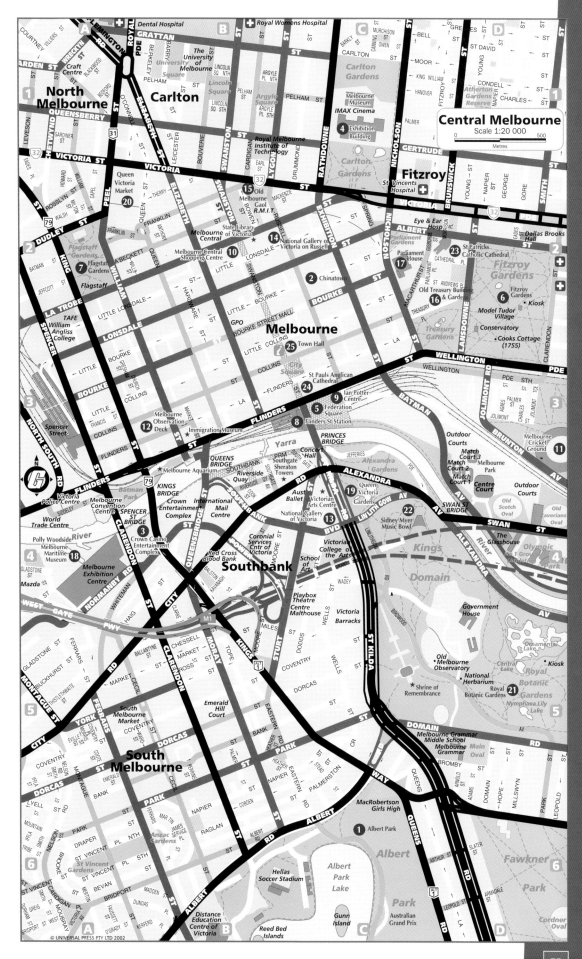

North of the River

The city centre's broad, straight streets are easily negotiated on foot. In busy Collins Street, which is lined with trees lit with fairy lights, business is concentrated at the western end and shopping at the eastern end. At Rialto Towers, visitors can take a lift to the 55th floor and savour the city's most spectacular panorama from the **Melbourne Observation Deck**; Ph: (03) 9629 8222.

While the National Gallery of Victoria's St Kilda Rd site is closed for refurbishment (see p.78), its permanent collection as well as visiting interstate and international exhibitions are being housed at the **National Gallery of Victoria on Russell**; fee for special exhibitions, Ph: (03) 9208 0222. Nearby, **Old Melbourne Gaol**, Victoria's oldest prison, preserves memorabilia of the 19th-century penal system including the death masks of executed murderers. Bushranger Ned Kelly was hanged here in 1880. Night tours, lit by candles, are especially atmospheric; entry fee, Ph: (03) 9663 7228.

Queen Victoria Market is packed with food stalls, many selling snacks and flavoursome deli produce of Greek, Italian and Polish origin; go early for the freshest fare. Vendors of clothing and other goods also trade noisily here. The markets are closed Mon and Wed. Guided tours, including sampling, are available; fee, Ph: (03) 9320 5822.

Most of **Swanston Street**, Melbourne's original major north–south thoroughfare, is now open only to pedestrians, trams and commercial vehicles with permits.

Shopping for fruit and vegetables at Queen Victoria Markets

A magnet for shoppers, the precinct is enlivened by buskers and refreshed by cosmopolitan food outlets. The **Town Hall**, at the intersection with Collins Street, houses a pipe organ of rare distinction; musical and other events are presented here and free behind-the-scenes tours are available; Ph: (03) 9658 9658.

A hallowed venue for test cricket, **Melbourne Cricket Ground**, established in 1854, also hosts the Australian Rules Football Grand Final. It has a seating capacity of about 100 000, and was the central focus of the 1956 Olympic Games. The site's Australian Gallery of Sport and Olympic Museum holds numerous historical artefacts of the sporting world; Ph: (03) 9657 8879.

The Melbourne Cup

The running of the Melbourne Cup at Flemington Racecourse brings most of the nation to a virtual standstill for several minutes. But the city of Melbourne comes to a halt for a whole day. First run in 1861, the event is now one of the world's great handicap horse-races. As well as heavy betting, the meeting is marked by huge hats, frivolous fashions and copious amounts of champagne.

Parks and Gardens

Melbourne's parks and gardens spread across a quarter of the city. Mostly established in the second half of the 19th century, they now display historical monuments and botanical diversity, and supply shade, recreational facilities, splendid scenery and wide, open spaces.

The skilfully landscaped **Royal Botanic Gardens**, designed by noted botanist Baron Ferdinand von Mueller and home to more than 51 000 plants, are best entered by Observatory Gate on Birdwood Ave. Tours, including a Garden Highlight Walk, Aboriginal Heritage Walk and visit to the observatory begin from the visitor centre; Ph: (03) 9252 2300. The adjacent **Kings Domain** features fountains, silver birches, a floral clock and the **Shrine of Remembrance**, which has the Grave of the Unknown Soldier as its centerpiece and, nearby, a statue of Simpson, a World War I stretcher-bearer. **Government House** stands atop the hill. Some rooms are open to the public but guided tours must be booked; Ph: (03) 9654 5528. The much humbler Governor La Trobe's Cottage, a prefabricated, timber-clad building brought from England in 1839 and now managed by the National Trust, is also open to inspection.

Albert Park, 3km south of Melbourne's CBD and currently home to the Australian Formula 1 Grand Prix, has always attracted sports enthusiasts. Its facilities include a boating lake, an 18-hole public golf course and ample walking tracks; Parks Victoria, Ph: 131 963.

Picnicking beside the Yarra River

Fitzroy Gardens are distinguished by huge elm trees that line avenues laid out in the shape of the Union Jack. **Cook's Cottage**, which was transported here from Yorkshire, England, in 1934 to mark Melbourne's centenary, once housed the famous captain's parents.

Flagstaff Gardens, opposite Queen Victoria Market, contain tennis courts and a bowling club. Originally a signalling point for approaching sailing ships—hence the name—the land was later allocated to gardens; tall elm trees now tower above lawns and flowerbeds.

Temple of the Four Winds, Royal Botanic Gardens

Southbank

Plans formulated in the 1980s led to the highly successful redevelopment of a large area south of the Yarra River as a residential and recreational centre focusing principally on entertainment. One pleasant way of reaching Southbank is via the walkway linking it to Melbourne's CBD.

The district's roomy shopping precinct, **Southgate**, is laid out on multiple levels and encompasses restaurants, cafes, ferry wharves and scores of stylish shops; outdoor performers make good use of the spacious pavements and plazas. To the west, additional shops and eateries surround the **Crown Entertainment Complex**, which has upmarket restaurants, cinemas, live shows and gaming facilities; Ph: (03) 9292 8888.

The **National Gallery of Victoria (NGV)** is due to re-open in 2003 following extensive refurbishment of the original 1968 building, which could no longer accommodate its ever-expanding collection. The transformed NGV will house international works; the outstanding Australian collection will soon be displayed in its own elegant complex at the **Ian Potter Centre** in Federation Square (due to open in late 2002); free entry, Ph: (03) 9208 0222.

The cultural heart of the city, the **Victorian Arts Centre** is distinguished by its 115m spire and a reputation for hosting outstanding local and international artists. It is home to the Melbourne Theatre Company and the Australian Ballet, and is the hub of the Melbourne Festival. Performance spaces include theatres and concert halls, which may be toured by visitors during the day; Ph: (03) 9281 8000. The Performing Arts Museum within the centre preserves theatre clothing and stage sets; free entry, Ph: (03) 9281 8000.

The Belfast-built *Polly Woodside* first set sail in 1885, made many journeys around Cape Horn and carried freight across Australasian waters. Today, this iron-hulled barque, meticulously restored and permanently moored, forms the centrepiece of the **Polly Woodside Melbourne Maritime Museum**. Historic photographs and exhibits displayed aboard and in old cargo sheds nearby emphasise Melbourne's intriguing seaport heritage. Ph: (03) 9699 9760.

Crown Entertainment Complex, Southbank

Luna Park funfair, St Kilda

Down the Yarra to the Sea

The muddy **Yarra River** winds through the centre of Melbourne on its journey from the slopes of the Great Dividing Range westward to **Port Phillip**. Spanned by numerous bridges and plied by a range of pleasure-craft, its busy waters are often the venue for spectacular events ranging from rowing regattas to Dragon Boat Festivals.

River cruises offer a different perspective on Melbourne's landmarks. Most depart from Southgate or Princes Walk (near **Princes Bridge**) and chug gently downstream under the modern Bolte and West Gate bridges to Dockland. On cruises upstream from the city, you can break your journey at South Yarra for a 15min uphill walk and a tour of Como House, an elegant 19th-century mansion built using profits from the wool industry; entry fee, Ph: (03) 9827 2500.

Parks dotted along the Yarra attract cyclists and walkers, and in recent years regeneration of the waterway and its banks has led to the return of many native bird and other animal species. The Main Yarra Trail, which is suitable for bikers and hikers, follows the river for 33.5km from **Southbank** through **Yarra Bend Park**, to Westerfolds Park in **Templestowe**. You can picnic in a park or take Devonshire tea in a local cafe, then hire a canoe or rowing boat to explore the river further. Boats can be hired at either historic Studley Park Boathouse at **Kew**, Ph: (03) 9853 1972, or Fairfield Boathouse at **Fairfield**, Ph: (03) 9486 1501.

Melbourne's bayside beaches stretch east and south from Albert Park around Port Phillip Bay. Although the water can look murky after rain, it is reasonably clean and safe for swimming; there is no surf, however. **St Kilda**'s beach and palm-lined foreshore, cycleway and vibrant eateries (most notably on Fitzroy and Acland Sts) are busy year-round. Visitors can stroll to the end of St Kilda Pier, which dates from 1853, for a different view of the city, or try the thrills and spills of Luna Park; free entry, fee for rides, Ph: (03) 9525 5033.

Also worth visiting are the surprisingly pristine city beaches of **Port Melbourne**, **Albert Park** and **Middle Park**; **Brighton**, with its colourful bathing boxes; pretty Half Moon Bay in **Hampton**; and the secluded beaches at **Black Rock**.

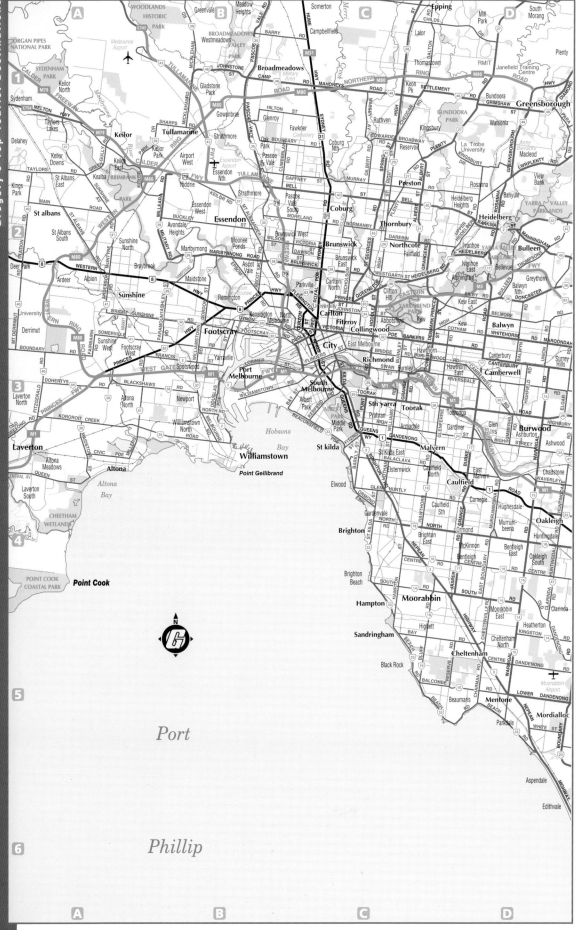

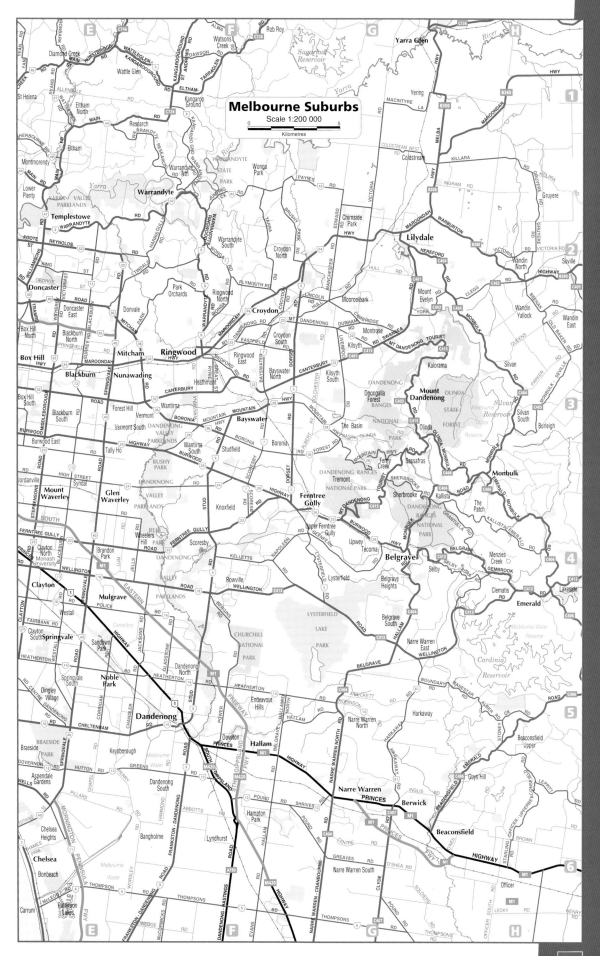

Melbourne Suburbs

Scale 1:200 000

Kilometres

The Bellarine Peninsula

Best time to visit: Year-round for heritage, food and wine; summer for beach activities and festivals; winter for log fires and cosy B&Bs

Average daily temperatures: Jan 14–25°C, Apr 10–20°C, Jul 5–16°C, Oct 12–22°C

Getting there: By road from Melbourne via Princes Hwy (M1) to Geelong (75km); by rail from Melbourne to Geelong (V-Line, Ph: 136 196); by passenger/vehicle ferry from Sorrento to Queenscliff, Ph: (03) 5258 3244, and by passenger-only ferry from Sorrento to Portsea and Queenscliff, Ph: (03) 5984 1602

Festivals and events:

Jan: Festival of Sail and Waterfront Geelong Festival, Geelong (sailing regatta, food and wine and entertainment); Spray Farm Summer Festival, Spray Farm Vineyard, Bellarine; Rip View Swim Classic, Point Lonsdale front beach

Feb: Australian International Airshow (odd years only), Avalon Airport, near Geelong

Mar: International Seafood Fair, Geelong

Jun: National Celtic Festival, Geelong

Sep: Momenta, Arts Geelong

Oct: Geelong Show; International Horse Trials, Spray Farm Vineyard, Bellarine

Nov: Queenscliff Music Festival; Wallington Strawberry Fair

Activities: Swimming, surfing, fishing, boating, sailing, snorkelling, diving, bushwalking, bird-watching, cycling, horseriding, wine-tasting, hot-air ballooning, golf

Highlights: Waterfront Geelong's cafes and free entertainment; Queenscliff's heritage buildings and eateries; dolphin cruises; Rip and bay views from Point Lonsdale; Bellarine Peninsula Railway steam-train ride between Queenscliff and Drysdale, Sun only, fee, Ph: (03) 5258 2069

Tip: For a colourful introduction to Geelong, follow the more than 100 large painted bollards, representing figures from Geelong's past, along the waterfront; 4km, 1hr one way walking, 20min cycling.

Kids' stuff: Eastern Beach swimming complex, Waterfront Geelong, Ford Discovery Centre, Geelong, entry fee, Ph: (03) 5227 8700; A Maze 'n' Things (3D maze), Wallington, entry fee, Ph: (03) 5250 2669; Adventure Park, Wallington, entry fee, Ph: (03) 5250 2756; Marine Discovery Centre (touch tank, exhibits), Queenscliff, school holidays only, entry fee, Ph: (03) 5258 3344

Further information: Geelong—National Wool Museum, cnr Moorabool and Broughton Sts, Geelong, Vic 3220, Ph: (03) 5222 2900 or 1800 620 888; Geelong and Great Ocean Road Visitor Centre, Stead Park, Princes Hwy, Corio, Vic 3214, Ph: (03) 5275 5797 or 1800 620 888

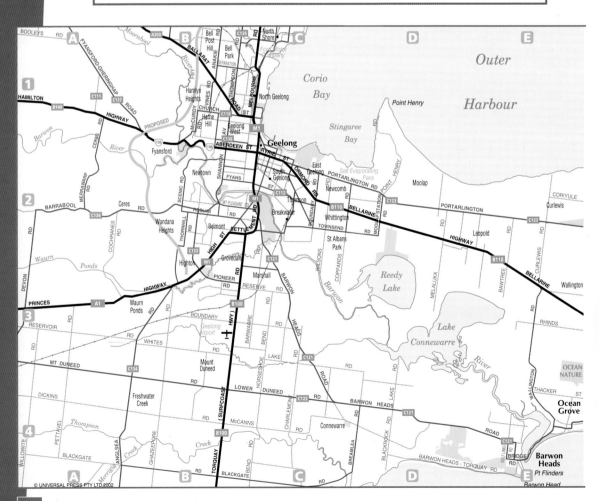

© UNIVERSAL PRESS PTY LTD 2002

A popular daytrip from Melbourne, the Bellarine Peninsula combines bay and ocean beaches, boating and the vibrant Waterfront Geelong entertainment and eating precinct with peaceful bayside villages, wineries and tranquil rural hinterland. The peninsula's wide range of accommodation includes boutique hotels, excellent B&Bs and numerous caravan parks and camping grounds.

Geelong's wide streets and imposing bluestone buildings are a legacy of the economic boom of the 1860s and 1870s, when this waterfront was one of the busiest in the country. In summer, locals and visitors enjoy Eastern Beach's Art-Deco pool complex. Inland, along the Barwon River, a network of walking and cycle tracks provides access to leafy parks. The Geelong Art Gallery holds an out-standing Australian collection, including Frederick McCubbin's *A Bush Burial*; entry fee (free on Mon), Ph: (03) 5229 3645.

Elegant **Queenscliff**, preserved almost unchanged from its 1890s heyday, is known for its stylish eateries, heritage hotels and historic fortifications. From

Point Lonsdale Lighthouse

Point Lonsdale Lighthouse there are impressive views over the notorious Rip, the turbulent passage of water at the entrance to Port Phillip Bay.

The twin seaside towns of **Ocean Grove** and **Barwon Heads** have access to both riverfront and surf beaches and are a popular destination for summer holiday-makers; Barwon Heads has the added attraction of being the setting for the popular television series *SeaChange*.

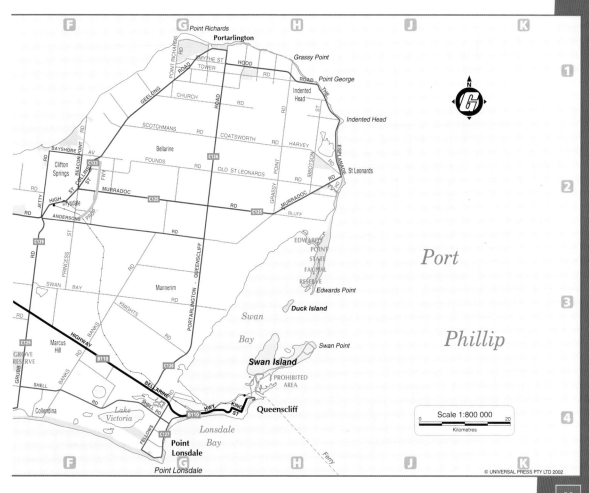

The Dandenongs

Best time to visit: Year-round: spring for colourful flower festivals; summer for picnics and BBQs; autumn for mountain mists; winter for brisk walks and cosy open fires

Average daily temperatures: Jan 11–22°C, Apr 9–15°C, Jul 3–8°C, Oct 7–15°C

Getting there: By road from Melbourne via Maroondah Hwy to Lilydale (38km) or via Burwood Hwy to Ferntree Gully (35km); by rail to Lilydale, Upper Ferntree Gully and Belgrave

Festivals and events:

Feb–Mar: Dandenong Folk Festival, Olinda

Mar: Grape Grazing Festival, Yarra Valley (celebrating the vintage with food and music)

Apr: Great Train Race (runners compete with the Puffing Billy steam train over 25km between Belgrave and Emerald)

Jun–Aug: Dandenong Ranges Winter Festival (open fires and Christmas fare)

Jul: Winter Wood-fest, Warburton

Aug: Spring Floral Festival, Olinda

Sep–Oct: Tesselaar's Tulip Festival, Silvan

Nov: Monbulk Jazz Festival

Activities: Bushwalking, birdwatching, fishing, visiting gardens and plant nurseries, wining and dining, scenic drives, picnicking, horseriding, mountain biking, browsing galleries and craft and antique shops, hot-air ballooning

Highlights: Puffing Billy train ride from Belgrave to Emerald and Gembrook Lake through thick forest and over timber trestle bridges, fee, Ph: (03) 9754 6800 or 1900 937 069 for recorded timetable; William Ricketts Sanctuary sculpture gallery, Mt Dandenong, set among fern gardens and waterfalls, entry fee, Ph: 13 19 63; National Rhododendron Gardens, Olinda, entry fee, Ph: (03) 9751 1980; superb view from Kalorama over Silvan Reservoir

Tip: Take a coat—mountain temperatures are 4–5°C colder than Melbourne or the foot of the ranges. The area is most crowded during weekends in spring and autumn.

Kids' stuff: Emerald Lake Park (with wading pool, aqua-bikes for hire, waterslide), entry fee per car, Ph: (03) 5968 4667; Emerald Lake Model Railway, entry fee, Ph: (03) 5968 3455

Further information: Dandenong Ranges and Knox Visitor Information Centre, 1211 Burwood Hwy, Upper Ferntree Gully, Vic 3156, Ph: (03) 9758 7522 or 1800 645 505, www.yarraranges tourism.com

The forested slopes, fern gullies and picturesque villages of the Dandenong Ranges are just 1hr, but a world away, from Melbourne's city streets. A favoured daytrip and short-break destination, the ranges offer a cool green retreat in summer and beckon with cosy tearooms and open fires in winter. Scenic, sun-dappled roads wind between towering mountain ash and forests of oaks, elms and poplars to intriguing craft galleries and grand public gardens. Farm-gate sales provide an opportunity to stock up on fresh produce ranging from berries and asparagus to potatoes. Bushwalkers can explore a 300km network of marked tracks. The region is also famed for its boutique accommodation, including secluded and luxurious cottages, charming B&Bs and picturesque heritage guesthouses.

Puffing Billy *steam train*

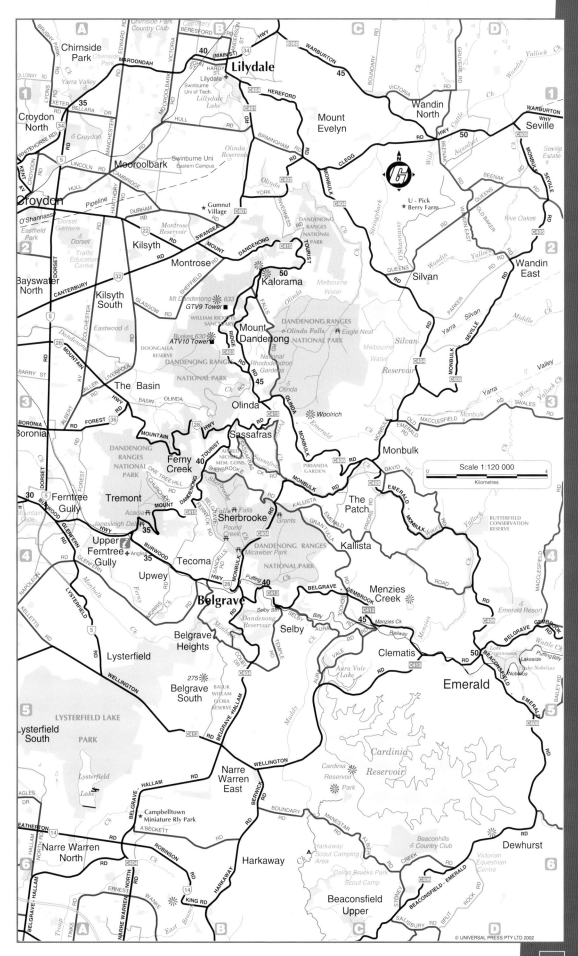

The Gippsland Lakes

Best time to visit: Year-round; summer for beach activities; spring for wildflowers

Average daily temperatures: Jan 14–27°C, Apr 10–21°C, Jul 5–16°C, Oct 12–22°C

Getting there: By road from Melbourne via Princes Hwy (A1) to Bairnsdale (280km), Lakes Entrance (315km); by rail from Melbourne to Bairnsdale (V-Line, Ph: 136 196)

Festivals and events:

Jan: Foothills Festival, Buchan

Feb: Bruthen Blues Bash, Bruthen; Paynesville Jazz Festival

Mar: Metung Classical Music Festival; Marlay Point to Paynesville Overnight Yacht Race

Mar–Apr: Buchan Rodeo

Apr: All Australian Line Dancing Championship, Bairnsdale

May: Buskers Harvest Festival, Lakes Entrance

Jun: Gippsland Wool and Fibre Festival, Bairnsdale

Nov: Sale and District Agricultural Show

Activities: Swimming, surfing, fishing, windsurfing, sailing, jet-skiing, water-skiing, canoeing, bird-watching, bushwalking, cycling, horseriding, whitewater rafting

Highlights: Exploring the waterways by boat; abundant, delicious seafood; ferry ride (free; passenger/vehicle ferry) from Paynesville to Raymond Island, site of koala colony and bush-walking tracks; prolific birdlife, with birdwatching hides for enthusiasts; waterside boardwalk from Metung to Legend Rock; walking along Ninety Mile Beach; walking or cycling the East Gippsland Rail Trail from Bairnsdale to Bruthen (30km, 3hr one way by bicycle); Buchan Caves, with elaborate formations, underground pools and nearby spring-fed swimming hole, entry fee, Buchan Caves Reserve, Ph: (03) 5155 9264

Tip: Boats can be hired by the hour, half-day or day; or, for sightseeing, you can join a cruise boat at Lakes Entrance or Lake Tyers.

Kids' stuff: Howitt Park, Bairnsdale (signposted off the Princes Hwy), a well-equipped public playground with flying fox, wire walk-bridge, swings, BBQ area; paddleboating at Lakes Entrance (Dec–Easter); swimming and paddling in the safe, shallow, lake waters of the Paynesville foreshore; koala-spotting, Raymond Island

Further information: Bairnsdale Visitor Information Centre, 240 Main St, Bairnsdale, Vic 3875, Ph: (03) 5152 3444; Central Gippsland Information Centre, 8 Foster St, Sale, Vic 3850, Ph: (03) 5144 1108; Lakes Entrance Visitor Information Centre, cnr Marine Pde and the Esplanade, Lakes Entrance, Vic 3909, Ph: (03) 5155 1966 or 1800 637 060

Sailing on the Gippsland Lakes

The Gippsland Lakes, Australia's largest network of inland waterways, consist of the Victoria, King and Wellington lakes, all of which are fed by rivers flowing from the high ranges. The lakes run roughly parallel to the sea and are separated from it by the long strip of shoreline and dunes known as **Ninety Mile Beach**. Much of the area is protected by the **Gippsland Lakes Coastal Park** and the **Lakes NP**. Famed for their fishing, the lakes also provide ideal venues for all kinds of watersports, on both still water and surf; the temperate climate (up to 6°C warmer than Melbourne) is an added attraction. This is a popular family holiday destination, with varied and plentiful accommodation (including numerous caravan parks) and an array of dining options ranging from fast-food outlets to stylish lakeside restaurants.

Bairnsdale, a busy regional centre on the Mitchell River, is known for its heritage architecture and its links with the high country (it is the coastal terminus of the Great Alpine Road). McLeods Morass, a freshwater marsh, has an outstanding birdwatching boardwalk.

Fishing boats on Cunninghame Arm, Lakes Entrance

In **Mitchell River NP**, about 50km inland from Bairnsdale, a walking track (1km, 1hr return) leads through sheltered patches of temperate rainforest to the Den of Nargun. In traditional Aboriginal mythology, this shallow cave, reached via natural stepping stones, was the lair of a half-human, half-stone creature. The deep and rugged Mitchell River gorge is popular for whitewater canoeing and rafting, especially in spring.

Paynesville, which is virtually surrounded by water, is a centre for boating and fishing and a gateway to the **Lakes NP**, renowned for its spring wildflower displays and abundant wildlife. Further east, the attractive village of **Metung** fronts sandy beaches and busy jetties and marinas; offshore, yachts and motor cruisers ply glassy waters bounded by thickly wooded hills. **Lakes Entrance** is both a major fishing port (you can buy rock lobster, prawns and scallops fresh off the boats at the Fishermen's Co-op on Bullock Island) and an attractive, long-established holiday destination.

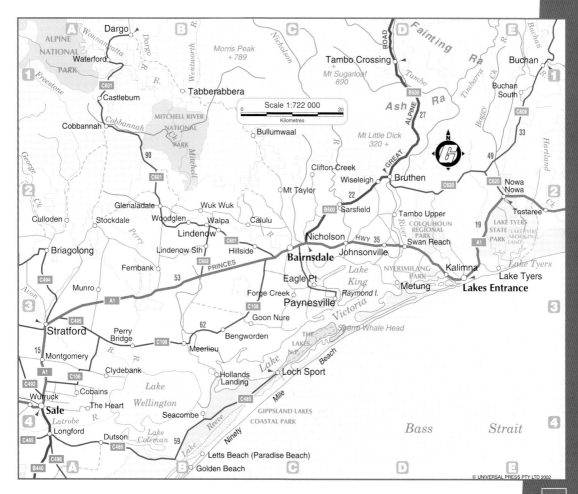

The Goldfields

This region was the site of some of the largest and most frenetic goldrushes of the 1850s, events that brought about momentous changes in Australia, including the generation of fabulous wealth, the political upheaval of the Eureka Rebellion, and rapid population growth. Evidence of the sudden rush of riches can be seen in the majestic Victorian architecture, cultural treasures and grand gardens of the boomtime centres of **Ballarat**, **Bendigo**, **Castlemaine** and **Maryborough**. Mining activities also uncovered the mineral springs that led to the growth of the spa towns of **Daylesford** and **Hepburn Springs**.

In the scenic foothills of the **Pyrenee Range**, a cluster of fine wineries offers tastings and cellar-door sales; many also have restaurants that showcase local produce. The region's range of accommodation includes luxurious heritage buildings, vineyard cottages, old-style guesthouses and upmarket resorts.

The Goldfields region also boasts a remarkable concentration of exceptional regional art galleries. Ballarat Fine Art Gallery has Eureka memorabilia and artworks by Sidney Nolan, Tom Roberts and the Lindsay family; Ph: 1900 937 425 (24hr Infoline). Artists represented in Bendigo Art Gallery's collection include Arthur Streeton and Margaret Preston; Ph: (03) 5443 4991. The Castlemaine Art Gallery and Historical Museum houses works by Frederick McCubbin and Russell Drysdale and also provides a fine introduction to the area's rich Aboriginal heritage; Ph: (03) 5472 2292.

Sovereign Hill, Ballarat's re-creation of an early goldrush town

The Eureka Rebellion

In 1854, an attempt by the government to collect a licence fee from miners created smouldering resentment that quickly flared into rebellion. As well as the abolition of the fee, miners demanded the right to vote and an opportunity to buy land. At a meeting in Ballarat, hundreds burnt their licences and, flying the Eureka Flag, determined to fight for their rights from a make-shift stockade. On 3 Dec, at least 25 miners and 4 troopers died in a predawn battle. Although the miners were defeated, strong public support saw their aims eventually realised. The Eureka Stockade Centre, Ph: (03) 5333 1854, now stands on the site of the stockade; the original Eureka Flag is on display at the Ballarat Fine Art Gallery.

History comes to life at **Sovereign Hill**, in Ballarat, a re-creation of an 1860s goldmining township, with hotel, black-smith's shop, printing shop and bakery, all operated by staff in period costume; entry fee; Ph: (03) 5331 1944, www.sovereignhill.com.au. Bendigo displays re-minders of the sizable Chinese presence in the goldfields, including the Joss House and Golden Dragon Museum (the 100m-long Sun Loong imperial dragon makes an annual outing during the Easter Fair); entry fee, Ph: (03) 5441 5044. The 'time-capsule' town of **Maldon** is almost unchanged in appearance from goldrush times. Also of interest is the small historic town of **Clunes**, where the discovery of gold in 1851 triggered the local rushes. Several impressive buildings here testify to the fortunes made.

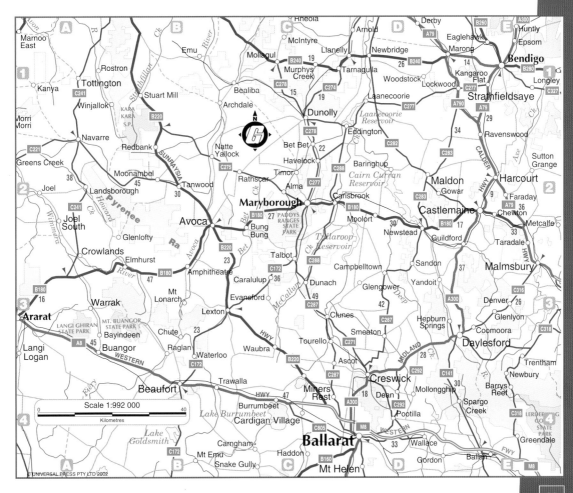

The Grampians

Rising abruptly from the flat plains of western Victoria, the grand and rocky fortress of the Grampians harbours a host of colourful wildflower species (some found nowhere else), prolific wildlife and a rich heritage of rock art (Aboriginal presence here dates back more than 10,000 years). All of this is now protected by the **Grampians NP**.

The spectacular scenery includes bare peaks, sheer-sided cliffs (which attract rockclimbers of all abilities), plunging valleys sheltering stands of river red gums, fern-filled gullies, and wooded ridges. A 160km network of marked walking trails, ranging from easy to challenging, threads through the park. The sealed Mt Victory Rd leads to the attractions of **Boroka Lookout**, **Reed Lookout** (a short walk away from the jutting Balconies rock formation), **Mackenzie Falls** (reached via a steep walk from the car park) and **Zumstein** (a grassy area where large numbers of kangaroos congregate). Several companies offer adventure activities, including rockclimbing, abseiling, canoeing and horseback tours; plan and book ahead to guarantee a place on the tour of your choice—Action Adventure, Ph: (03) 5356 4654; Base Camp and Beyond, Ph: (03) 5356 4300; Grampians Adventure Services, Ph: (03) 5356 4556. Camping grounds are plentiful or, if you prefer a roof over your head, **Halls Gap** offers a wide range of accommodation and eateries.

Mountain vista, Grampians NP

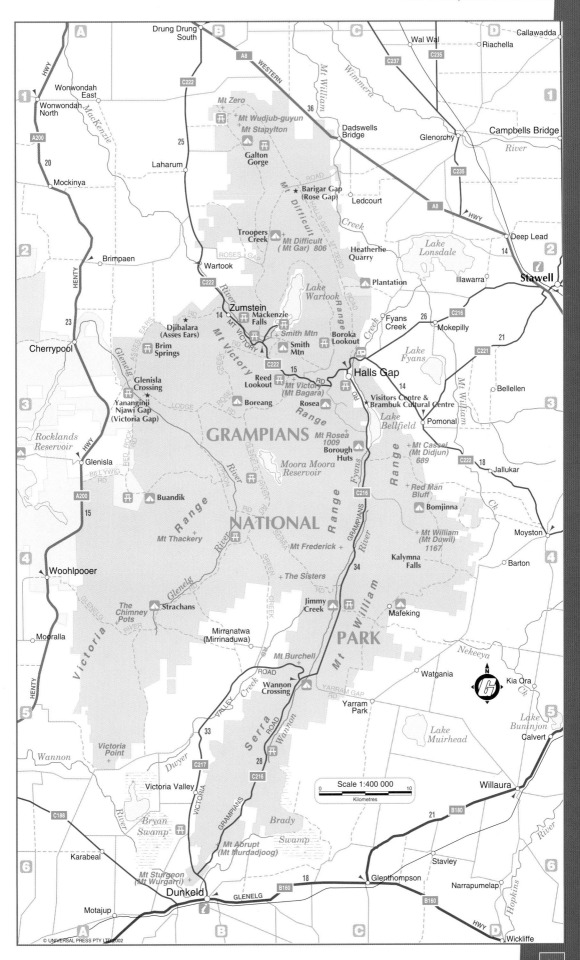

Scale 1:400 000

Kilometres

© UNIVERSAL PRESS PTY LTD 2002

The Great Ocean Road

Best time to visit: Year-round; spring for wildflowers and muttonbirds; summer for beach activities; winter for whalewatching

Average daily temperatures: Jan 14–22°C, Apr 11–18°C, Jul 8–14°C, Oct 11–19°C

Getting there: By road from Melbourne via Princes Hwy (M1) and Great Ocean Road (B100) to Warrnambool (355km), or via Princes Hwy to Warrnambool (265km) and Port Fairy (295km); by rail from Melbourne to Warrnambool

Festivals and events:

Jan: Pier to Pub Swim, Lorne

Feb: Wunta Wine and Food Fiesta, Warrnambool

Mar: Apollo Bay Music Festival; Port Fairy Folk Festival

Apr: Easter Surfing Classic, Torquay

Jun: Rhapsody in June Music Festival, Port Fairy; Fun 4 Kids, Warrnambool

Aug: Winter Blues Festival, Port Campbell

Oct: Spring Music Festival, Port Fairy; Warrnambool Agricultural Show

Activities: Surfing, swimming, fishing, diving, bushwalking, birdwatching, whalewatching, canoeing, cycling, mountain biking, horseriding, hanggliding, enjoying great local produce

Highlights: Teddy's Lookout, Lorne; Marriner's Lookout, Apollo Bay; 12 Apostles; Loch Ard Gorge; whalewatching, Logans Beach, Warrnambool; Tower Hill, south of Warrnambool; historic Port Fairy waterfront; view over crater lakes from Red Rock Lookout (NW of Colac); early-morning platypus-spotting canoe trip, Forrest, fee, Ph: (03) 5236 2119

Tip: If you have your own transport, consider an overnight stop in Port Campbell to allow a visit to the 12 Apostles at sunrise, when the crowds that descend later in the day are absent.

Kids' stuff: Lake Pertobe Adventure Playground, Warrnambool (paddleboats, maze, fort, flying fox, giant slides, sandpit); Flagstaff Hill Maritime Museum, Warrnambool (recreated 1850s port, with lighthouses), entry fee, Ph: (03) 5564 7841; Surfworld Museum, Torquay, entry fee, Ph: (03) 5261 4606

Further information: Geelong and Great Ocean Road Visitor Centre, Stead Park, Princes Hwy, Corio, Vic 3214, Ph: (03) 5275 5797 or 1800 620 888; Great Ocean Road Visitor Information Centre, Foreshore, Apollo Bay, Vic 3233, Ph: (03) 5237 6529; Lorne Visitor Information Centre, 144 Mountjoy Pde, Lorne, Vic 3232, Ph: (03) 5289 1152; Warrnambool Visitor Information Centre, cnr Raglan Pde (Princes Hwy) and Kepler St, Warrnambool, Vic 3280, Ph: (03) 5564 7837

View from Teddy's Lookout, Lorne

As well as the spectacular drive along the Great Ocean Road itself, one of the country's most scenic routes, this region offers a multitude of attractions. Dense forests and wildflower heathlands fringe the coastline. Further inland are volcanic plains, dramatic crater lakes and historic towns. Each winter, Warrnambool's Logans Beach plays host to female right whales and their calves. Fabulous local fare includes crayfish (rock lobster) from Apollo Bay, Timboon cheeses, and organic vegetables grown in the rich, volcanic soils of the Otway Ranges. The region's wide range of accommodation includes beachfront resorts, B&Bs with sweeping ocean views, and forest guesthouses.

The Great Ocean Road hugs the coast for 240km from the surfing industry town of **Torquay** to the former port of **Warrnambool**. Along the way, it takes in stunning vistas, charming seaside towns, swimming and surfing beaches, rainforest bushwalking trails and excellent eateries. **Jan Juc**, **Bells Beach** and **Johanna Beach** are renowned surfing destinations. **Aireys Inlet** is hemmed in by delightful rainforest and wildflower-speckled heath. **Lorne** is an elegant beach-resort town, with boutiques and a stylish cafe strip; picturesque **Apollo Bay** retains the charm of a fishing village. Inland, **Angahook–Lorne State Park** is known for its wildflowers and walking trails, **Otway NP** for its towering trees and rainforest gullies.

Those who climb to the observation deck of the lighthouse at **Cape Otway** are rewarded with breathtaking views across the powerful swells of the Southern Ocean. To the west, rugged slopes give way to gigantic jagged cliffs falling sheer to the pounding sea, an awe-inspiring shoreline known as the Shipwreck Coast; viewing platforms allow visitors to experience nature's fearsome grandeur.

Loch Ard Gorge, in Port Campbell NP, was the location of both a tragic wreck and the remarkable survival of 2 of those on board (as well as a porcelain peacock, now on display at Warrnambool's Flagstaff Hill Museum). Themed walking tracks here explore the environmental and human history of the site; in places, the ground fairly trembles under the onslaught of the surging ocean. The landmark sea stacks of the **12 Apostles** and **London Bridge** (one of whose immense arches recently collapsed) are striking testament to the processes that constantly reshape the coastline.

London Bridge, soon after the sudden collapse of the larger arch in 1990

How Many Apostles?

You won't be able to count 12. Only 8, including 1 partly obscured by a headland, are visible from public lookouts; another 2 stand out of sight on Gibsons Beach. The missing Apostles may have disappeared since the group was named, or perhaps never actually existed. One thing is certain, however: the waves will eventually claim all those visible today while carving new stacks from the cliffs.

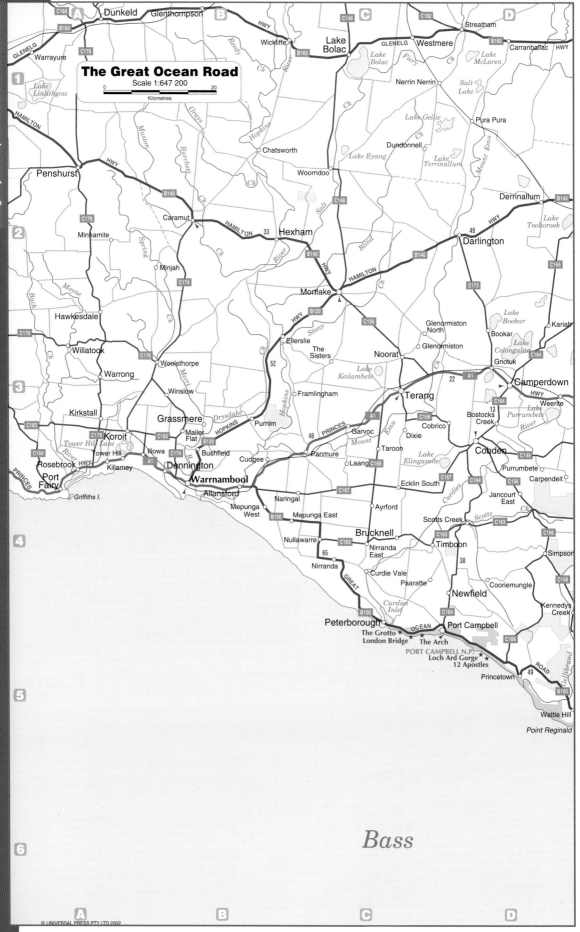

The Great Ocean Road

Scale 1:647 200

0   20

Kilometres

Bass

© UNIVERSAL PRESS PTY LTD 2002

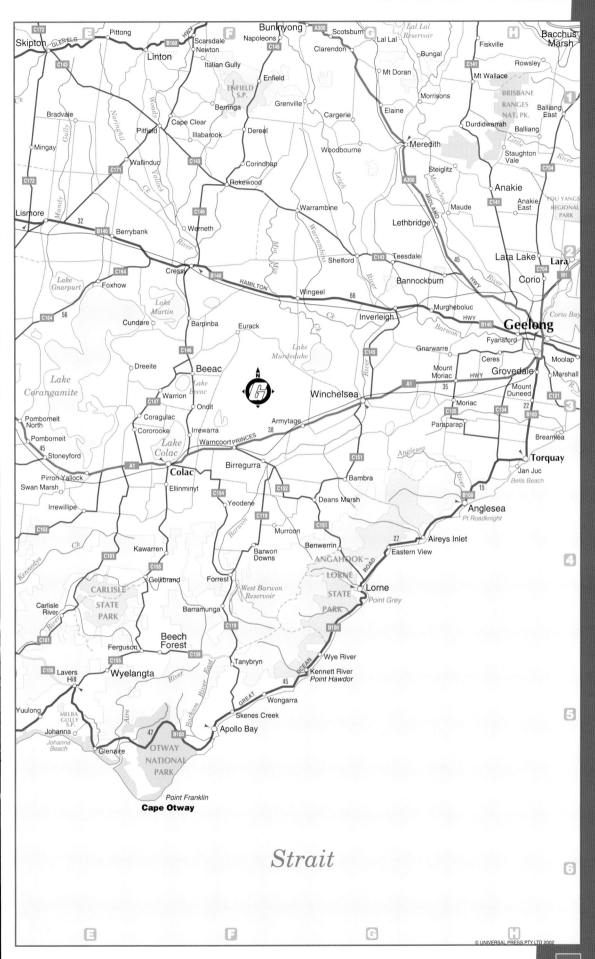

Strait

The Mornington Peninsula

Best time to visit: Year-round; summer for beach activities and watersports; winter for uncrowded beaches and wild ocean vistas

Average daily temperatures: Jan 13–25°C, Apr 11–19°C, Jul 7–14°C, Oct 11–20°C

Getting there: By road from Melbourne via Nepean Hwy to Frankston (50km) and Sorrento (100km); by rail from Melbourne to Frankston (V-Line, Ph: 136 196); by passenger/vehicle ferry from Queenscliff to Sorrento, Ph: (03) 5258 3244, and by passenger-only ferry from Queenscliff to Sorrento and Portsea, Ph: (03) 5984 1602

Festivals and events:

Jan: Frankston on the Sea Festival; Sail Melbourne (yachting regatta), Port Phillip Bay

Feb: Schnapper Point Classic, Mornington Yacht Club

Mar: Peninsula Pinot Week (food and wine festival), various locations; Frankston Heritage Festival

Apr: Frankston International Guitar Festival

Jun: Winter Wine Festival, various locations

Oct: Mornington Food and Wine Festival

Nov: Heronswood Garden Festival, Dromana

Activities: Swimming, surfing, boating, sailing, fishing, diving, beachcombing, bushwalking, birdwatching, cycling, horseriding, hang-gliding, paragliding, wine-tasting, golf

Highlights: Riding the chairlift to the summit of Arthurs Seat for sweeping views; swimming with Port Phillip Bay's bottlenose dolphins—Moonraker Charters, Sorrento, Ph: (03) 5984 4211, Polperro Dolphin Swims, Sorrento, Ph: (03) 5988 8437; seal-watching cruises; boutique wineries and restaurants of Red Hill; wild coastline of Mornington Peninsula NP; koala spotting, French Island

Tip: Take the ferry trip between Sorrento and Queenscliff for wonderful bay vistas. Peninsula ocean beaches can be dangerous; choose patrolled beaches and swim between the flags.

Kids' stuff: Ashcombe Maze, Shoreham, entry fee, Ph: (03) 5989 8387; Arthurs Seat Maze, entry fee, Ph: (03) 5981 8449; beach horseriding, Gunnamatta Trail Rides, Rye, fee, Ph: 1800 801 003; learn-to-surf classes, Sorrento Back Beach, fee, Ph: (03) 5988 6143

Further information: Peninsula Visitor Information Centre, Point Nepean Rd, Dromana, Vic 3936, Ph: (03) 5987 3078 or 1800 804 009

The Mornington Peninsula has been a favourite holiday destination for generations of Melburnians. A string of resort towns curves west from Frankston around the sheltered and sandy shores of Port Phillip Bay to **Portsea**. Along the narrow spit of land at the end of the peninsula, calm 'front' beaches line the bay while more rugged 'back' beaches face the great ocean swells of the Bass Strait. The oceanside strip is part of **Mornington Peninsula NP** and has excellent coastal walking tracks and surf beaches. To the east are the quiet shores of Western Port and the undulating, fertile hinterland, site of a developing wine industry. The peninsula is ideal for daytrips from Melbourne: distances between main attractions are short and the roads are excellent—a number of scenic routes take in both coastal and hinterland attractions. There is a wide choice of accommodation, including luxury resorts, friendly B&Bs and caravan parks, and a full range of dining options.

Busy **Mornington** has been a seaside resort since the 1880s, when tourism began to displace fishing as the town's main source of income. The old centre retains much of its early fishing-village atmosphere and is still home to a fishing fleet, as well as a yacht club; there is good swimming at nearby beaches.

Bush-clad Arthurs Seat, the highest point on the peninsula and centrepiece of **Arthurs Seat State Park**, offers sweeping views back towards Melbourne and westward over the Rip to the Bellarine Peninsula. The summit can be reached via a scenic drive or an exhilarating ride on the state's longest chairlift—open Sep–Jun and weekends and school holidays in winter, Ph: (03) 5987 2565—

Sailboats on Port Phillip Bay

Red Hill Estate Winery

followed by a climb up the viewing tower. Walking tracks lead through nearby Seawinds Gardens, with its stands of birch and pine trees, to other parts of the park. You're sure to see brightly coloured rosellas flitting through the branches here, and may even come across a wallaby.

To the east are the vineyards, wineries, restaurants and galleries of **Red Hill**. The wineries are best known for their pinot noir, though other varieties are being produced in increasing quantities; most establishments offer cellar-door tastings (fee, refunded with purchase).

The oldest town on the peninsula, elegant **Sorrento** was the site of Victoria's first settlement, a short-lived convict camp set up in 1803, of which only a gravesite remains. The town's grand limestone hotels date from the 1870s and 1880s, when steamers crossed from Melbourne carrying daytrippers and holidaymakers eager for salt air and golden beaches. Today's visitors have the added attractions of smart cafes and restaurants. Sorrento is also the departure point for the Queenscliff ferry and a number of scenic cruises around the bay.

Point Nepean

Fear of a Russian invasion in the early 1880s prompted the fortification of the western tip of the Mornington Peninsula to safeguard the entrance to Port Phillip Bay. The complex remained in service until 1945, and although it fired only 2 shots in anger, its presence certainly protected adjacent fragile habitat from development. Visitors can inspect tunnels leading to gun emplacements and bunkers, and take in magnificent views west over the Rip and south over wild Cheviot Beach, where Prime Minister Harold Holt disappeared in 1967. Fee (includes transport to fort); bookings recommended as daily visitor numbers are strictly limited; Ph: (03) 5984 4276.

The Mornington Peninsula
Scale 1:200 000

0   10

Kilometres

Portarlington

Grassy Point

HOOD

TOWER   RD   ROAD   Point George

Indented Head

Indented Head

COATSWORTH   HARVEY   RD

St Leonards

LEONARDS   IBBOTSON

MURRADOC

C125   BLUFF   RD

EDWARDS POINT STATE FAUNAL RESERVE

Edwards Point

Swan Bay

Duck Island

Swan Point

Swan Island

PROHIBITED AREA

Queenscliff

Nepean Bay

Ticonderoga Bay

Portsea

POINT   Point Franklin

Point King

HOTHAM   NEPEAN   RD

Sorrento

MORNINGTON

West Sister

East Sister

Sorrento Back Beach

MELBOURNE   RD

B110

Blairgowrie

Rye

ROAD   B110

Tootgarook

PENINSULA

ROAD

BROWNS

DUNDAS   ST

BROWNS   RD

TRUEMANS   RD

SANDY

St Andrews Beach

Gunnamatta Beach

NATIONAL

TRUEMANS   RD

Port

Phillip

Balcombe

Balcombe Point

C783

Mt Martha

ESPLANADE   HEARN   RD

Martha Point

Dromana Bay

Safety Beach

C783

Dromana

ROAD   MARINE   NEPEAN   HWY

B110   C789

11

McCrae

BOUNDARY   RD

C787

Dromana South

ARTHURS SEAT STATE PARK

Rosebud

Rosebud West

NEPEAN   B110

EASTBOURNE

POINT   RD

ARTHURS SEAT STATE PARK

PENINSULA

SEAT   ARTHURS

Red Hill

11

PURVES

C789

Rosebud South

C777

JETTY   RD

MORNINGTON

Boneo

LIMESTONE

BROWNS   RD

BROWNS   RD

Main Ridge

Creek

SHANDS   RD

BALDRYS

TUCKS

Boneo

C777

MORNINGTON PENINSULA NATIONAL PARK

MEAKINS   RD

MUSK CREEK

MORNINGTON - FLINDERS   RD

C787   BOYDS   RD

KEYS

C787

BONEO

Main

C777

PARK

Cape Schanck

CAPE SCHANCK

Cairns Bay

Bass   Strait

Bushrangers Bay

Picnic Point

Cape Schanck

A   B   C   D

1 2 3 4 5 6

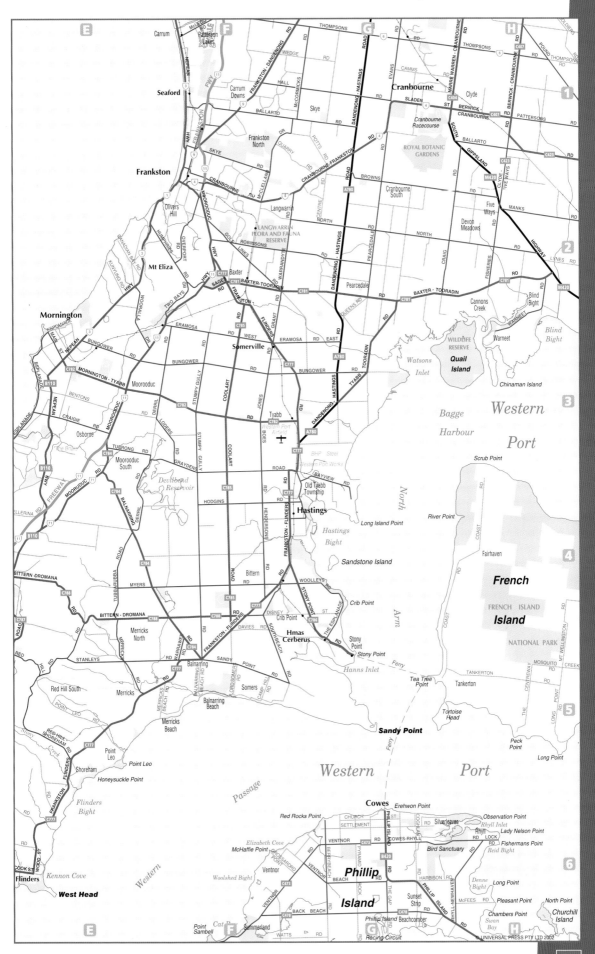

The Murray River

Best time to visit: Year-round; summer for swimming and water activities

Average daily temperatures: Jan 15–31°C, Apr 10–29°C, Jul 5–16°C, Oct 17–27°C

Getting there: By road from Melbourne via Hume Fwy (M31) and Northern Hwy (B75) to Echuca (205km), then via Murray Valley Hwy (B400) to Swan Hill (355km)

Festivals and events:

Feb: Border Flywheelers Rally, Barham Lakes (restored farm vehicles and machinery); Model Boat Regatta, Barham Lakes; Club Marine Southern 80 Waterski Race, Echuca; Riverboats Jazz, Food and Wine Festival, Echuca

Mar: World's Longest Lunch, Echuca–Moama and Nagambie Lakes (part of the Melbourne Food and Wine Festival celebrations)

Apr: Port of Echuca Sail Pasts and Fireworks Display

Jun: Rotary, Steam, Horse and Vintage Rally, Echuca

Jul: Winter Blues Festival, Echuca

Oct: Port of Echuca Heritage Steam Festival

Dec: Murray Marathon (5-day canoe race from Yarrawonga to Swan Hill)

Activities: Boating (houseboats, sailing, cruising), canoeing, water-skiing, fishing, swimming, birdwatching, bushwalking, 4WD touring, cycling, horseriding, browsing craft and antique shops, wine-tasting, hot-air ballooning, golf

Highlights: Riverboat cruise; Echuca's historic wharf; magnificent sunsets; red gums and bird-rich wetlands of Barmah Forest and Gunbower Island; cruising the Kerang wetlands; river delicacies of yabby, trout and Murray cod

Tip: Handcrafted red-gum furniture and craftworks are a local speciality.

Kids' stuff: Sharp's Magic Movie House and Penny Arcade, Echuca, Ph: (03) 5482 2361; Echuca Farm Yard (touch and feed a range of farm animals), Ph: (03) 5480 7334

Further information: Echuca–Moama Visitor Information Centre, 2 Heygarth St, Echuca, Vic 3564, Ph: (03) 5480 7555 or 1800 804 446, www.echucamoama.com; Golden Rivers Country Visitor Information Centre, 15 Murray St, Barham, NSW 2732, Ph: (03) 5453 3100 or 1800 621 882, www.goldenrivers.com.au

The abundance of waterways centred on the mighty Murray—Australia's most important river and the border between Victoria and New South Wales—shaped this region's colourful history and now provides a year-round water playground. Wide rivers, tranquil lakes, and sparkling weirs and wetlands are the venues for activities of all kinds, ranging from water-skiing to paddling in a sandy river bend and casting a line for the Murray's prized fish. The river's rich heritage of paddlesteamers and inland ports can be experienced in Echuca (still a working port) and Swan Hill. The Murray is also renowned for its stands of towering red gums and plentiful birdlife. Adjacent plains, irrigated with river waters, yield rich harvests of fruits and vegetables, and wineries open cellar-doors for tastings and sales. Riverside restaurants showcase the best of local produce, or you can fill a picnic basket and choose your own location for a waterfront feast. Accommodation includes stylish B&Bs, golf resorts, family holiday apartments, houseboats (wake to the sound of gentle lapping waves) and caravan parks.

A steady flow of tourists makes the carefully restored port of **Echuca** as busy today as it was at the height of river trading a century ago. Boats operating out of the port offer a range of cruises, from 1hr to overnight. The old port area is now managed as a tourist attraction including the old red-gum wharf, a collection of restored paddlesteamers, the Wharf Museum and historic buildings such as

Historic wharf at Echuca

Up the Lazy River

Historic paddlesteamers operating out of Echuca today include the *Alexander Arbuthnot* (1916), Ph: (03) 5482 4248; *Canberra* (1912), Ph: (03) 5482 2711; *Pevensey* (1909–11), Ph: (03) 5482 4248; and *Pride of the Murray* (1924), Ph: (03) 5482 5244; all offer 1hr river cruises. The wood-fired PS *Emmylou* (whose engine dates from 1906) takes visitors on 90min and overnight cruises, Ph: (03) 5480 2237, while the MV *Mary Ann* is a fully licensed floating restaurant offering lunch and dinner cruises, Ph: (03) 5480 2200. The PS *Adelaide* (1866), one of the oldest steam-driven boats in the world, is moored in the wharf area but is not used for cruises.

the Bridge and Star hotels; entry fee, Ph: (03) 5482 4248. For motor-car enthusiasts, the National Holden Motor Museum is stocked with more than 40 meticulously restored Holden vehicles showing the development of this Australian icon; Ph: (03) 5480 2033, entry fee.

Downstream, **Swan Hill**'s Pioneer Settlement is a re-creation of a paddle-steamer-era riverside port. Visitors can tour a working blacksmith's workshop, bakery and general store and enjoy short cruises along the river on the PS *Pyap*; entry fee, Ph: (03) 5032 1093.

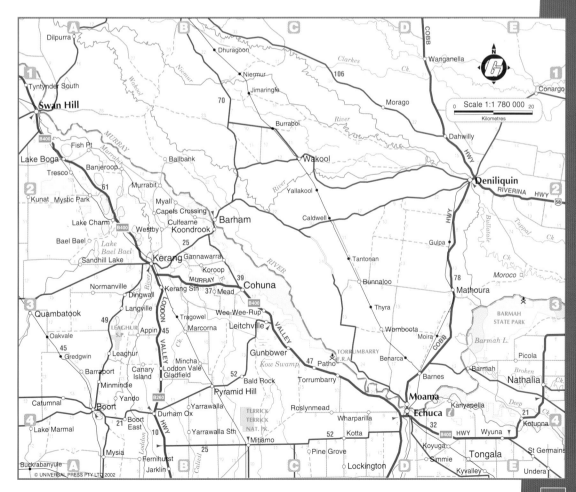

The Northern Wine Country

Best time to visit: Autumn for harvest festivals; summer for rose blooms and water activities

Average daily temperatures: Jan 15–31°C, Apr 8–22°C, Jul 4–15°C, Oct 11–25°C

Getting there: By road from Melbourne via Hume Fwy (M31) to Benalla (190km) and Wangaratta (235km); by rail from Melbourne to Benalla and Wangaratta; by air from Melbourne to Albury

Festivals and events:

Mar: Tastes of Rutherglen (9-day food and wine festival); Myrtleford Tobacco, Hops and Timber Festival (food, wine and entertainment)

Apr: Brown Brothers Easter Festival, Milawa (regional produce); Australia Felix Benalla Easter Arts Festival

Jun: Rutherglen Winery Walkabout

Oct: Benalla Agricultural Show

Nov: Wangaratta Jazz Festival; Brown Brothers Wine and Food Festival, Milawa; Benalla Rose Festival

Activities: Wine-tasting, exploring historic towns, browsing craft and antique shops, bushwalking, horseriding, cycling, 4WD touring, boating, fishing, water-skiing, birdwatching, hang-gliding, gliding, hot-air ballooning, watching motor races, gem-fossicking

Highlights: Milawa's gourmet foods; fine wines of Milawa, Glenrowan and Rutherglen; Ned Kelly history; Benalla Rose Gardens and statue of local son and World War II hero Edward 'Weary' Dunlop

Tip: Cycle Rutherglen's gentle and scenic Muscat Trail, which links 10 wineries and provides access to a number of picturesque riverside picnic spots; for bicycle hire, contact the Visitor Information Centre, Ph: (02) 6032 9166, or Walkabout Cellars, Ph: (02) 6032 9784.

Kids' stuff: Cycling paths of Wangaratta, Rutherglen and Benalla (bicycle hire and trail details from local visitor centres); canoeing on Rutherglen's Lake Moodemere (it has virtually no current and is therefore ideal for learners)

Further information: Benalla Visitor Information Centre, 14 Mair St, Benalla, Vic 3672, Ph: (03) 5762 1749; Mansfield Visitor Centre, 167 Maroondah Hwy, Mansfield, Vic 3722, Ph: (03) 5775 1464 or 1800 060 686; Rutherglen Visitor Information Centre, 13/27 Drummond St, Rutherglen, Vic 3685, Ph: (02) 6032 9166; Wangaratta Visitor Information Centre, cnr Tone Rd and Handley St, Wangaratta, Vic 3677, Ph: (03) 5721 5711 or 1800 801 065

This part of Victoria is famed for its exceptional regional produce, particularly wines, cheeses, mustards, honey and farm-fresh fruit and vegetables. Additional attractions include its historic gold-rush towns, rich bushranger heritage—outlaw and folk hero Ned Kelly was born, raised and roamed here—and magnificent rose gardens. **Benalla** is also the site of Australia's largest gliding centre—visitors can take a joy flight or enrol for lessons, Ph: (03) 5762 1058—and of the Winton Motor Raceway. To the west lies the Goulburn Valley, which is dotted with orchards and dairy farms and is one of the richest agricultural areas in the state. A host of fine eateries showcases local fare; accommodation includes upmarket B&Bs in heritage buildings, comfortable motels and tranquil caravan parks.

Kelly Country

In 1878, Benalla's Commercial Hotel became the headquarters for police hunting the Kelly gang, after Ned Kelly was outlawed for the murder of 3 policemen at Stringybark Creek, south of Tatong. For nearly 2 years, Kelly and his men took refuge in the rugged Warby and Wombat Ranges. In June 1880, planning to derail a police train next day, they spent a night at Glenrowan inn. Tipped off, the police surrounded the inn and finally captured Kelly after a fierce shootout during which the outlaw appeared in his famous armour. Today, Glenrowan features a 6m statue of Kelly in his armour; a replica of the Kelly homestead; a Kelly Museum, entry fee, Ph: (03) 5766 2448; the Cobb & Co Museum (with more Kelly memorabilia), entry fee, Ph: (03) 5766 2409; and Ned Kelly's Last Stand, a computerised re-enactment of the siege, entry fee, Ph: (03) 5766 2367. Plaques around the town describe the events of the siege.

Wine-tasting at Brown Brothers Milawa Vineyard

Gourmet wine and food producers are concentrated around **Milawa** and **Oxley**. Perhaps the best-known establishment is Brown Brothers Milawa Vineyard. In operation since 1889, it has cellar-door sales, a restaurant, BBQ facilities and a children's playground; Ph: (03) 5720 5547. At the Milawa Cheese Company, visitors can taste and buy award-winning cheeses, including a variety of sheep-and goat's-milk cheeses; Ph: (03) 5727 3588. In the centre of town is Milawa Mustards, Ph: (03) 5727 3202.

Rutherglen, to the north, has been making wine since the 1850s. Today it is known especially for its fortified wines but also produces high-quality red and white table wines; the durif grape is a local speciality. There are 17 wineries here, many with excellent restaurants.

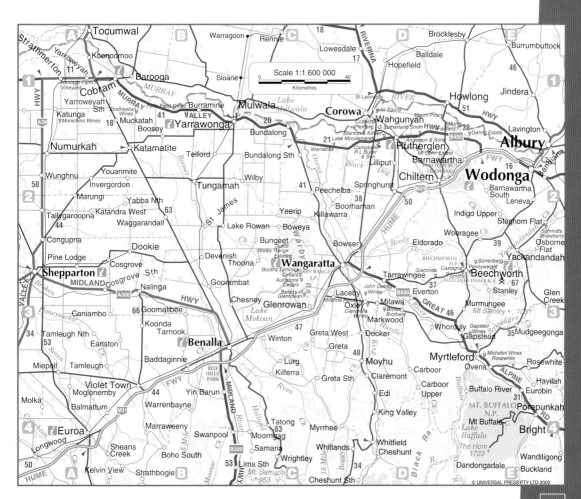

Phillip Island

Best time to visit: Spring for baby koalas; summer for watersports and festive buzz; spring to autumn for muttonbirds and seals

Average daily temperatures: Jan 14–23°C, Apr 11–19°C, Jul 7–13°C, Oct 11–19°C

Getting there: By road from Melbourne via South Gippsland Hwy (M420) and Bass Hwy (A420) to Newhaven (125km) and Cowes (140km); by ferry from Stony Point, on Mornington Peninsula, to Cowes; by V-Line coach from Melbourne's Spencer St Station to Cowes

Festivals and events:

Jan: Phillip Island Swim Classic, Cowes; Kilcunda Lobster Festival

Feb: San Remo Channel Challenge

Mar: Championship Series V8 Super Cars

Oct: Australian 500cc Motorcycle Grand Prix

Activities: Swimming, surfing, fishing, bay cruises, birdwatching and wildlife spotting, bushwalking, picnicking, cycling, hang-gliding, scenic flights, motorbike and classic-car races, golf

Highlights: Penguin parades in Phillip Island Nature Park; seal-watching cruises from Cowes to Seal Rocks, Ph: (03) 5678 5642; walk from the Nobbies to the Blowhole; Cape Woolamai surf beach; Koala Conservation Centre near Cowes; fish and chips from the San Remo Fishing Co-op

Tip: Bookings are essential for the penguin parades; weekends and holiday periods are especially popular. Consider purchasing the Rediscover Nature Ticket, which includes entry to the Koala Conservation Centre and historic Churchill Island as well as the parade; Ph: 1300 366 422.

Kids' stuff: A Maze 'n' Things, south of Cowes, entry fee, Ph: (03) 5952 2283; Wildlife Wonderland (Gippsland giant worms, white shark display), Bass (just off the island), entry fee, Ph: (03) 5678 2222

Further information: Phillip Island Information Centre, Phillip Island Rd, Newhaven, Vic 3925, Ph: (03) 5956 7447 or 1300 366 422

Easy access from Melbourne and a fine array of both sheltered swimming beaches (on the northern shores) and superior surfing beaches (in the SE) have made Phillip Island a popular weekend and holiday destination for more than a century. Today, it offers the fascinating mixture of holiday towns, major motorsports events, and intriguing wildlife.

The penguin parade at **Summerland Beach**, the island's greatest drawcard, has become one of Australia's most popular attractions. The world-famous Phillip Island Grand Prix Circuit is open to visitors wishing to relive the history of motor sport on the island; entry fee, Ph: (03) 5952 9400. **Cowes,** the island's main town, has safe swimming at sandy beaches, cinemas and other entertainments, and a wide range of eateries, with fresh lobster and other seafood featuring strongly on menus. It is also the arrival point for ferries from the Mornington Peninsula, and the departure point for bay cruises. The island's plentiful and varied accommodation is concentrated around Cowes and includes luxury apartments, secluded cottages, heritage guesthouses, holiday parks and caravan parks.

Churchill Island, reached by a narrow wooden vehicle bridge, is the location of a historic homestead, gardens and orchard, Ph: (03) 5956 7214; it also has several walking tracks. At the **Koala Conservation Centre**, Ph: 1300 366 422, a raised boardwalk brings visitors face-to-face with sleepy koalas. From Sep–Nov, you may also spy young koalas that have grown too big for their mother's pouch clinging to the fur on her back.

Coastline near the Nobbies

Penguin Parade

Fairy penguins nest in burrows above the high-water mark. At dawn, they take to the ocean for a day's fishing, returning, with remarkable punctuality, minutes after sunset to waddle back up the sands. At Summerland Beach in Phillip Island Nature Park, viewing platforms and floodlights allow spectators to observe the penguins' activities. Early risers can 'Breakfast with the Penguins' as they set off at daybreak; those taking a more leisurely approach can enjoy the ever-popular evening 'Penguin Parade'. Displays in the adjacent visitor centre show life inside the burrows. From spring to autumn, the viewing platforms also provide fine views of muttonbirds swooping back to shore. Visitor numbers are limited and income from fees goes towards protecting the penguins' natural habitat. Entry fee; Ph: 1300 366 422.

Seal Rocks is home to more than 16 000 fur seals—Australia's largest colony—with numbers peaking during the Oct–Dec breeding season. A viewing platform at the **Nobbies** provides clear sightings of these creatures basking on rocks. Close-up images of their antics are beamed live to the nearby Seal Rocks Sea Life Centre; entry fee, Ph: 1300 367 325. The Nobbies is also the starting point of a raised walkway that skirts thundering seas on its short but spectacular route to the **Blowhole**. The spouting water of the Blowhole is at its most impressive during high tide and heavy seas; views stretch south from here along the coast.

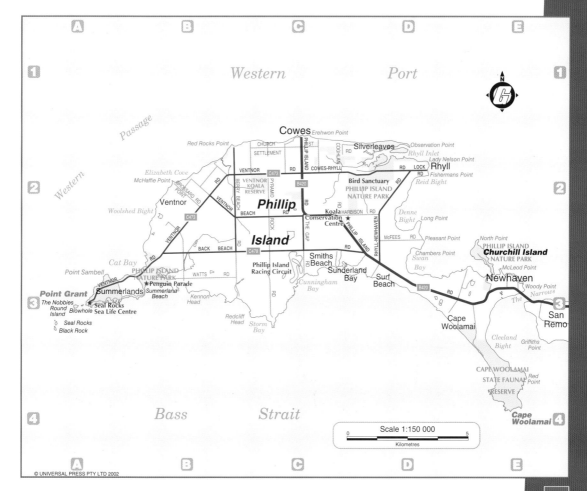

The Victorian Alps

Best time to visit: Year-round; winter for downhill skiing, cross-country skiing and snowboarding; summer for bushwalking

Average daily temperatures: Beechworth: Jan 13–27°C, Apr 8–22°C, Jul 4–15°C, Oct 11–25°C; Mt Buffalo Jan 7–16°C, Apr 4–10°C, Jul 2.5–2°C, Oct 7–11°C

Getting there: By road from Melbourne via Hume Fwy (M31) to Wangaratta then via Great Alpine Road (B500) to Bright (320km) and Mt Hotham (370km); by air from Melbourne to Albury and from Melbourne and Sydney to Mt Hotham

Festivals and events:

Jan: Opera in the Alps, Mt Buffalo

Feb: Blues and Roots Festival, Mt Buffalo

Mar: Mighty Mitta Muster, Mitta Mitta; Music in the Mountains, Falls Creek

Apr: Bright Autumn Festival; Mt Beauty Music Muster; Beechworth Golden Horseshoes Festival; Geebung Polo Match, Dinner Plain

May: Beechworth Harvest Celebration (food and wine stalls)

Jun: Back to Back Wool Challenge, Omeo

Jul: Mt Hotham to Dinner Plain Cross-Country Race (14km); FIS World Aerials, Mt Buller (freestyle skiing competition); Falls Creek Ski School International Ball

Aug: International Kangaroo Hoppet, Falls Creek

(cross-country skiing event); Dog Sled Races, Dinner Plain

Oct: Mt Buffalo Spring Ball

Activities: Skiing (downhill, cross-country), snowboarding, ice-skating, bushwalking, cycling, horseriding, mountain biking, caving, abseiling, canoeing, hang-gliding, trout-fishing, browsing craft and antique shops

Highlights: Great Alpine Road, a 300km scenic drive from Wangaratta across the mountains to the coast at Bairnsdale; Beechworth's antique shops; Myrtleford to Bright (94km) Rail Trail, which follows the railway line and can be enjoyed in sections on foot, bicycle or horseback

Tip: Weather conditions in alpine areas can change rapidly at any time of year; even in summer, you should wear or carry warm clothing including a windproof and waterproof jacket, hat and gloves.

Kids' stuff: Lotsafun Amusement Park, Bright (roller-skating, dodgem cars), Ph: (03) 5755 1137; skiing and snowboarding classes for beginners at Mt Buffalo

Further information: Beechworth Visitor Information Centre, Ford St, Beechworth, Vic 3747, Ph: (03) 5728 3223; Bright Visitor Information Centre, 119 Gavan St, Bright, Vic 3741; Mt Buller Visitor Information Centre, Mt Buller, Vic 3723, Ph: (03) 5777 6622; Victorian Snow Line, Ph: 13 28 42

The vast and rugged expanse of the Victorian Alps is the southernmost section of the Great Dividing Range. Known as the high country, this is a spectacularly scenic region of peaks, alpine plains and forested slopes, dotted with historic towns and lively ski resorts.

Ovens River Bridge at Bright in autumn

In summer, the region offers magnificent walking-trails including the Australian Alps Walking Track, a section of which crosses the **Bogong High Plains**, where huts built a century ago by cattlemen still stand. Awaiting exploration in the foothills are the gold towns of **Beechworth** (with 32 buildings classified by the National Trust), **Yackandandah**, charming **Bright**, known for its autumn colours, and **Omeo**, once the centre of the toughest and most remote goldfield in Victoria. (For information on the wineries and gourmet treats of Milawa, see p.103).

In winter, snowsports are the main drawcard; the official ski season runs from Jun–Oct. **Falls Creek** is regarded as the state's most exclusive resort. It caters for skiers and snowboarders of all abilities, with gentle slopes for beginners, broad pistes to suit intermediates, and some of the steepest and most challenging runs in Australia; cross-country enthusiasts can enjoy 40km of trails, all of which are groomed daily. This is one of the few resorts in Australia where visitors can ski directly from their lodges to the lifts and slopes; facilities include ski and snowboard hire, a ski school, discos, nightclubs, restaurants, supermarkets, cafes and pubs. Ph: 1800 232 557, www.fallscreek.com.au.

Ski classes for children and the over-40s are a speciality at **Mt Buffalo**, making it an ideal resort for families. There are downhill pistes for skiers of all abilities, snowboarding areas and toboggan runs, and fine cross-country skiing (13km of marked trails and 20km of more remote, unmarked trails). Ph: 1800 037 038.

Mt Buller is Australia's largest and Victoria's most popular ski resort. It offers slopes to suit skiers and snow-boarders of all grades, and cross-country trails that extend to Mt Stirling. Other facilities include ski and snowboarding schools, ice rinks, discos, pubs, restaurants, cafes, equipment hire, and bars. There is a wide range of accommodation. Ph: (03) 5777 6052 or 1800 039 049.

Mt Hotham, the highest of Victoria's resorts, has abundant natural snow and, with nearby **Dinner Plain** and **Mt Feathertop**, offers an extensive network of runs for snowboarding, downhill and cross-country skiing. It caters for begin-

ners upwards, and nearly all slopes are accessed by chairlifts. Mt Hotham has its own airport, 20min away at Horsehair Plain, with flights from Melbourne and Sydney. Ph: (03) 5759 4444.

Skiing at Mt Buller

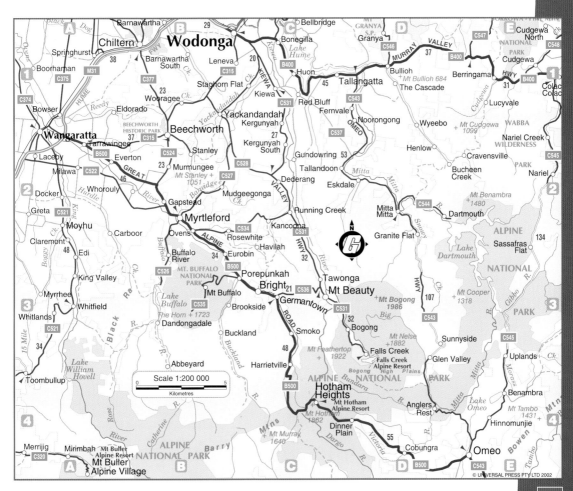

Wilsons Promontory

Best time to visit: Spring for abundant wildflowers; summer for beaches; autumn for ideal walking temperatures

Average daily temperatures: Jan 14–20°C, Apr 13–17°C, Jul 8–13°C, Oct 11–17°C

Getting there: By road from Melbourne via South Gippsland Hwy (A420) to Meeniyan, then C444 to Tidal River (230km)

Festivals and events:

Mar: Toora Festival (music, food, children's entertainment and King of the Mountain footrace)

Activities: Bushwalking, beachcombing, swimming, surfing, fishing, picnicking, birdwatching and wildlife spotting, diving, whalewatching

Highlights: Tidal River to Squeaky Beach walk (3hr return); Mt Oberon walk (panoramic views from summit, 2hr return); excellent swimming in the shallow waters of Sealers Cove

Tip: The promontory, especially Tidal River, is extremely crowded during peak holiday periods.

Kids' stuff: Paddling in the sandy shallows at Tidal River; summer outdoor cinema, Tidal River; ranger-led activities during school holidays

Further information: Prom Country Information Centre, South Gippsland Hwy, Korumburra, Vic 3950, Ph: (03) 5655 2233 or 1800 630 704

The storm-battered, granite-shouldered mountains of Wilsons Promontory are linked to the mainland by the sandy plain of **Yanakie Isthmus**. Aboriginal middens in the area date back many thousands of years, and in the 1800s sheltered coves here were used by sealers and whalers. The southernmost point of mainland Australia, this peninsula is now protected by **Wilsons Promontory NP**.

There is vehicle access to **Tidal River**, site of a stunning, sandy surf beach, cafe, store and information centre. Many of the 30 or so well-maintained walking tracks that criss-cross the park's rugged beauty start here. They range from easy half-day family rambles to the classic 3-day 'Prom' circuit, a 44km trail that crosses to **Sealers Cove** and returns via **Refuge Cove** and **Kersop Peak** (a good vantage point for winter whale sightings); along the way, it takes in stunning seascapes, mountains, forests and fern gullies. Prolific and frequently seen wildlife includes kangaroos, emus, wombats and crimson rosellas; the surrounding waters, which are protected by **Wilsons Promontory Marine Park**, support an array of colourful sea life and provide wonderful diving opportunities.

Accommodation on the promontory is available only at Tidal River; it includes self-contained cabins, huts, group lodges and a camping ground; Ph: 13 1963 (Parks Victoria Information Centre) for bookings. Plentiful accommodation and a range of eateries can also be found in nearby mainland townships.

Giant boulders at Whisky Bay

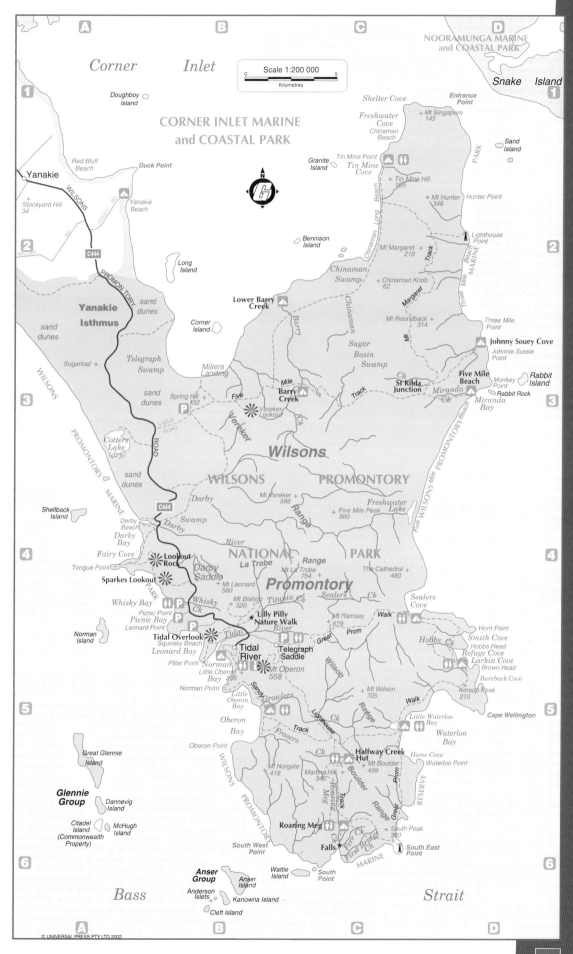

Stonehaven Bay, Hook Island, Whitsundays

Queensland

Queensland's famed sunshine and abundant and varied attractions make it Australia's premier holiday destination. The state's 3000km-long eastern coastline stretches from the cosmopolitan beaches and bright lights of the Gold Coast to the pristine sands and rainforested slopes of the Daintree and remote Cape York. For most of its length, the coast is fringed by the Great Barrier Reef, a wonderland of tropical islands, colourful reefs and coral atolls. The Reef islands, most of which are protected by national parks, are the site of exclusive retreats and family resorts, and also offer idyllic cruising. Further south is Fraser Island, the world's largest sand island, where the high dunes hold crystal-clear freshwater lakes. To the west of the Great Dividing Range are the rolling pastoral lands, scattered towns and wide horizons of the Outback. The capital, Brisbane, is a friendly, outdoor-oriented city, with attractive riverfront parklands, alfresco restaurants and, on its doorstep, the coastal playground of Moreton Bay.

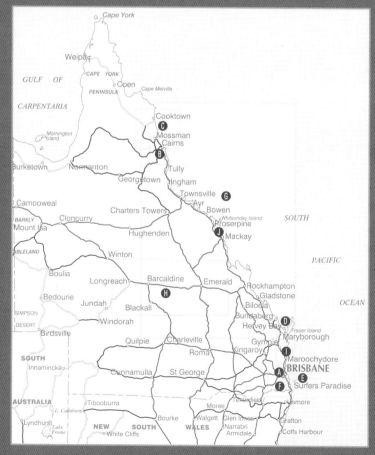

Tourist Information

Queensland Government Travel Centre
30 Makertson St
Brisbane
Qld 4000
Ph: 13 88 33
www.queenslandtravel.com.au

Top Tourist Destinations

- A Brisbane
- B Cairns
- C The Daintree
- D The Fraser Coast
- E The Gold Coast
- F The Gold Coast Hinterland
- G The Great Barrier Reef
- H Outback Queensland
- I The Sunshine Coast
- J The Whitsunday Coast

Brisbane

Best time to visit: Year-round

Average daily temperatures: Jan 20–30°C, Apr 14–25°C, Jul 9–22°C, Oct 15–27°C

Getting there: Linked by air to all state capitals; daily rail services from Sydney (970km)

Festivals and events:

Jan: Australia Day fireworks

Mar–Apr: Streets of Brisbane (festival of street theatre), South Bank Parklands

May: Queensland Jazz Carnival, various inner-city venues; Brisbane River Fun Run; Caxton St Seafood and Wine Festival, Paddington; Paniyiri Greek Festival, West End

May–Jun: Queensland Winter Racing Festival (combination of carnival and horseracing), Eagle Farm and Ascot; DÄR Indigenous Arts and Culture Festival, various venues

Jun: Queensland Day; Out of the Box Festival of Early Childhood (even years only); Lantern and Music Festival (start of whalewatching season), Point Lookout, North Stradbroke Island

Aug: Royal Brisbane Show, Fortitude Valley; Straddie Fishing Classic, North Stradbroke Island

Aug–Sep: Riverfestival (includes Dragon Boat Regatta, fireworks), riverside venues

Sep: Spring Hill Fair (food, street entertainment); Brisbane Festival (multi-arts event, even years only), various inner-city venues

Oct: Brisbane Writers Festival

Activities: Museums and galleries, wining and dining, river cruises, riverside markets, swimming, sailing, fishing, abseiling, cycling

Highlights: River cruise; South Bank precinct; cycleways along City Botanic Gardens foreshore; view from Mt Coot-tha; Boondall Wetlands; Moreton Bay dolphin cruises; dolphin feeding at Tangalooma, Moreton Island; whalewatching from Point Lookout, North Stradbroke Island, and Cape Moreton, Moreton Island

Tip: Ride the elevator to the top of the 91m-high clock tower of City Hall for panoramic views of central Brisbane and beyond; Ph: (07) 3403 8888.

Kids' stuff: Swimming lagoon at Breaka Beach, South Bank Parklands; Roma St Parklands playground with rock-lined dry creekbed for games and exploration; Top's Amusement Centre, CBD, entry fee, Ph: (07) 3221 9177; Queensland Sciencentre (interactive displays), entry fee, Ph: (07) 3220 0166; New Farm Park, New Farm (playgrounds with massive fig trees, tennis courts, sports and picnic area); riverside cycleways; Lone Pine Koala Sanctuary, Fig Tree Pocket, entry fee, Ph: (07) 3378 1366

Further information: Brisbane City Council Call Centre, Ph: (07) 3403 8888, www.brisbane.qld.gov.au; Brisbane Marketing, 15 Adelaide St, Brisbane, Qld 4000, Ph: (07) 3006 6200; Brisbane Visitor Information Centre, Queen St Mall, Brisbane, Qld 4000, Ph: (07) 3006 6290, www.visitbrisbane.com.au

The subtropical city of Brisbane offers a warm welcome year-round. The meandering Brisbane River is the city's focal point; parklands of lush vegetation and walkways fringe its banks, passenger ferries and cruise boats constantly ply its waters, and no fewer than 7 bridges, including the graceful, 1940 Story Bridge, cross it. The CBD is contained within one large river bend and includes **Queen St Mall**, the city's shopping and dining hub, and the forests and fields of Roma St Parklands. The **Riverside Centre**, on the eastern side of the CBD, is the site of cruise boat wharves. Popular eateries line nearby **Eagle St Pier**, which is also the location of weekend craft markets. **South Bank**, on the southern shore, is the city's cultural and leisure precinct. The hilly, inner-city suburbs to the north of the CBD—Paddington, Milton ('Little Italy'), Petrie Terrace and Spring Hill— are known for their restaurants and wonderful mixture of traditional 'Queenslander'-style buildings, ranging from workers' cottages to colonial mansions. Hills and leafy valleys stretch west; to the east, the city's outer suburbs are edged by the calm waters of Moreton Bay, which are ideal for sailing, fishing and other watersports.

Places of Interest

Anzac Square (1)

Brisbane Convention and Entertainment Centre (2)

Brisbane Cricket Ground (The Gabba) (3)

City Botanic Gardens (4)

City Hall (5)

Eagle St Pier and Markets (6)

Kangaroo Point (7)

Old Government House (8)

Old Windmill (9)

Parliament House (10)

Queen St Mall (11)

Queensland Art Gallery and Museum (12)

Queensland Cultural Centre (13)

Queensland Sciencentre (14)

Riverside Centre (15)

Roma St Parklands (16)

South Bank Parklands (17)

St Johns Anglican Cathedral (18)

Treasury Casino (19)

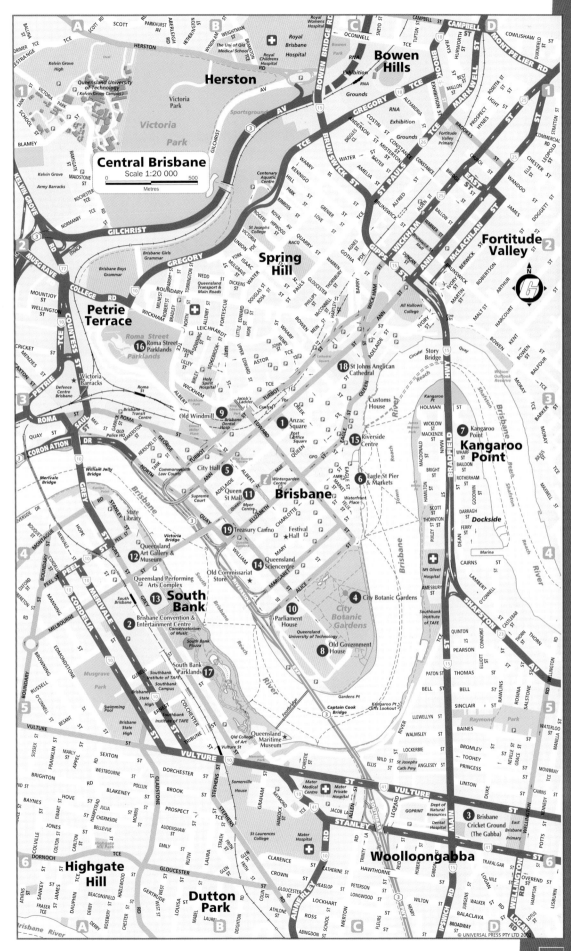

Central Brisbane

Scale 1:20 000

0   500
Metres

© UNIVERSAL PRESS PTY LTD 2002

Brisbane's CBD and the Brisbane River

South Bank

The state's most important arts and cultural institutions are grouped together on the south side of the river in the handsome **Queensland Cultural Centre**, an integrated complex of modern buildings surrounded by gardens and plazas adjacent to Victoria Bridge. Housed in one building are the Queensland Museum (natural history and cultural heritage), fee for special exhibitions, Ph: (07) 3840 7555, and the Queensland Art Gallery (European, Aboriginal, Asian and Pacific works), entry fee for special exhibitions, Ph: (07) 3840 7303. A neighbouring building contains the Queensland Performing Arts Complex, the state's premier venue for music and theatre; tours are available, Ph: 136 246.

A short and pleasant stroll eastward leads to the **South Bank Parklands**, the transformed site of the 1988 World Expo and now a magnificent riverfront recreation area. Frequented by buskers and street entertainers, it encompasses popular Breaka Beach (see below), gardens and fountains, playgrounds, boardwalks, cafes and restaurants, a cycleway, cinema, and BBQ and picnic areas.

Breaka Beach

The highlight of South Bank Parklands is the artificial lagoon area of Breaka Beach, which includes one large swimming lagoon (with a depth of 0.9–1.8m), and 2 smaller and shallower children's pools. The spacious surrounds are covered in white sand dredged from Moreton Bay and edged with palm trees. Chlorinated fresh water is pumped through sand filters and recirculated every 6hr. The beach is packed at the weekend and also busy on weekday evenings. There are changing rooms with showers, and lifeguards are on duty 7 days a week. Free entry, Ph: (07) 3867 2051.

Parks and Gardens

The riverfront **City Botanic Gardens** occupy a site cleared by convict labour in 1828 for a fruit and vegetable garden; paths and cycleways here thread through rainforest, majestic palms and huge Moreton Bay Figs; Ph: (07) 3403 0666. **Old Government House**, on the edge of the gardens, dates from the 1860s and now houses the offices of the National Trust; Ph: (07) 3229 1788. **Roma St Parklands'** 16ha of subtropical garden cover the former goods yards in the heart of the city; features include themed gardens, a forest with boardwalks that cross waterfalls, a lake, and a large grassy area for outdoor events; Ph: (07) 3006 4545.

At the foot of **Mt Coot-tha**, 7km west of the city centre, the 52ha of Brisbane Botanic Gardens–Mt Coot-tha display more than 20 000 plants from 5000 species in a range of themed areas. Self-guided walking tours lead visitors through rainforest, along an Aboriginal food trail, and into a formal Japanese garden, a cactus and bromeliad house, a bonsai house, and the futuristic-looking Tropical Display Dome, where thousands of plants thrive in artificial humidity; Ph: (07) 3403 2535. Drive to the lookout on top of Mt Coot-tha for sweeping views across the city to Moreton Bay.

Spreading west from Mt Coot-tha is the 28 000ha mountain forest of **Brisbane Forest Park**, where there are picnic and BBQ facilities and opportunities for bushwalking, birdwatching, horseriding and cycling; Ph: (07) 3300 4855.

The shimmering **Boondall Wetlands**, situated between Nudgee Beach and the suburb of Boondall on Brisbane's north-eastern outskirts, include more than 1000ha of tidal flats, open forest and melaleuca swamps. Bushwalking tracks and boardwalks lead to birdwatching hides in the forest and on the foreshore, and there is also a cycleway. The complex network of creeks can be explored by canoe—obtain a detailed brochure on the wetlands' Canoe Trail (showing routes, times and highlights) from the visitor centre; Ph: (07) 3865 5187.

Historic **Cleveland Point**, to the SE of the CBD, on the edge of Moreton Bay, is one of Queensland's earliest European settlements. Buildings surviving from colonial times include the unusual octagonal wooden lighthouse, which now stands in a reserve 30m away from its original waterfront site; the magnificent vista from here across the bay to Stradbroke and Moreton islands is best viewed in the late afternoon. Ferries operate daily between nearby Cleveland and North Stradbroke Island.

City Botanic Gardens, Brisbane

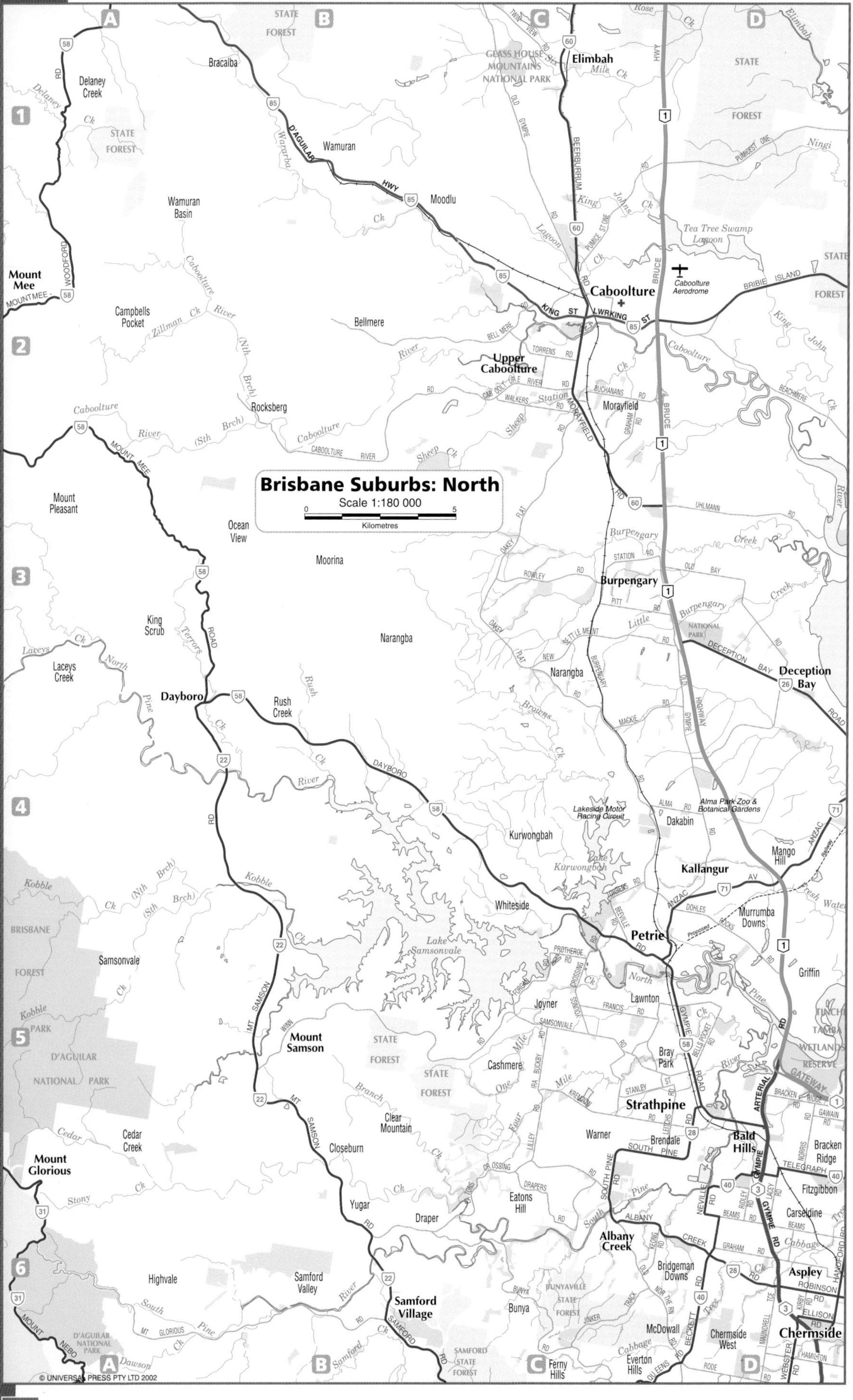

Brisbane Suburbs: North

Scale 1:180 000

0 _____ 5
Kilometres

A | B | C | D

1
2
3
4
5
6

Mount Mee
Delaney Creek
Bracalba
STATE FOREST
STATE FOREST
Wamuran
Wamuran Basin
Moodlu
D'AGUILAR HWY
Elimbah
GLASS HOUSE MOUNTAINS NATIONAL PARK
STATE FOREST
Ningi
BEERBURRUM
Tea Tree Swamp Lagoon
Campbells Pocket
Bellmere
Caboolture
Caboolture Aerodrome
BRIBIE ISLAND
STATE FOREST
Rocksberg
Upper Caboolture
KING ST
LWR KING ST
Morayfield
Mount Pleasant
Ocean View
Moorina
Burpengary
Caboolture River
Narangba
Burpengary
STATION
King Scrub
Laceys Creek
Dayboro
Rush Creek
Narangba
NATIONAL PARK
DECEPTION BAY
Deception Bay
BRISBANE FOREST
Samsonvale
Kurwongbah
Lake Kurwongbah
Lakeside Motor Racing Circuit
Dakabin
Alma Park Zoo & Botanical Gardens
Mango Hill
Kallangur
Murrumba Downs
Fresh Water
Kobble PARK
D'AGUILAR NATIONAL PARK
Mount Samson
STATE FOREST
Whiteside
Petrie
Griffin
Joyner
Lawnton
Cashmere
Bray Park
TINCHI TAMBA WETLANDS RESERVE
Mount Glorious
Cedar Creek
Clear Mountain
Closeburn
Strathpine
Warner
Brendale
Bald Hills
Bracken Ridge
Highvale
Yugar
Draper
Eatons Hill
Albany Creek
Bridgeman Downs
Fitzgibbon
Carseldine
Aspley
Samford Valley
Samford Village
Bunya
BUNYAVILLE STATE FOREST
McDowall
Chermside West
Everton Hills
Chermside
Ferny Hills
SAMFORD STATE FOREST

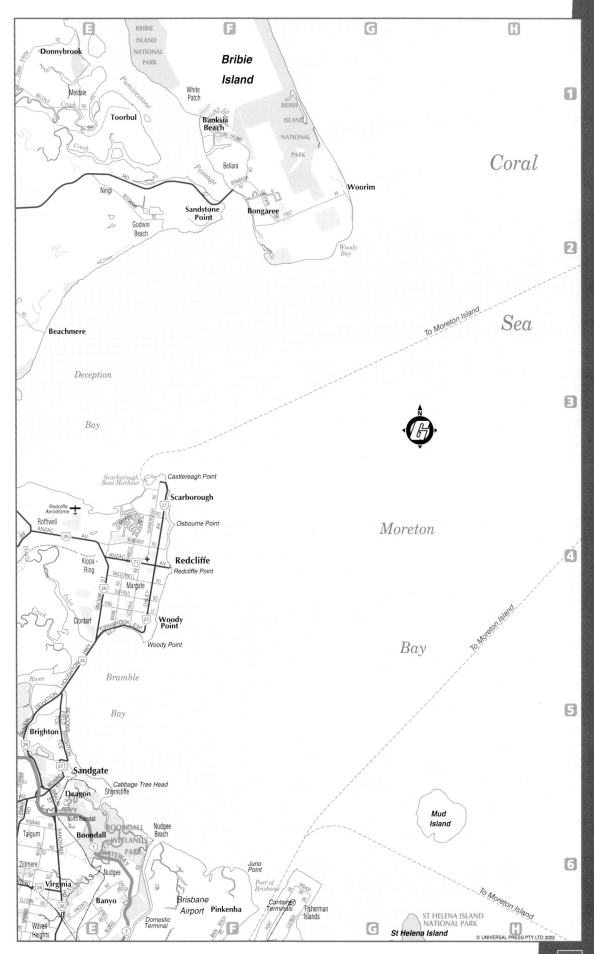

E F G H

1

Bribie Island

BRIBIE ISLAND NATIONAL PARK

Donnybrook

Meldale

Toorbul

White Patch

Banksia Beach

BRIBIE ISLAND NATIONAL PARK

Bellara

Woorim

Coral

2

Ningi

Sandstone Point

Bongaree

Godwin Beach

Woody Bay

Beachmere

To Moreton Island

Sea

Deception

3

Bay

N

Scarborough Boat Harbour

Castlereagh Point

Scarborough

Redcliffe Aerodrome

Rothwell

ANZAC

Osbourne Point

Moreton

4

Kippa-Ring

Redcliffe

Redcliffe Point

Clontarf

Margate

Woody Point

Woody Point

To Moreton Island

Inlet

Creek

Bramble

Bay

River

Bay

5

Brighton

Sandgate

Cabbage Tree Head

Shorncliffe

Deagon

North Boondall

Taigum

BOONDALL WETLANDS PARK

Nudgee Beach

Mud Island

6

Zillmere

Boondall

Nudgee

Juno Point

Virginia

Banyo

Brisbane Airport

Pinkenba

Port of Brisbane

Container Terminals

Fisherman Islands

To Moreton Island

Wavell Heights

Domestic Terminal

ST HELENA ISLAND NATIONAL PARK

St Helena Island

E F G H

© UNIVERSAL PRESS PTY LTD 2002

BRISBANE

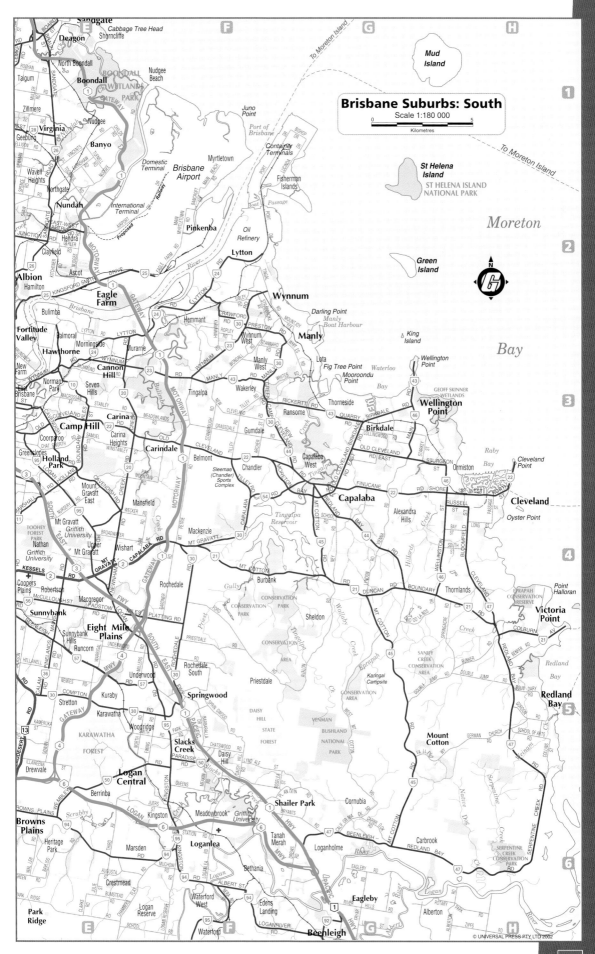

Brisbane Suburbs: South
Scale 1:180 000

0 _____ 5
Kilometres

© UNIVERSAL PRESS PTY LTD 2002

The Islands of Moreton Bay

Moreton Bay is sheltered by an arc of 3 large sand islands and dotted with numerous smaller islands. Its wide waters are home to more than 400 bottlenose dolphins and are visited in winter by humpback whales during their annual migration to tropical waters. Passenger and vehicular ferries cross to both Moreton Island and North Stradbroke Island; since 1963, Bribie Island has been linked to the mainland by a long bridge. A wide range of accommodation is on offer on the main islands.

Low-lying **Bribie Island** is edged by white-sand beaches and patches of mangrove. Tranquil Pumicestone Passage is ideal for swimming and windsurfing; Woorim, which lies on the east coast but is sheltered by Moreton Island, has gentle surf. Easy bushwalking tracks lead through **Bribie Island NP** in the north of the island. Bribie Island Tourist Information, Ph: (07) 3408 9026.

Almost all of sandy **Moreton Island** is national park; there are no sealed roads and visitors must travel by 4WD or on foot. The island's towering dunes are some of the tallest in the world and hold high freshwater lakes fringed by pure white sand, including the dazzling Blue Lagoon. Children can have fun climbing up and sliding down the Big and Little sandhills in the south of the island. Birdlife is prolific, but marsupials are few (the bandicoot is the island's largest). Guests at Tangalooma Wild Dolphin Resort can participate in hand-feeding dolphins each evening in the shallows. Permits are required for camping. Moreton Island Visitors Information Centre, Ph: (07) 5474 8400.

North Stradbroke Island's long, white, east-coast surfing beaches, its freshwater lakes and its renowned fishing combine to draw large numbers of holidaymakers. Brown Lake (the colour comes from its peaty bottom) is a short drive by conventional vehicle from Dunwich and has good picnic and BBQ facilities. Blue Lake, with its clear, deep water and white-sand bed, is reached via a 2.5km walk from the Trans-Island Rd; the surrounding **Blue Lake NP** protects forested hills, heathlands and marshes and is home to wallabies and birds. The cliffs at Point Lookout, the most easterly place in the state, are a favoured whalewatching spot; turtles and huge stingrays are also seen frequently. Bookings are essential for campsites. Stradbroke Island Visitor Centre, Ph: (07) 3409 9555.

For information on **South Stradbroke Island**, see p.136.

Cylinder Beach, North Stradbroke Island

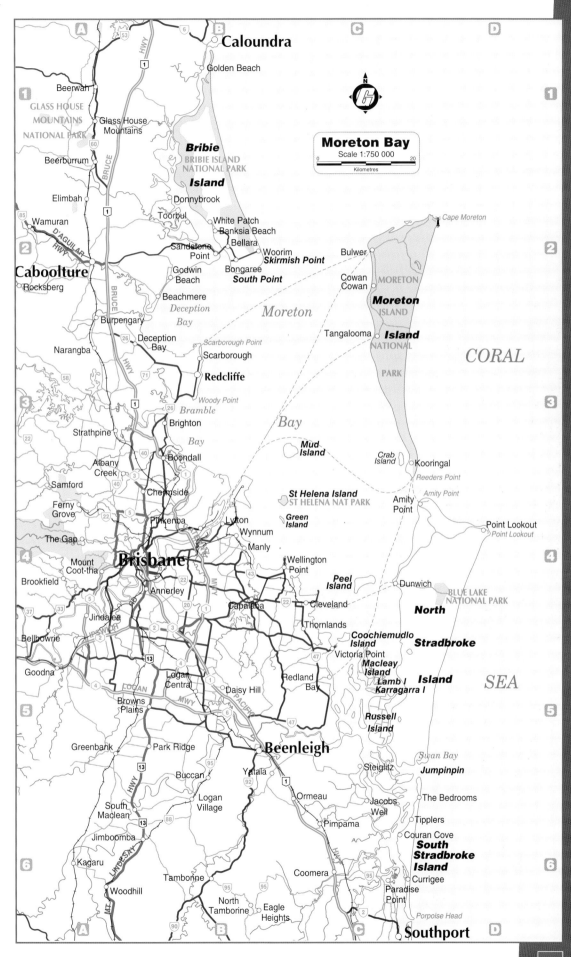

A1 B1 C1 D1

Caloundra

Golden Beach

Beerwah

GLASS HOUSE
MOUNTAINS
NATIONAL PARK

Glass House
Mountains

Beerburrum

Bribie
BRIBIE ISLAND
NATIONAL PARK
Island

Elimbah

Donnybrook

Wamuran

Toorbul

White Patch
Banksia Beach
Bellara

D'AGUILAR HWY

Sandstone
Point

Woorim
Skirmish Point

Bulwer

Moreton Bay
Scale 1:750 000
0   20
Kilometres

Cape Moreton

Caboolture

Rocksberg

Godwin
Beach

Bongaree
South Point

Cowan
Cowan

MORETON

Beachmere

Moreton

Burpengary

Deception
Bay

Moreton

ISLAND

Tangalooma

Island

Narangba

Deception
Bay

Scarborough Point

NATIONAL

PARK

CORAL

Scarborough

Redcliffe

Woody Point

Strathpine

Bramble

Bay

Brighton

Bay

Albany
Creek

Boondall

Mud
Island

Crab
Island

Kooringal

Samford

Chermside

Reeders Point

Ferny
Grove

Pinkenba

St Helena Island
ST HELENA NAT PARK

Amity Point

The Gap

Lytton

Wynnum

Green
Island

Amity
Point

Point Lookout
Point Lookout

Mount
Coot-tha

Brisbane

Manly

Wellington
Point

Peel
Island

Dunwich

BLUE LAKE
NATIONAL PARK

Brookfield

Annerley

Capalaba

Cleveland

North

Jindalee

Thornlands

Stradbroke

Bellbowrie

Coochiemudlo
Island

Goodna

Logan
Central

Daisy Hill

Redland
Bay

Victoria Point
Macleay
Island
Lamb I
Karragarra I

Island

SEA

Browns
Plains

Russell
Island

Greenbank

Park Ridge

Beenleigh

Steiglitz

Swan Bay

Jumpinpin

Buccan

Yatala

Ormeau

Jacobs
Well

The Bedrooms

South
Maclean

Logan
Village

Pimpama

Tipplers

Jimboomba

Couran Cove
South
Stradbroke
Island

Kagaru

Tamborine

Coomera

Currigee

Woodhill

North
Tamborine

Eagle
Heights

Paradise
Point

Porpoise Head

Southport

Cairns

Best time to visit: Autumn, winter and spring (Mar–Oct, the dry season) for beaches and diving; in summer (the Wet), rainfall and humidity are high and presence of deadly box jellyfish makes ocean swimming unsafe

Average daily temperatures: Jan 24–31°C, Apr 21–29°C, Jul 17–26°C, Oct 20–30°C

Getting there: By road from Brisbane via Bruce Hwy (1735km); by rail from Brisbane; by air from most state capitals

Festivals and events:

May: Far North Queensland Tropical Flora Festival, Cairns; Port Douglas Carnivale; Far North Queensland Folk Festival, Kuranda

Aug: Country Music Festival, Mossman; Mareeba Multicultural Festival

Sep: Cairns Amateurs (week-long carnival of racing, fashion, art, food and balls); Kuranda Spring Arts Festival

Oct: Marlin Fishing Classic, Cairns; Reef Festival of Cairns–Fun in the Sun

Activities: Swimming, snorkelling, diving, fishing (beach, reef, game and inland), beach activities, windsurfing, jet-skiing, sailing, reef cruises, hang-gliding, cycling, horseriding, 4WD touring, white-water rafting, bushwalking, birdwatching, golf

Highlights: Reef and island cruises; diving on the reef; Skyrail journey over rainforest canopy; Kuranda Scenic Railway; scenic flights over the Reef; coastal drive between Cairns and Port Douglas and view from Rex Lookout; Four Mile Beach, Port Douglas, at dawn; Barron Gorge NP; tropical produce and carnival atmosphere of Port Douglas Sat market

Tip: For panoramic views of rainforest slopes, Barron Gorge and distant tropical sea, take the Kuranda Scenic Railway, fee, Ph: (07) 4038 1555 or 1800 620324, to Kuranda and return over the forest canopy to the coast on the Skyrail Rainforest Cableway, fee, Ph: (07) 4036 9249.

Kids' stuff: Shallow, warm waters of Four Mile Beach, Port Douglas; Rainforest Habitat Wildlife Sanctuary, Port Douglas, entry fee, Ph: (07) 4099 3235; Hartley's Creek Crocodile Farm (crocodile show and feeding 11.00am and 3.00pm), entry fee, Ph: (07) 4055 3576

Further information: Tourism Tropical North Queensland, 51 The Esplanade, Cairns, Qld 4870, Ph: (07) 4031 7676; Port Douglas Daintree Tourism Association, Reef Anchor House, Port Douglas, Qld 4871, Ph: (07) 4099 4588, www.pddt.com.au

The city of Cairns is the main gateway for tourist traffic to Tropical North Queensland and an excellent base for exploring the region's varied riches of reef, rainforest and Outback. Hundreds of tours, including cruises, fishing charters and dive excursions to the **Great Barrier Reef** and day tours and safaris to coastal and inland regions, depart daily from here. The city is also the location of much of the region's accommodation (ranging from 5-star hotels to backpacker hostels) and offers an array of eateries, shops and nightlife.

Some of the most accessible dive sites on the Reef lie between Cairns and Port Douglas, and dive vessels catering for all levels of experience and budget operate out of both centres. **Green Island**, a 30min cruise from Cairns, is ideal for those seeking an easy daytrip destination on the Great Barrier Reef. **Fitzroy Island**, 45min away, offers unspoilt wilderness with camping, bunkhouse and cabin accommodation. Further afield, tiny Michaelmas Cay, 2.5hr north of Cairns, is home to thousands of seabirds and offers excellent diving and snorkelling.

West of Cairns lie the cool heights, scenic lakes and tropical wetlands of the **Atherton Tableland**; to the south, the rainforest, high peaks, waterfalls and rapids of **Wooroonooran NP**, part of the Wet Tropics World Heritage Area.

Trinity Wharf complex, Cairns

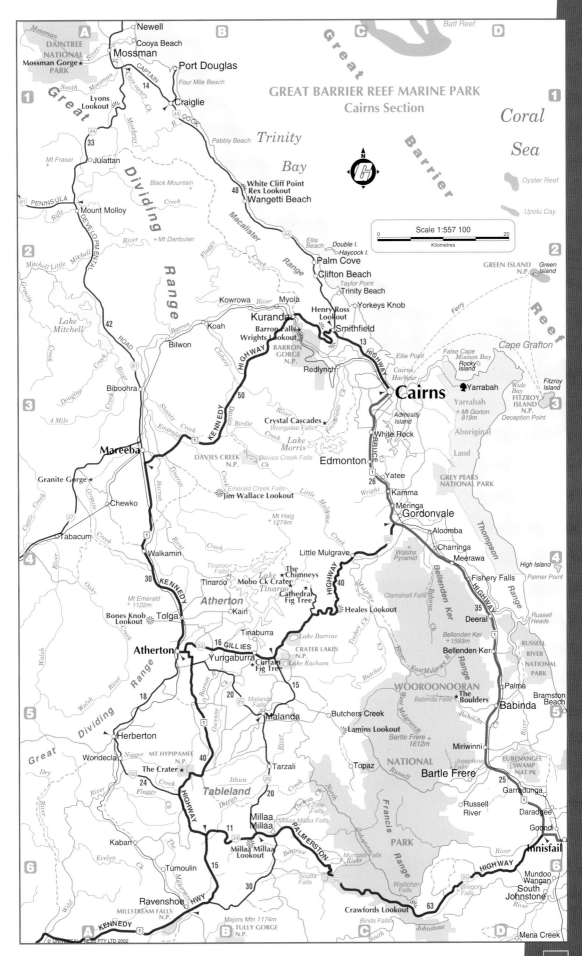

GREAT BARRIER REEF MARINE PARK
Cairns Section

Scale 1:557 100
Kilometres

Kuranda markets

Upland Rainforests

The mountain village of **Kuranda** perches on the edge of a wild, rainforest-filled valley 25km from Cairns. In the early 1900s, settlers used the village as a summer retreat from the humidity of the coast; in the 1960s and 1970s, alternative lifestylers were drawn to its tree-shaded streets and picturesque timber buildings. Today, Kuranda attracts visitors year-round to its country market (Thu–Sun), eateries, galleries and shops. Other attractions include the daily Heritage Market for handcrafts; the Tjapukai Aboriginal Cultural Park (with dance theatre and displays of Aboriginal artefacts), entry fee, Ph: (07) 4036 9249; 2 walk-through aviaries; and the Australian Butterfly Sanctuary, which houses more than 2000 tropical butterflies, entry fee, Ph: (07) 4093 7575. Rainforest walks surround the village, and a cruise boat

and a guided forest walk depart from the banks of the Barron River, nearby.

Getting to Kuranda is part of the experience. Those who choose to drive will enjoy spectacular views back to the coast as the road climbs through rainforest. Alternatively, visitors can travel on the Kuranda Scenic Railway; Ph: (07) 4038 1555 or 1800 620324. This 90min journey in historic carriages takes you up the steep escarpment, across gorges and ravines via century-old steel bridges and through 15 hand-hewn tunnels. The third option is the Skyrail, an exhilarating 7.5km ride that sweeps high over the rainforest canopy and Barron Gorge. Both the train and the Skyrail provide views of **Barron Falls**, 3km south of Kuranda, which cascade for 250m. The volume of water has been reduced by the construction of a local hydro-electric scheme, but the falls remain an awesome sight when swollen by wet-season rains.

Railway Safari

One of Australia's great railway journeys, the Savannahlander leaves Cairns once a week for the 4-day, 850km, return trip to remote Forsayth, a dot on the map in Queensland's vast Gulf Savannah. The train climbs out of Cairns along the same route as the Kuranda Scenic Railway, continuing on through majestically beautiful terrain ranging from lush rainforest to broad tropical grasslands. Along the way, passengers can explore several frontier townships; the train also stops at selected vantage points to make the most of photographic opportunities. Traveltrain (Queensland Railways), fee, Ph: (07) 3235 1122 or 1800 620324.

Northern Beaches

Pristine beaches and continually unfolding vistas of rainforested slopes and shimmering tropical waters make the drive between Cairns and Port Douglas a sheer delight. Just north of the city lies a series of long, white-sand beaches, each with its own township, including **Yorkeys Knob** and **Trinity**, **Clifton** and **Ellis** beaches. Take your time here and stop for a paddle—most of the beaches have summer swimming enclosures that protect against box jellyfish—or to savour the balmy air and spectacular views. From the heights of **Rex Lookout**, a long line of jutting headlands, interspersed with pale scalloped beaches and backed by purple ranges can be seen stretching south towards Cairns.

Although transformed in the 1980s by upmarket tourist developments, **Port Douglas** remains a family holiday destination offering a wide range of accommodation and eateries, a friendly atmosphere and an exquisite location between lush tropical forest and broad white beaches. Drive to the top of Flagstaff Hill (where the breezes are often harnessed by hang-gliders) for a fine view south over palm-fringed **Four Mile Beach**. Cruise, dive and fishing boats depart daily from Port Douglas for the Inner and Outer Great Barrier Reef. Popular destinations include the Low Isles, a coral cay topped by a historic lighthouse and surrounded by coral reefs, and the Agincourt Reefs, situated on the edge of the continental shelf and considered one of the best dive sites in the region.

Marina at Dickson Inlet, Port Douglas

The Daintree

Best time to visit: Autumn, winter and spring (Mar–Oct, the dry season) for beaches and diving; in summer (the Wet), rainfall and humidity are high and presence of deadly box jellyfish makes ocean swimming unsafe

Average daily temperatures: Jan 24–31°C, Apr 23–29°C, Jul 19–25°C, Oct 22–29°C

Getting there: By road from Cairns via Captain Cook Hwy to Daintree River ferry crossing (110km), Cape Tribulation (145km) and Cooktown (250km); 4WD essential beyond Cape Tribulation

Festivals and events:

Jun: Cooktown Discovery Festival; Aboriginal Dance and Cultural Festival (dance, music, traditional sports; odd years only), Laura

Oct: Lizard Island Black Marlin Classic

Activities: River cruises, bushwalking, birdwatching, horseriding, sea-kayaking, fishing (check restrictions in Daintree NP with QPWS), reef trips, beach activities, swimming, 4WD safaris

Highlights: Stunning coastal vista from lookout at Cape Tribulation; crocodile cruises on Daintree River; guided night-time wildlife-spotting walks; empty white-sand beaches; scenic flights over the Reef to Cape Tribulation; Quinkan rock-art galleries, Laura; sampling exotic fruits

Tip: During the peak season (Jun–Oct and Easter), it is advisable to book car hire in advance. Note that some car-hire companies prohibit 2WD vehicles being taken further north than the Daintree River Ferry; travel north of Cape Tribulation requires a 4WD vehicle.

Kids' stuff: Daintree Rainforest Environmental Centre (boardwalk through rainforest canopy, displays on flora and fauna); rainforest trail rides; swimming in cool rainforest pools

Further information: Tourism Tropical North Queensland, 51 The Esplanade, Cairns, Qld 4870, Ph: (07) 4031 7676; Port Douglas Daintree Tourism Association, Reef Anchor House, Port Douglas, Qld 4871, Ph: (07) 4099 4588, www.pddt.com.au; Queensland Parks and Wildlife Service (QPWS), McLeod St, Cairns, Qld 4870, Ph: (07) 4052 3096; Daintree Tourist Information Centre, 5 Stewart St, Daintree, Qld 4873, Ph: (07) 4098 6120; Cooktown Tourism Association, PO Box 605, Cooktown, Qld 4871, Ph: (07) 4069 6100

Rainforest in Daintree NP

Centred on the river of the same name, the Daintree is an enchanting region of ancient lowland rainforests and pristine coastline. Spectacular scenery abounds here: deserted, palm-fringed beaches of white sand; jungle slopes soaring to rugged, cloud-misted heights; and wide-mouthed tidal rivers inhabited by crocodiles. Among the region's highlights is Cape Tribulation, the only place in Australia where rainforest and fringing coral reef can be seen side by side. Visitors to this region can spend active days on rainforest treks and 4WD safaris, or simply laze alongside the tropical sea. Accommodation options range from backpacker hostels to luxury retreats. A wide range of tours covers all the main sights, or you can hire a vehicle and explore independently. Daytrippers to Cape Tribulation can choose from eateries at Cow Bay and Cape Tribulation.

White-lipped tree frog, Daintree NP

Crocodile Cruises

Like most other coastal waterways of Cape York, the Daintree River is the haunt of huge and dangerous saltwater crocodiles. At Daintree village, you can join one of the numerous cruise boats that glide along the river and, from the safety of your vessel, spot wild crocs basking on the banks. Cruise options include adventure safaris with a maximum of 4 passengers, specialised birdwatching cruises, and estuary cruises; all offer informative commentaries. In the cooler months (Apr–Sep), crocodile sightings are virtually guaranteed. Trips range from 1–2hr.

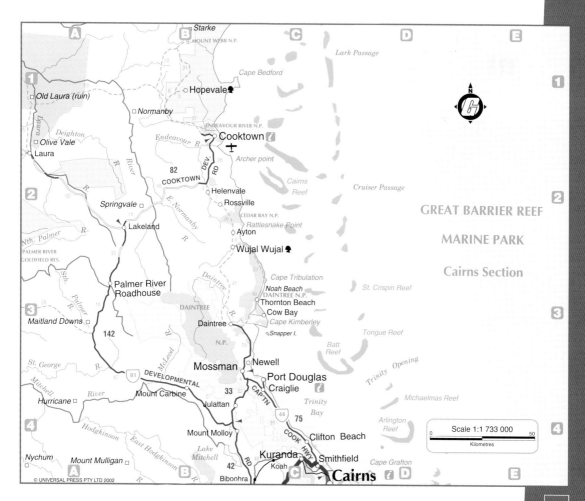

Daintree National Park

Two of the world's richest ecosystems, coral reefs and tropical rainforests, meet in 76 000ha **Daintree NP**, part of the Wet Tropics World Heritage Area. Offshore, the fringing reefs are home to approximately 400 different types of coral, more than 1500 species of fish and 4000 types of colourful molluscs. Prolific birdlife crowds onto coral cays, and dugong, green turtles and dolphins cruise the warm waters. Inland, the rainforest harbours an astonishingly rich variety of flora, including a high concentration of the most ancient flowering plants on Earth. It is also home to the greatest diversity of wildlife in Australia, ranging from brilliantly coloured butterflies as large as a human hand to tiny tree frogs and the endangered cassowary, a fruit-eating forest bird that stands up to 2m tall. Many rainforest creatures, especially mammals, are nocturnal, and the best way to see them is to join a night-time wildlife-spotting excursion.

Daintree NP is divided into 3 sections. The largest, the **Mossman Gorge Section**, lies just outside the town of Mossman. In the gorge itself, a 3km circuit walking track winds through rainforest to refresh-ing swimming holes. Guided tours conducted in this area by the Kuku Yalanji community provide a unique insight into the rainforest environment and Aboriginal culture; allow 1hr, Ph: (07) 4098 1305. To the north, the **Cape Tribulation Section** consists of a narrow coastal strip, where tangled rainforest tumbles down steep slopes to magnificent beaches and fringing reefs. The offshore **Snapper Island Section** lies at the mouth of the Daintree River, 20km north of Port Douglas, and is surrounded by the protected waters of the Great Barrier Reef Marine Park; access is by private boat or by private charter with local tour companies. A national park campsite is situated at Noah Beach, 8km south of Cape Tribulation; Ph: (07) 4098 0052. There are also 4 campsites on Snapper Island, Ph: (07) 4052 3096.

Numerous specialist tours are on offer locally, including ranger-guided walks, Aboriginal interpretative tours and nature safaris with commentaries by qualified biologists. Before walking in rainforest, it is wise to apply insect repellent to your shoes, socks and exposed skin in order to discourage leeches. Please leave flowers, shells, stones and wood in the park where they belong; all are protected by law.

Mossman Gorge area, Daintree NP

Horseriding on the beach at Cape Tribulation

Cape Tribulation and Beyond

The region north of the Daintree River attracts nature lovers and backpackers seeking a true wilderness experience. Beyond the ferry crossing, the road climbs to the crest of the Alexander Range (site of a lookout with dramatic views) then descends through dense rainforest to the small settlement of **Cow Bay**, which has accommodation and eateries and, 5km away along an un-sealed road, a tranquil beach. The Daintree Rainforest Environmental Centre, just south of Cow Bay, has a canopy boardwalk and interpretative displays which provide the perfect intro-duction to the tropical-rainforest en-vironment; entry fee, Ph: (07) 4098 9171.

Beyond Cow Bay, the main road con-tinues through the lowland rainforest of the Cape Tribulation Section of Daintree NP. At the Valley of the Palms, an easy and delightful track threads through a thicket of fan palms; at **Thornton Beach** the road emerges from the rainforest and levels out to run for a short distance along the edge of white sands.

Breathtakingly scenic **Cape Tribulation** is the end of the road north for most tour groups and self-drive visitors. There is no centralised settlement here, just small pockets of development strung along the road. From the main parking area, the Kulki Lookout Walk (400m one-way) leads through the rainforest to the head-land, which provides stunning views across the bay. The beaches are wide and sandy, and the water astonishingly blue. A number of other walking tracks wind inland through valleys swathed in rain-forest and traversed by cool streams.

The road north of Cape Tribulation is known as the Bloomfield Track and is for 4WD vehicles only. It is steep, dusty and often closed by rain (check current con-ditions before leaving Cairns); the views, however—over verdant rainforest to off-shore reefs—are majestic.

Leaving Cape Tribulation, the track climbs through dense forest over the Great Dividing Range, crosses the Bloomfield River, then winds on to the tropical outpost of **Cooktown**. A century before the town was founded, Captain James Cook's ship *Endeavour* beached here for repairs after being holed on coral near Cape Tribulation. In the 19th century, Cooktown developed as a port serving inland goldmines; today, it is a quiet tourist retreat with a number of interesting historic buildings. It is also the gateway to Cape York and remote Lizard Island, the furthest north of the Great Barrier Reef resort islands. Edged by more than 20 superb beaches and well-preserved reefs, Lizard offers splen-did and luxurious isolation at its single (expensive) resort. Cod Hole, a world-class diving site located just off the island, is renowned for its huge potato cod.

About 130km inland from Cooktown, just outside **Laura**, are the remarkable Quinkan rock-art galleries. Consisting of 1200 sites scattered around gorges that were once the wet-season home of the Guju-Minni people, the galleries consti-tute one of the largest assemblages of prehistoric rock art in the world. Most of the paintings are large, colourful depic-tions of humans and wildlife, and some record early contact with European set-tlers. This is rugged and remote country, accessible by 4WD only, but a wide range of organised tours is available.

The Fraser Coast

Best time to visit: Spring for warm, sunny days, cool nights and wildflowers; summer can be crowded; autumn and winter for cool, dry weather; Aug–Nov for whalewatching

Average daily temperatures: Jan 20–30°C, Apr 14–25°C, Jul 9–22°C, Oct 15–27°C

Getting there: By road from Brisbane via Bruce Hwy to Hervey Bay (290km); by rail to Maryborough with connecting bus to Hervey Bay; by air to to Hervey Bay. Fraser Island is reached by vehicle ferry—Hervey Bay to Kingfisher Bay, Ph: 1800 072 555; Hervey Bay to Wanggoolba Creek, Ph: (07) 4125 4444; Rainbow Beach to Hook Point, Ph: (07) 5486 3154; Hervey Bay to Moon Point, Ph: (07) 4125 4444. QPWS permits are needed for vehicles and for camping on Fraser Island, Ph: (07) 3227 8185

Festivals and events:
Feb: Yag'ubi Multicultural and Youth Culture Festival, Hervey Bay
Apr: Easter Family Fishing Contest, Hervey Bay
May: Bay to Bay Yacht Race (Tin Can Bay to Hervey Bay)
Jul: Rainbow Beach Fishing Classic
Aug: Whale Festival
Oct: Hervey Bay Seafood Festival

Activities: Sailing, yachting, canoeing, sea-kayaking, lake and bay swimming, fishing, whalewatching, water-skiing, scuba-diving, bushwalking, birdwatching

Highlights: Whalewatching; Fraser's Lakes McKenzie and Wabby and Eli Creek; driving along an ocean beach; charter flights, Air Fraser Island, Ph: 1800 627 583

Tip: Hire a houseboat to explore the safe, calm waters of the Great Sandy Strait and the sheltered west coast of Fraser Island; you can enjoy a spot of fishing while keeping an eye out for dolphins, rays and other marine life.

Kids' stuff: Whalewatching cruises; Eli Creek 'waterslide'; dolphin viewing, Tin Can Bay; Hervey Bay Natureworld (touch and feed native animals), entry fee, Ph: (07) 4124 1733

Further information: Hervey Bay Visitor Information Centre, cnr Urraween and Maryborough Rds, Hervey Bay, Qld 4655, Ph: (07) 4124 2912 or 1800 811 728, www.herveybay tourism.com.au; Fraser Coast–South Burnett Regional Tourism Board, 388 Kent St, Maryborough, Qld 4650, Ph: (07) 4122 3444 or 1800 444 155, www.frasercoast.org.au

Located 3.5hr north of Brisbane by road, Hervey Bay is one of the world's top whalewatching spots. It is also the main access point for World Heritage-listed Fraser Island, Earth's largest sand island, which is renowned for its crystal-clear lakes perched high in ancient dunes, abundant birdlife and majestic rainforest. For travel on Fraser, 4WD is essential. Vehicles can be hired at Hervey Bay, and daily 4WD coach tours to the island operate from Hervey Bay, Noosa Heads, Rainbow Beach and Brisbane. Fraser's long ocean beach—the main north–south thoroughfare—is subject to normal road rules; it also doubles as a landing strip for charter planes. Between the island and mainland lie the shimmering, sheltered waterways of the **Great Sandy Strait**, home to turtles, dolphins and dugongs, and an ideal location for a wide range of watersports.

Lake MacKenzie, Fraser Island

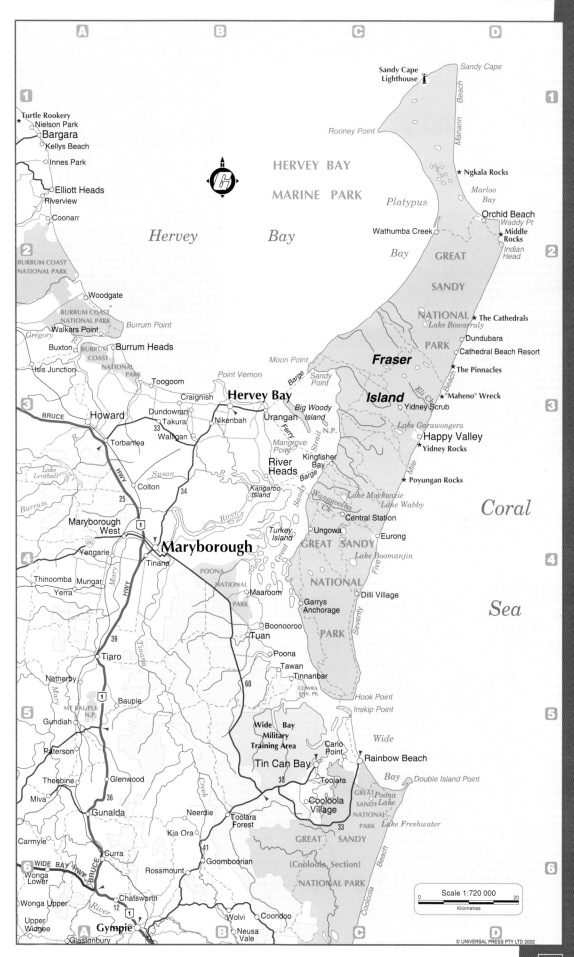

© UNIVERSAL PRESS PTY LTD 2002

Mainland Sights

Every winter an estimated 2000 humpback whales break the long journey between their northern calving grounds and their Antarctic feeding grounds to rest and frolic in the calm waters of Platypus Bay, about an hour by boat north of **Hervey Bay**. More than 15 tour operators based in **Urangan** offer half-, three-quarter- or full-day whalewatching excursions. Usually several pods are in the bay at any one time, so sightings are virtually guaranteed; many become close encounters as the massive creatures, measuring up to 15m long, cruise, leap and dive beside the tour boats.

In summer, Hervey Bay's sandy beaches offer safe and crowd-free swimming. A network of foreshore pathways and boardwalks makes this region one of the most wheelchair-accessible tourist destinations in Queensland.

Historic **Maryborough**, the regional centre, dates from 1847; its river port was once a major point of entry for migrants. Walking and driving tours of heritage sites take in the restored wharf precinct and the city's many grand 'Queenslander' houses, built of local timber.

At **Tin Can Bay**, dolphins are regular visitors to the wharf, and the wetlands along the foreshore bristle with birdlife. Visitors can hire houseboats and small boats to explore and fish the tranquil waters of **Great Sandy Strait**, which is famed for catches of bream, whiting, flathead, mackerel, tailor and mangrove jack, as well as sand and mud crabs.

Picturesque **Rainbow Beach** offers the safest surfing in the region; it is protected by shark nets and during summer weekends is patrolled by lifesavers. Ferries crossing to Fraser Island's **Hook Point** leave from **Inskip Point**, just to the north along an unsealed track.

Humpback whale breaching in Platypus Bay, Hervey Bay Marine Park

Wanggoolba Creek, Fraser Island

Fraser Island

Sands washed northward by ocean gradually accumulated over a period of 800 000 years to form 120km-long Fraser Island. It is not only the largest sand island in the world, but also one of the few places where rainforest grows on sand. **Central Station**, now the site of a museum and grassy picnic area, was once the headquarters of the island's timber industry and home to a workforce of more than 100 people. Nearby, a boardwalk follows silent **Wanggoolba Creek** through luxuriant rainforest and some of the tallest trees on the island.

Fast-flowing **Eli Creek** is the island's largest stream; young and old alike can ride this natural waterslide as it rushes to the beach along a white-sand channel fringed with pandanus. Boardwalks follow both banks from the beach to a bridge where you enter the creek.

The most famous, and most accessible, of Fraser's shipwrecks, the *Maheno*, lies rusting on the sands about halfway along the island's eastern side. This former trans-Tasman liner was blown ashore in 1935 during a cyclone while being towed to Japan to be scrapped. Further north are the enchanting **Cathedrals**, ancient sands bound together by clay, coloured red, pink, orange and yellow by leaching oxides, and carved by the elements into multihued spires and towers.

You can camp, fish and paddle on Fraser's extensive, spray-misted ocean beaches, but treacherous currents—and sharks—put surfing out of the question. However, swimming in the island's rain-fed perched lakes, possibly in the company of 2 or 3 saucer-sized short-necked freshwater turtles, can be an unforgettable experience. Crystal-blue waters, shimmering white sands, verdant forest and a general air of tranquillity make **Lake McKenzie** one of Fraser's most popular spots. **Lake Wabby**, the deepest lake on the island, is separated from the ocean to the east by an enormous, steep-sided dune and the shifting sands of Hammerstone Sandblow. Year-round, this is a fine place to sprawl in the sun or splash in the cool, blue-green waters.

Don't Feed the Dingoes

Feeding Fraser Island's wild dingoes is not only dangerous but also prohibited and could result in a hefty fine. Dingoes are wild animals, and should be regarded with extreme caution. Always keep your distance. Enticing dingoes closer with food leads to them becoming dependent on humans; it also decreases their natural wariness and can make them aggressive in their demands for food.

The Gold Coast

Best time to visit: Year-round

Average daily temperatures: Jan 20–28°C, Apr 16–26°C, Jun 10–21°C, Oct 15–25°C

Getting there: By road from Brisbane via Pacific Hwy (Hwy 1) to Coolangatta (85km) and Surfers Paradise (75km); by rail from Brisbane (Citytrain, Ph: 131 230); by air to Coolangatta from most capital cities

Festivals and events:

Jan: Magic Millions Racing Carnival (held over 10 days), Bundall

Feb: Billabong Boost Junior Series surfing competition, Burleigh Heads

Apr: Australian Surf Lifesaving Championships, Kurrawa Beach

May–Jun: Wintersun Festival, 10 days of rock'n'roll, various locations

Jul: American Independence Day Street Parade Festival (American Football, cheerleaders, US car displays), Surfers Paradise; Gold Coast City Marathon

Aug: Sydney–Gold Coast Classic, Southport Broadwater; Gold Coast Show, Parklands Showgrounds

Sep: Asia Pacific Masters Games (mature-age sports), Southport

Oct: Honda Indy 300, Surfers Paradise; Tropicarnival (food, fireworks, all-nations parade), Surfers Paradise

Nov–Dec: Schoolies' Week

Activities: Nightlife, theme parks, beach activities, swimming, surfing, canoeing, sea-kayaking, windsurfing, sailing, parasailing, water-skiing, jet-skiing, diving, fishing (beach, small boat and charter boat), bushwalking, golf

Highlights: Bars, nightclubs and restaurants of Broadbeach and Surfers Paradise; beach walk from Main Beach to the Spit; sandy coves, rewarding fishing and tranquil hinterland of South Stradbroke Island; watersports on the Broadwater; bushwalking in Burleigh Head NP; boat cruise of rivers and canalways; Currumbin Wildlife Sanctuary, Ph: (07) 5534 1266; theme parks

Tip: From mid-Nov to mid-Dec, hordes of students arrive from NSW and Vic to celebrate the completion of exams. Special events are staged including free beach concerts and sporting activities. Arrange your visit for another time if this is not your scene.

Kids' stuff: The calm, shallow waters of Greenmount Beach, Coolangatta, the protected beaches of the Broadwater, and the river and creek inlets at Tallebudgera and Currumbin are ideal for family swimming.

Further information: Gold Coast Tourism Bureau, Cavill Ave, Surfers Paradise, Qld 4217, Ph: (07) 5538 4419, or (07) 5536 7765 www.gold coasttourism.com.au

Aerial view of Surfers Paradise

A concentration of natural and purpose-built attractions makes the 70km-long Gold Coast an enticing holiday destination. Surfers Paradise and adjoining Broadbeach are known for their wide range of dining options, lively after-dark scene, great shopping and 5-star hotels. Beyond the commercial strip, grand mansions line intriguing canal-way developments. Superb surfing beaches stretch north and south and, along with the extensive, sheltered waters of the Broadwater at Southport, allow for all types of water- and beach-based activities. The coastline is also studded with theme parks, championship golf courses and wildlife sanctuaries. Accommodation ranges from luxurious suites in high-rise hotels to guest houses, tourist parks with cabins, and hinterland farm resorts.

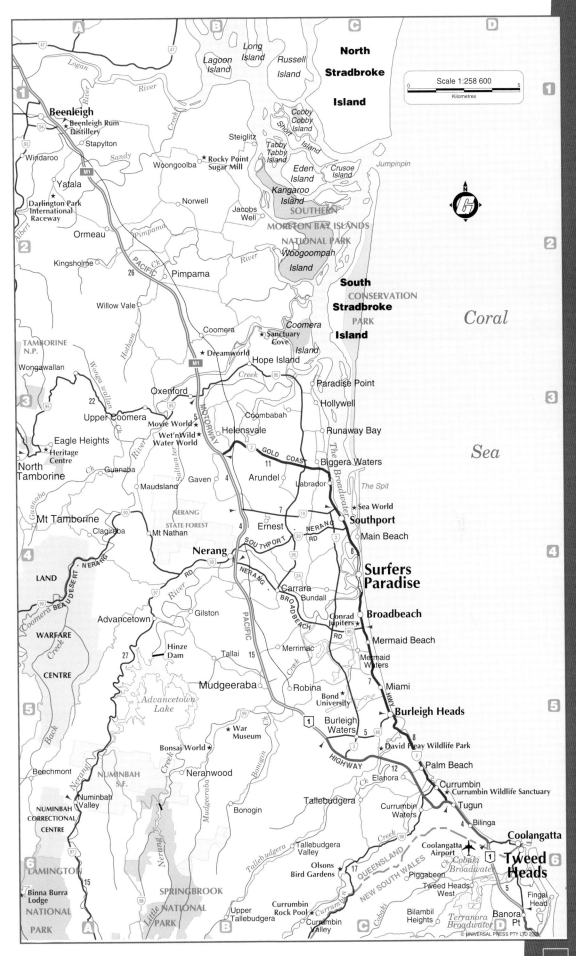

Golden Sands

Most of the Gold Coast's 40 beaches are well equipped, with open-air showers, drinking water and adjacent parklands with picnic and BBQ facilities and playground equipment. The majority are patrolled year-round, with additional lifesavers on duty during summer.

At **Southport**, the calm expanse of the **Broadwater** is ideal for all types of watersports, particularly sailing and fishing; its sheltered beaches also offer safe swimming. On its eastern edge, the **Spit**, home to the Sea World theme park, has one of the few areas of natural habitat close to Surfers Paradise; walking tracks lead through grasslands and coastal scrub, and there is a long jetty favoured by anglers as well as a surf beach. To the south, **Main Beach** is reckoned to be the best local beach for windsurfing. A mecca for sunbathers, **Surfers Paradise** offers great swimming, free beach volleyball and the lively atmosphere of its Cavill Ave strip; **Broadbeach** adds to the fun with its fairground. **Palm Beach** and nearby **Currumbin** have reliable surf and spectacular views, while the pretty beaches of **Coolangatta**, to the south, have gentle, child-friendly surf.

Further afield, **South Stradbroke Island** is a 22km-long sandbar lying just north of the Spit. It was joined to North Stradbroke Island until 1898, when a shipwreck and pounding seas caused a permanent breach. You can cross the Broadwater to the island by Fast Cat ferry from Runaway Bay (then hire a bicycle to get around) or hire a boat, pack a picnic and lots of sunscreen and anchor at one

Parasailing, Surfers Paradise

of Stradbroke's many sandy beaches. Wildlife includes friendly wallabies, pelicans and, at low tide, armies of soldier crabs. There are 4 camping grounds and 2 resorts, all on the bay side.

Burleigh Head NP, at the mouth of **Tallebudgera Creek**, south of **Burleigh Heads**, protects a small but diverse area of coastal vegetation including pandanus palms, tussock grassland and rainforest. Many of the park's volcanic rock formations hold strong spiritual significance for the local Aboriginal population. Walking trails around the rocky headland (some wheelchair accessible) provide magnificent views of beach and ocean; Ph: (07) 5576 0271. Burleigh Beach, just to the north, is the site of one of the east coast's legendary surfing breaks—for experienced board riders only.

Ocean view from Burleigh Head NP

Theme Parks

The Gold Coast is the theme-park capital of Australia. Most attractions have a single entry fee (family tickets are available), which, although fairly expensive, usually covers all rides and shows and so provides a full day's activities and entertainment.

At **Warner Bros. Movie World** you can stroll through movie sets (including re-created sets from *Harry Potter and the Philosopher's Stone*), watch actors and stunt-artists in action at the Police Academy Stunt Show and the Looney Tunes Show, and participate in demonstrations of movie tricks (such as back projection), before heading for the main attraction—an array of movie-based rides that seem to get bigger, faster and scarier each year. They include the Roadrunner Rollercoaster, Looney Tunes River Ride, Batman Adventure—the Ride 2, and the fast and furious Lethal Weapon. Ph: (07) 5573 3999, www.movieworld.com.au.

Dreamworld is Australia's answer to Disneyland. It has 12 themed areas, including Koala Country, Gum Tree Gully, Gold Rush Country and Australian Wildlife Experience. There are also Imax movies, an island reserve housing rare Bengal tigers, a bushranger show, opportunities to cuddle a koala, waterslides and dodgem cars, and a host of thrilling rides (including the daunting Tower of Terror and the Giant Drop). Ph: 1800 073 300, www.dreamworld.com.au.

Sea World is a 25ha marine park offering a combination of shows, attractions and funpark rides. The action includes performing dolphins and seals, spectacular water-skiing displays, and aqua-ballet. At Polar Bear Shores, underwater viewing windows allow you to come face-to-face with these large Arctic carnivores; you can also visit a dolphin nursery pool. Cartoon Beach is an adventure playground with roving cartoon characters and children's rides; more challenging rides elsewhere include the triple-loop Corkscrew Roller Coaster and the rollicking Pirate Ship. Ph: (07) 5588 2205, www.seaworld.com.au.

Wet'n'Wild Water World is a 10ha, water-based playground set in a subtropical garden with grassy grounds, picnic and BBQ facilities and snack bars. Attractions include waterslides and a freshwater wave pool. There's something here to suit all members of the family: the Double Screamer toboggan drop and the Speed Coaster, Mammoth Plunge and Twister waterslides are meant for adults and older children; younger children will enjoy Buccaneer Bay's pirate galleon with water cannon, flying-fox swing and 'crocodile' rides. Lifeguards are on duty throughout the park. Ph: (07) 5573 6233, www.wetnwild.com.au.

Roadrunner Rollercoaster, Warner Bros. Movie World

The Gold Coast Hinterland

Best time to visit: Autumn and spring; summer is wet and winter can be chilly

Average daily temperatures: Jan 18–30°C, Apr 14–27°C, Jul 6–19°C, Oct 13–27°C

Getting there: By road from Brisbane via Pacific Hwy to Nerang (72km) for North Tamborine, Springbrook, the Numinbah Valley and Binna Burra; from Brisbane via Lindsay Hwy to Beaudesert (65km) for North Tamborine; from Brisbane via Ipswich (30km) and Cunningham Hwy to Main Range NP (120km); by air to Coolangatta

Festivals and events:

Apr: Rathdowney Heritage Day (bush band, parade, food stalls)

Jun: Beaudesert Country and Horse Festival (rodeo, country-and-western concert)

Aug: Tamborine Mountain Flower and Garden Festival

Sep: Beaudesert Show

Oct: Canungra Hang-Gliding Classic

Activities: Rainforest walks, birdwatching, abseiling, horseriding, mountain biking, browsing galleries and craft shops, 4WD touring, fishing, wine-tasting

Highlights: Circuit walks through rainforest at entrances to Lamington NP; views from Wunburra, Purlingbrook Falls and Best of All lookouts, Springbrook NP

Tip: Go spotlighting after dark on a rainforest trail to see possums and other mountain marsupials.

Kids' stuff: Treetop boardwalk at O'Reilly's Rainforest Guesthouse (open to day visitors, free); glow worms at Natural Bridge

Further information: Ipswich Visitors and Tourist Information, cnr Brisbane St and d'Arcy Doyle Pl, Ipswich, Qld 4305, Ph: (07) 3281 0555; Tamborine Mountain Information Centre, Doughty Park, North Tamborine, Qld 4272, Ph: (07) 5545 3200

The green wall of mountains that forms a backdrop to the Gold Coast is part of a series of ranges that sweeps south to the Queensland–New South Wales border. Known collectively as the Scenic Rim, these ranges encompass quiet villages, tearooms, country markets, boutique wineries, lookouts with panoramic views, cascading waterfalls and extensive rainforest walking trails. The region can be explored on an easy daytrip from either Brisbane or the Gold Coast, and has much to offer keen bushwalkers as well as those simply seeking a change from busy coastal resorts. Anglers can even participate in a spot of inland fishing at Advancetown Lake (also known as Hinze Dam) on the way to the mountains.

Much of the hinterland's natural environment is protected by wild and bea-

Rainforest walk in Lamington NP

utiful national parks; some are included in the extensive Central Eastern Rainforests of Australia World Heritage Area.

Lamington NP, in the heart of the World Heritage Area, features tumbling waterfalls, mountain streams and ancient rainforests. Native wildlife includes marsupials such as red-necked pademelons, colourful parrots and butterflies, water dragons and carpet pythons, and the bizarre spiny crayfish, a blue, white and red crustacean that forages on the forest floor. There's great bushwalking including short walks for day visitors. For those wishing to stay longer, accommodation is available at campgrounds or in the historic lodges at the 2 park entrances—**Binna Burra Mountain Lodge**, Ph: (07) 5533 3521 or 1800 074 260, where a ride on a flying-fox cableway is part of the accommodation package, and **O'Reilly's Rainforest Guesthouse**, at Green Mountains, which features a superb treetop walkway, Ph: (07) 5544 0644. Ranger, Ph: (07) 5544 0634.

The rugged and often cloud-covered plateau protected by **Springbrook NP** is a weathered remnant of a huge volcano that was once centred on Mt Warning. The park is known for its lookouts (with sweeping views to the coast), waterfalls and ancient forests, which are reached via a series of walking tracks ranging from easy to challenging; some are wheelchair accessible. The park visitor centre, which has displays on the area's timber-getting past, is located in Springbrook township's original 1911 schoolhouse. The popular **Natural Bridge** section of the park is named after an imposing, natural stone arch that straddles a mountain stream; a colony of glow-worms lives beneath it. Campsites are available. Ph: (07) 5533 5147.

Tamborine NP offers panoramic views, pretty picnic spots and short bushwalks to hinterland forests, waterfalls and lookouts. The park is fragmented into 14 sections, each providing habitat for a wide range of birds and animals, including the rare Albert Lyrebird. Camping is not permitted, but there is plenty of private accommodation nearby. Ranger station, Ph: (07) 5545 1171.

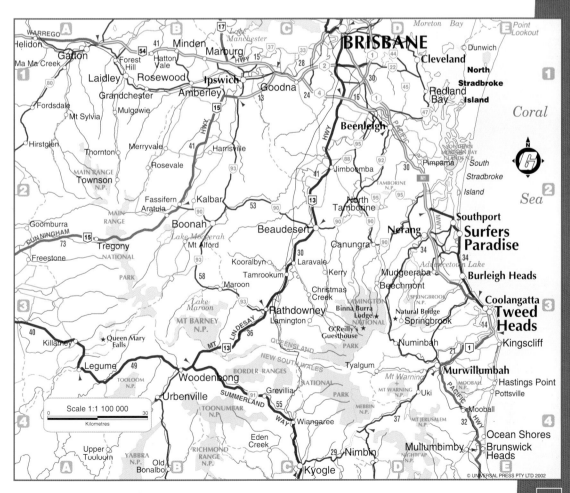

The Great Barrier Reef

Best time to visit: Autumn to spring (Apr–Oct, the dry season) for beaches, diving and bushwalking; in summer (the Wet), rainfall and humidity are high and presence of deadly box jellyfish makes ocean swimming unsafe

Average daily temperatures: Jan 25–31°C, Apr 22–30°C, Jul 15–24°C, Oct 21–28°C

Getting there: By road from Brisbane via Bruce Hwy to Mackay (995km), Townsville (1385km), Ingham (1500km), Innisfail (1650km), Cairns (1735km); by rail from Brisbane; by direct air services from most capital cities to Cairns and Townsville (feeder air services from Cairns and Brisbane to Proserpine and Hamilton Island)

Festivals and events:

May: Australian–Italian Festival, Ingham; Charters Towers Country Music Festival

Jun: Ingham Country Music Festival

Jul: Australian Festival of Chamber Music (even years only); Tully and District Annual Show

Aug: Townsville Running Festival

Oct: Maraka Festival (cultural and sporting events, carnival), Ingham; Great Tropical Jazz Festival, Magnetic Island

Activities: Swimming, snorkelling, diving, beach activities, fishing (beach, reef and inland), reef cruising, sea-kayaking, windsurfing, para-skiing, sailing, jet-skiing, bushwalking, whitewater rafting, horseriding, birdwatching

Highlights: Reef cruises; snorkelling and diving on the Reef; scenic coastal drive past Hinchinbrook Island; mountain rainforest and palm-fringed beaches; whitewater rafting on Tully River

Tip: For the ultimate, 'with-the-works' Reef adventure, join a week-long cruise departing from Cairns and taking in Fitzroy Island, Cooktown, Lizard Island, Hedley Reef, the Hinchinbrook Channel and Dunk Island, with stops along the way for snorkelling, swimming, and strolling on empty island beaches. Shorter cruises are also available. Ph: (02) 9206 1122, www.captcookcrus.com.au.

Kids' stuff: Get close to marine life at an underwater observatory (on Green or Hook islands), at Reef HQ in Townsville, or in a glass-bottom boat; most resorts have 'kids' clubs' and programs of children's activities.

Further information: Hinchinbrook Visitor Centre, 21 Lannercost St, Ingham, Qld 4850, Ph: (07) 4776 5211; Innisfail Information Centre, 1 Edith St, Innisfail, Qld 4860, Ph: (07) 4061 7422; Magnetic Island Visitor Information Centre, Picnic Bay Mall, Magnetic Island, Qld 4819, Ph: (07) 4778 5155; Mission Beach Wet Tropics Visitor Information Centre, Porter Promenade, Mission Beach, Qld 4852, Ph: (07) 4068 7099; Rainforest and Reef Centre, Bruce Hwy, Cardwell, Qld 4849, Ph: (07) 4066 8601; Townsville Visitor Information, Flinders Mall, Townsville, Qld 4810, Ph: (07) 4721 3660

One of the wonders of the natural world, the Great Barrier Reef consists of about 3000 separate coral reefs and extends for approximately 2000km along the Queensland coast. In the south and for most of its length, it consists of a wide scattering of islands and reefs extending up to 200km offshore. Near Cairns, it becomes a more continuous barrier, and north of Port Douglas it meets the coast proper, creating the rare combination of rainforest and fringing coral reef. Dotted along its entire length are hundreds of mainly uninhabited islands, ranging from low coral cays to steep-sided and wooded 'continental' islands (actually the peaks of a submerged mountain range). The coastal strip is equally enchanting, with a string of idyllic beaches backed by lush tropical rainforest. Accommodation on both the coast and the islands ranges from budget to spare-no-expense, with options including remote and secluded luxury lodges, sophisticated resorts, caravan parks, family units and family-oriented island resorts.

For information on the northern section of the Great Barrier Reef, see pp.122–129; for information on the Whitsunday Coast, see pp.150–153. The following pages deal with the section between Cairns and Townsville.

Snorkelling, Great Barrier Reef

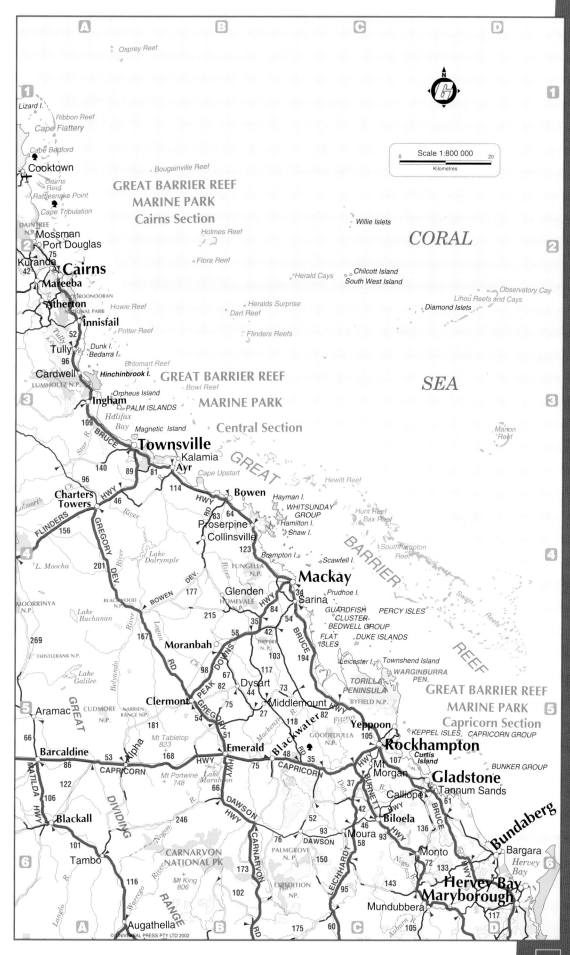

The Living Reef

Coral reefs are built up by coral polyps—tiny, primitive marine animals that are related to sea anemones. Each polyp produces a cement-like material that forms a hard exterior called an exoskeleton. When a polyp dies, a new polyp attaches itself to and builds on the remaining exoskeleton, and so the Reef slowly grows—the Great Barrier Reef has been expanding in this way for more than 2 million years. Inside its exoskeleton, the polyp is like a soft tube. It feeds at night by thrusting out clusters of tentacles that sweep in passing food particles. To survive, coral polyps need warm salt water (never less than 17.5°C) and sunlight—coral will not grow at depths to which the sun does not reach nor in muddy river mouths.

Nature's Wonderland

The ongoing work of countless millions of tiny sea animals called coral polyps (see above), the Great Barrier Reef is the largest structure in the world made by living organisms. Its coral passageways and caves are home to thousands of species of colourful fish, crustaceans and other marine creatures, while hundreds of bird species live on island, cay and mainland shores. The entire Reef is World Heritage-listed and protected by the Great Barrier Reef Marine Park.

The best way to see the Reef's wonders is by snorkelling or diving, or, if you wish to stay dry, from a glass-bottomed boat. There are also underwater observatories on Green Island (see p.122) and Hook Island in the Whitsundays (see p.152). A miniature version of the Reef, featuring a full range of tropical marine life, can be viewed at the Reef HQ aquarium in Townsville (see p.143).

Diver alongside a Maori wrasse

Breakwater Marina and Castle Hill, Townsville

The Tropical Coast

The coastal strip between Townsville and Cairns is a region of outstanding natural beauty. It is fringed by idyllic beaches and takes in parts of 2 World Heritage Areas—the southern section of the Wet Tropics and the central section of the Great Barrier Reef. It is also the wettest part of Australia, receiving as much as 4m of rain each year; this results in lush rainforest, spectacular waterfalls, and churning whitewater rapids.

The port city of **Townsville** is the gateway to Magnetic Island (see p.144); you can also travel west from here to the old gold towns of Charters Towers and Ravenswood, or north to the Tully River for fishing and whitewater rafting. Townsville's centre and waterfront are graced by elegant heritage buildings with iron-lace-decorated balconies, while its suburbs feature many fine examples of the highset, wooden, 'Queenslander' houses that are typical of the tropical north. Reef HQ (part of the Great Barrier Reef Marine Park Authority) is the largest coral-reef aquarium in the world; visitors can walk underwater through transparent viewing tunnels and observe hundreds of colourful fish and living corals in a self-supporting ecosystem. The tanks are open to the elements, and fish and corals reproduce and seek out food just as they would do on the real Barrier

Reef; entry fee, Ph: (07) 4750 0800. To experience the real thing locally, divers can head for the wreck of the SS *Yongala*; situated off Cape Bowling Green, just south of Townsville, it is covered in coral and teems with marine life.

Cardwell is one of the few places where the Bruce Hwy meets the sea; drivers enjoy magnificent views of waterways winding through mangrove forest in the shadow of Hinchinbrook Island. Ferries and organised tours depart for the island from Cardwell; you can also join a fishing charter here, or hire a yacht, motor cruiser or houseboat.

Mission Beach encompasses a string of settlements dotted along the coast between South Mission Beach and Bingal Bay. All front onto white-sand beaches and are surrounded by dense rainforest that in places stretches right down to the shore. Largely undeveloped, the area is ideal for holidaymakers looking for both unspoilt natural beauty and a relaxed and quiet getaway. Cassowaries—large, flightless birds standing up to 2m tall—are often seen in the rainforest here. The rushing waters of the nearby Tully River are ideal for whitewater rafting, with the more than 40 rapids providing almost continuous action; several operators offer full-day excursions. Mission Beach is the gateway to Dunk and Bedarra islands (see p.144), and daily Barrier Reef cruises also depart from here.

To the Islands

Its easy access from Townsville (it is only 8km away by daily passenger and vehicle ferry), sheltered beaches (some enclosed by coral reefs), national park wilderness areas and wide range of accommodation make **Magnetic Island** an excellent choice for affordable family holidays. More than two-thirds of the island is national park. Walking tracks wind through eucalypt forest and stands of hoop pine, which are home to koalas, rock wallabies, goannas and more than 100 species of birds. Accommodation options range from campsites and holiday flats to luxury resorts. Visitors can also join daily cruises from here to the Reef.

Hinchinbrook Island, the largest island on the Reef and the largest island national park in Australia, is ideal for walkers and lovers of wilderness. Rugged slopes cloaked with rainforest and tall eucalypts rise steeply from pristine beaches and mangrove swamps. The renowned 32km Thorsborne Trail winds along the island's east coast. A demanding multiday hike, it is for experienced, self-sufficient walkers only; bookings essential, Ph: (07) 4066 8601. Other than camping, the only accommodation on the island is a low-key resort. Access is by water taxi from Dungeness and Cardwell.

Ulysses butterfly

Dunk Island, located 4km off Mission Beach, is swathed with rainforest and home to a huge variety of plants and wildlife, including the large and beautiful, electric-blue Ulysses butterfly, the island's symbol. Most of Dunk is national park. Its resort offers privacy and a wide range of facilities and activities, including fitness groups and a kids' club, sailing, golf, bushwalking, windsurfing and archery. Access is by air from Cairns or Townsville, or by launch, ferry or water taxi from Mission Beach.

Just south of Dunk is smaller **Bedarra Island**, the location of the adults-only Bedarra Island Resort, which offers high-quality, high-price, tropical indulgence. Access is by water taxi from the mainland or from Dunk Island.

Aerial view of Magnetic Island

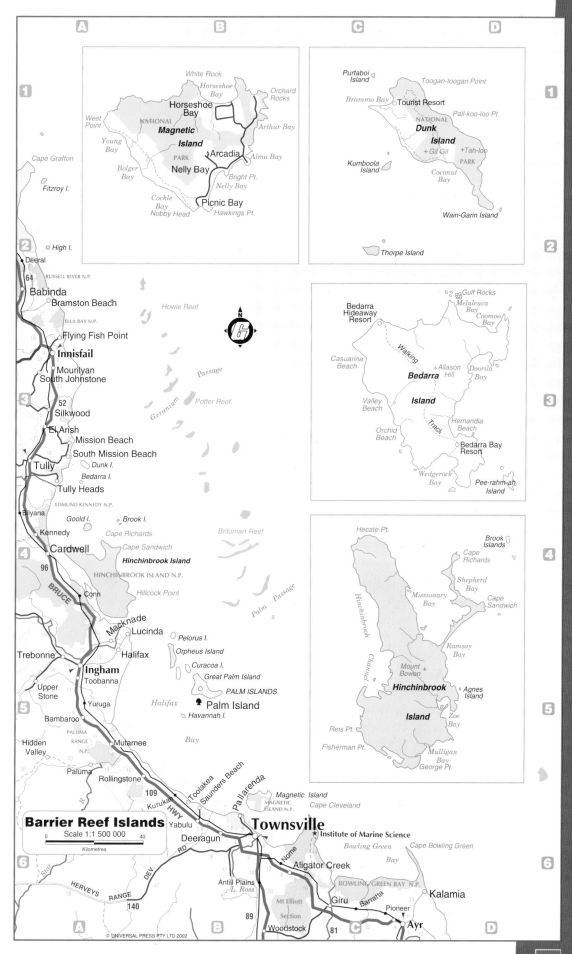

Barrier Reef Islands

Scale 1:1 500 000

0   40

Kilometres

© UNIVERSAL PRESS PTY LTD 2002

Magnetic Island (inset A1)

White Rock
Horseshoe Bay
Horseshoe Bay
Orchard Rocks
West Point
NATIONAL
Young Bay
Arthur Bay
Magnetic Island
Arcadia
Alma Bay
Bolger Bay
Nelly Bay
PARK
Bright Pt.
Nelly Bay
Cockle Bay
Picnic Bay
Nobby Head
Hawkings Pt.

Dunk Island (inset C1)

Purtaboi Island
Toogan-toogan Point
Brammo Bay
Tourist Resort
Pall-koo-loo Pt.
NATIONAL
Dunk Island
+Gil Gil
+Tah-loo
PARK
Kumboola Island
Coconut Bay
Wain-Garin Island
Thorpe Island

Bedarra Island (inset C3)

Gulf Rocks
Bedarra Hideaway Resort
Melaleuca Bay
Coomoo Bay
Casuarina Beach
Walking
+Allason Hill
Doorila Bay
Bedarra Island
Valley Beach
Track
Hernandia Beach
Orchid Beach
Bedarra Bay Resort
Wedgerock Bay
Pee-rahm-ah Island

Hinchinbrook Island (inset C5)

Hecate Pt.
Brook Islands
Cape Richards
Missionary Bay
Cape Sandwich
Shepherd Bay
Hinchinbrook
Channel
Ramsay Bay
Mount Bowen
Hinchinbrook Island
Agnes Island
Reis Pt.
Zoe Bay
Fisherman Pt.
Mulligan Bay
George Pt.

Cape Grafton
Fitzroy I.
High I.
Deeral
64
RUSSELL RIVER N.P.
Babinda
Bramston Beach
Howie Reef
ELLA BAY N.P.
Flying Fish Point
Innisfail
Mourilyan
South Johnstone
Passage
52
Silkwood
Potter Reef
El Arish
Geranium
Mission Beach
South Mission Beach
Dunk I.
Tully
Bedarra I.
Tully Heads
EDMUND KENNEDY N.P.
Bilyana
Goold I.
Brook I.
Kennedy
Cape Richards
Cardwell
Cape Sandwich
96
Britomart Reef
Hinchinbrook Island
BRUCE
Conn
HINCHINBROOK ISLAND N.P.
Hillcock Point
Palm Passage
Macknade
Lucinda
Pelorus I.
Trebonne
Orpheus Island
Halifax
Curacoa I.
Ingham
Toobanna
Great Palm Island
PALM ISLANDS
Upper Stone
Yuruga
Halifax
Palm Island
Bambaroo
Havannah I.
PALUMA
RANGE
Mutarnee
Bay
Hidden Valley
N.P.
Paluma
Rollingstone
109
Toolakea
Saunders Beach
Kurukan
HWY
Pallarenda
Magnetic Island
MAGNETIC ISLAND N.P.
Cape Cleveland
Yabulu
Townsville
★ Institute of Marine Science
Deeragun
RD
Nome
Bowling Green Bay
Cape Bowling Green
Aligator Creek
HERVEYS
RANGE
DEV.
Antill Plains
L. Ross
BOWLING GREEN BAY N.P.
Kalamia
140
Mt Elliott
Section
Giru
Barratta
Pioneer
89
Woodstock
81
Ayr

Outback Queensland

Best time to visit: Autumn, winter and spring; summer is hot and sometimes wet

Average daily temperatures: Jan 23–37°C, Apr 16–31°C, Jul 7–23°C, Oct 17–34°C

Getting there: By road from Brisbane via Bruce Hwy (Hwy 1) and Capricorn Hwy (Hwy 66) to Longreach (1190km) or via Warrego Hwy (Hwy 54) and Carnarvon Development Rd (Hwy 55) to Carnarvon Gorge (750km); by road from Rockhampton via Capricorn Hwy to Longreach (675km); by rail from Brisbane to Longreach via Rockhampton (twice weekly, Ph: 132 232); by air from Brisbane to Longreach

Festivals and events:

Mar–Apr: Easter in the Outback Festival, Longreach, Barcaldine, Ilfracombe and Winton

May: Outback Muster and Drovers Reunion (includes 'Outback Games', camp dinners, bronco branding), Longreach; Longreach Agricultural Show

Jun: Harry Readford Cattle Drive, Longreach

Jun–Jul: Artesian Festival (celebrates artesian water that sustains the region; goat races, concert, ball)

Jul: Diamond Shears (shearing competition), Longreach

Activities: 4WD touring, bushwalking, birdwatching, gem fossicking, fishing

Highlights: Australian Stockman's Hall of Fame and Outback Heritage Centre, Longreach; walking tracks and rock-art galleries of Carnarvon Gorge; platypus-spotting, Carnarvon Gorge; sunset river cruise, Thomson River, Longreach

Tip: Outback road travel can involve long drives; to save time and energy, consider joining a specialised tour.

Kids' stuff: Carnarvon Gorge Wilderness Lodge organises special programs for children during the school holidays.

Further information: Longreach Visitor Information Centre, Qantas Park, Eagle St, Longreach, Qld 4370, Ph: (07) 4658 3555; Barcaldine Information Centre, Oak St, Barcaldine, Qld 4725, Ph: (07) 4651 1724; Ranger Station, Carnarvon Gorge section, Carnarvon NP via Rolleston, Qld 4702, Ph: (07) 4984 4505

Outback Queensland is a realm of far horizons, rolling grasslands, vast starry skies, and wild beauty. Travelling here involves covering long distances, but the ample rewards include fascinating insights into the country's rich Aboriginal heritage and the lives of pioneering pastoralists, shearers and drovers, and legendary Outback hospitality.

The country between **Emerald** and **Longreach** holds sites of great Aboriginal and European significance. Still provid-

Aboriginal hand-prints, Carnarvon Gorge

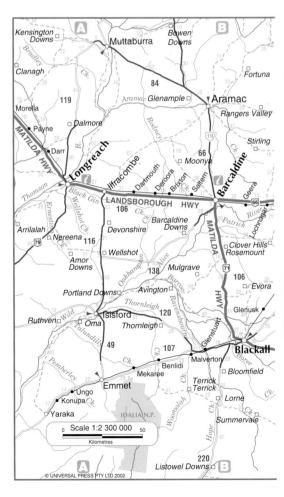

ing shade in **Barcaldine** is the Tree of Knowledge, the venue for meetings during the shearers' strike of 1891, which gave rise to the Australian Labor Party.

Longreach was the original headquarters of Qantas (the airline's name is an acronym of Queensland and Northern Territory Aerial Services). It is also the home of the Australian Stockman's Hall of Fame and Outback Heritage Centre, which pays tribute to the men and women of the Outback—from its original indigenous inhabitants to those of the present day. Accommodation options in Longreach include hotel-motels, host farms and caravan parks.

Wild and rugged **Carnarvon NP**, south of Emerald, protects the lush oasis of Carnarvon Gorge. Here, spring-fed creeks, ferns and palms support abundant wildlife (including platypuses), and overhangs and caves shelter extensive galleries of precious rock art. Most visitors stay at least 3 nights to walk the 21km of well-maintained tracks (walks range from easy strolls to more arduous treks). Accommodation is limited to 2

Australian Stockman's Hall of Fame

facilities outside the park—Carnarvon Gorge Wilderness Lodge (safari cabins and camping area), Ph: (07) 4984 4503, and Takarakka Bush Resort (campsites, amenities and covered kitchen and dining area), Ph: (07) 4984 4535—and bush camping inside the park at Big Bend (a 10km walk into the gorge), Ph: (07) 4984 4505. The former campground inside the park is now a day-use area.

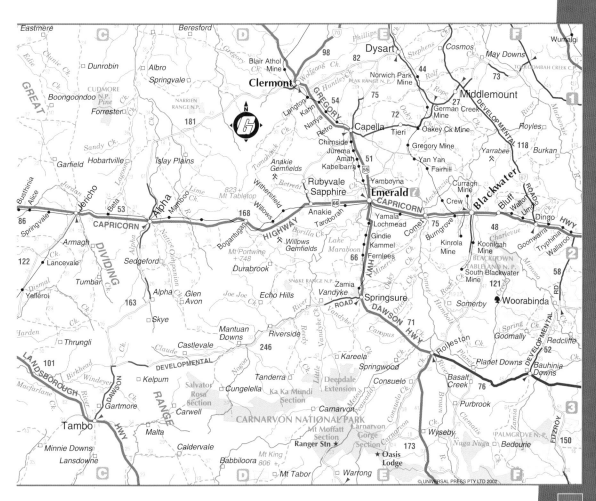

The Sunshine Coast

Best time to visit: Year-round; spring for warm days, cool nights and wildflowers; summer can be crowded; autumn and winter for cool, dry weather

Average daily temperatures: Jan 21–29°C, Apr 18–25°C, Jul 10–21°C, Oct 16–26°C

Getting there: By road from Brisbane via Bruce Hwy to Maroochydore (95km) and Noosa (145km); by rail to Nambour then Trainlink bus to Noosa, Ph 131 230; by air to Sunshine Coast Airport (north of Maroochydore)—direct flights from Sydney and Melbourne or via Brisbane

Festivals and events:

Apr: Sydney to Mooloolaba Yacht Race; Sea Week Festival, Mooloolaba

May: Caloundra City Show; Gympie Show

Jul: King of the Mountain Festival (foot race and all-day festival), Pomona

Aug: Sugar Festival, Nambour; Country Music Muster, Gympie

Aug–Sep: Noosa Jazz Festival

Oct: Gympie Gold Rush Festival

Activities: Swimming, canoeing, windsurfing, beach activities, sailing, sea-kayaking, water-skiing, snorkelling, diving, fishing, go-kart racing, golf, 4WD touring, bushwalking, birdwatching, rockclimbing, horseriding

Highlights: Noosa beach scene and Hastings St buzz; 4WD trip along Cooloola Beach; walking trails, sheltered coves and koalas in Noosa NP; surfing with dolphins

Tip: The Eumundi Markets (Wed, Sat) are among the best in the state, with more than 300 stalls offering fresh-grown fruits and vegetables, food, clothing and local arts and crafts (ranging from blown glass to bush furniture) in a delightful setting shaded by huge fig trees.

Kids' stuff: Maze Mania 4 Kids, Maroochydore (indoor playground for under 12s), entry fee, Ph: (07) 5479 5333; Underwater World, Mooloolaba (features a seal show), entry fee, Ph: (07) 5444 8488; the Big Pineapple (theme park on working pineapple plantation), Woombye (south of Nambour), fee for rides and tours, Ph: (07) 5442 1333

Further information: Maroochy Tourism Centre, Sixth Ave, Maroochydore, Qld 4559, Ph: (07) 5479 1566; Tourism Noosa Information Centre, Hastings St Roundabout, Noosa Heads, Qld 4567, Ph: (07) 5447 4988; Cooloola Regional Information Centre, Bruce Hwy, Kybong, Qld 4570, Ph: (07) 5483 5554

The Sunshine Coast starts just an hour's drive north of Brisbane. Clean white sands, broken by headlands and estuaries into beaches and coves, stretch north to Fraser Island (see p.133); inland are rainforested slopes, rich agricultural lands and colourful villages.

Seaside towns that have grown into major holiday centres—**Mooloolaba**, **Maroochydore**, **Coolum Beach** and **Noosa Heads**—offer fine dining and a wide choice of accommodation, ranging from 5-star resorts to backpacker hostels and beachfront campsites.

Much of the region's natural environment has been preserved, resulting in a winning combination of excellent holiday facilities and unspoilt beauty. At Noosa Heads, for example, you have a good chance of spotting a koala in **Noosa NP**, then rubbing shoulders with the rich and famous in lively Hastings St.

In **Great Sandy NP** (**Cooloola Section**), an extensive system of bushwalking tracks winds through banksia woodlands and wildflower-covered heathlands, while the park's enchanting waterways can be explored by canoe.

Noosa Heads and Noosa NP

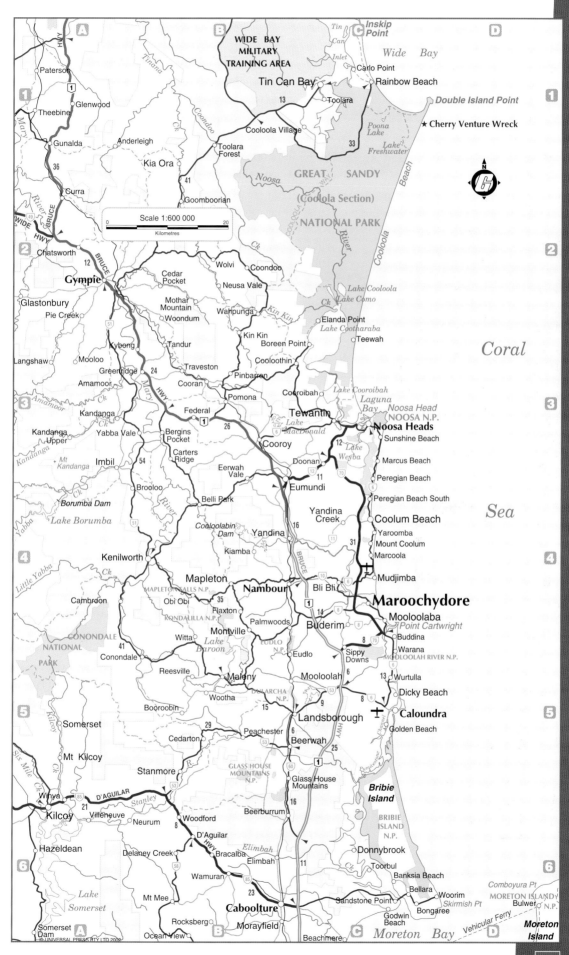

The Whitsunday Coast

Best time to visit: Year-round; autumn to spring (Mar–Nov) for beaches, diving and bushwalking; spring (Sep–Nov) for black marlin; in summer (the Wet), rainfall is high and presence of deadly box jellyfish makes ocean swimming unsafe

Average daily temperatures: Jan 24–30°C, Apr 22–28°C, Jul 17–23°C, Oct 19–27°C

Getting there: By road from Brisbane via Bruce Hwy to Mackay (995km) and Proserpine (1115km); by rail from Brisbane to Proserpine (then by connecting coach to Airlie Beach); by air from Brisbane, Cairns and Sydney to Mackay, Whitsunday Coast (Proserpine) and Hamilton Island; by ferry from Shute Harbour to all island resorts

Festivals and events:

Jul: Mackay Festival of Arts

Aug: Hogs Breath Race Week (yacht racing), Airlie Beach; Hamilton Island Race Week (yacht racing)

Sep: Airlie Beach Triathlon

Oct: Paddling through History (celebration of 6000 years of maritime history), Airlie Beach and South Molle Island

Nov: Reef Festival, Airlie Beach (incorporates Whitsunday Food and Wine Festival)

Activities: Sailing, swimming, snorkelling, diving, sea-kayaking, jet-skiing, parasailing, fishing, whalewatching, bushwalking, tandem skydiving, golf, horseriding

Highlights: Cruising through the archipelago; enjoying warm waters, white sands and coral reefs; scenic flights; whalewatching cruises

Tip: The warm, clear waters of the Whitsundays are a splendid place to learn to dive or improve your skills. Dive schools offer a range of courses and guided dives.

Kids' stuff: Hook Island Underwater Observatory; most island resorts cater well for children with well-organised, fun activities.

Further information: Whitsunday Information Centre, Bruce Highway, Proserpine, Qld 4802, Ph: (07) 4945 3711 or 1800 801 252, www.whitsundayinformation.com.au; Queensland Parks and Wildlife Services (QPWS), Whitsunday Information Centre, Airlie Beach, cnr Shute Harbour and Mandalay Rds, Qld 4802, Ph: (07) 4946 7022; Tourist Information Centre, The Mill, 320 Nebo Rd, Mackay, Qld 4740, Ph: (07) 4952 2677

The 74 islands that dot the **Whitsunday Passage** are the peaks of a coastal range that was submerged by rising seas at the end of the last ice age. Most are still cloaked with pine forest and rainforest, and blessed with glorious sandy beaches and fringing coral reefs. Almost all of the islands are national parks, and networks of walking trails allow visitors to get close to nature. Eight islands have resorts, and there are 30 campsites (permits must be obtained from the QPWS).

On the mainland, **Airlie Beach**, the gateway to the Whitsundays, is itself a popular year-round destination, with a shaded, white-sand beach, artificial waterfront swimming lagoon, a wide range of accommodation and services, and a backdrop of rainforested ranges. Nearby, the busy port of Shute Harbour and its Abel Point Marina bustle with yachts, charter cruises and fishing vessels. Walking trails lead from here to rugged **Conway NP**, which encompasses peaks that were once part of the same range as the islands. **Mackay**, to the south, has fine beaches, heritage-listed buildings and trawler-fresh seafood. Inland, 83km from Mackay, lies the untouched wilderness of **Eungella NP**.

Airlie Beach Lagoon

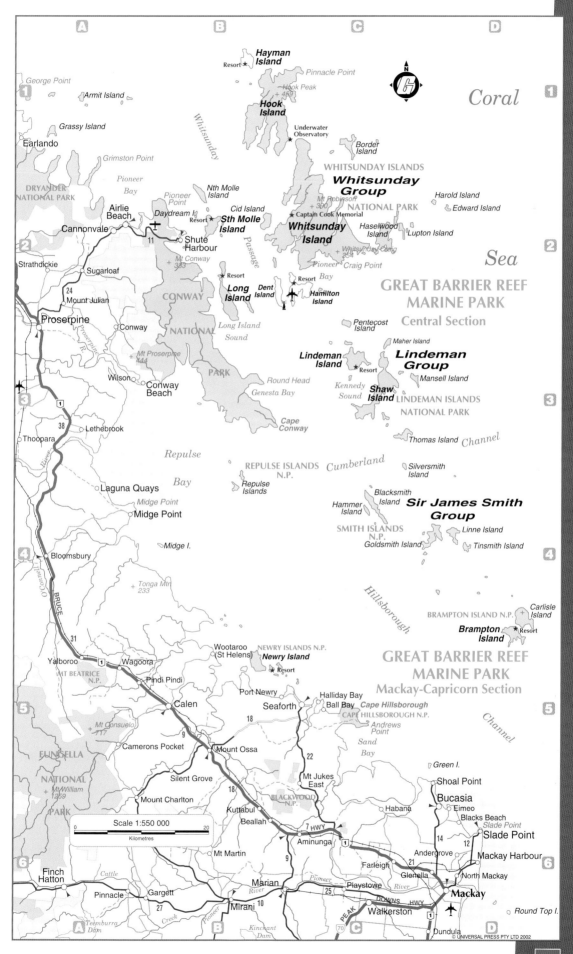

The Whitsunday Islands

Brampton Island, at the southern entrance to the Whitsunday Island Group, has white-sand beaches, walking trails and coral reefs. Packages at the island's resort include all meals and nonmotorised watersports. Brampton and nearby **Carlisle Island** (which are linked by a sandbar at low tide) are included in Brampton Island NP. Camping is available on Carlisle Island.

Daydream Island is the smallest of the settled islands. Its single resort was recently upgraded and now offers a coral reef, 3 swimming pools, 4 restaurants, a kids' club, a state-of-the-art spa centre and an outdoor cinema.

Hamilton Island offers a wide range of accommodation, from budget bungalows to self-contained apartments and villas and luxury hotels. It also has myriad eateries, shops, entertainment venues and its own airport. There are several secluded, coral-fringed beaches and stunning views from walking trails.

Hayman Island is the most northerly of the Whitsunday Group and closest to the Great Barrier Reef. It combines the natural beauty of its rugged timbered hills and fringing coral reef with the opulence of a 5-star resort.

Hook Island is characterised by beautiful beaches and rolling, forested hills. Its affordable beachside campground, cabins and dormitories are especially popular with budget travellers. The Hook Island Wilderness Resort has its own underwater coral observatory, which provides visitors with close-up views of dozens of reef-dwelling fish and coral species; entry fee, Ph: (07) 4946 9380.

The sprawling **Lindeman Group** is protected by Lindeman Islands NP, which offers self-sufficient camping on Lindeman, Shaw and Thomas islands. Lindeman Island has rainforest walking tracks and several viewpoints with spectacular vistas; it is also home to Australia's first Club Med, an ideal destination for especially active holidaymakers.

Long Island is a national park and has 13km of walking trails, many of which pass through lush tropical rainforest and provide magnificent views of the Whitsunday Pasage. Each of the island's 3 resorts has its own sandy beach.

South Molle's resort, situated in a sheltered bay at the foot of Mt Jeffreys, is especially popular with families. As well as watersports and safe swimming, the island has a golf course and 16km of graded walking trails threading through unspoilt national park.

Whitsunday Island, the largest island in the group, is a pristine, mountainous national park visited only by daytrippers and campers with permits. One of its highlights is exquisite Whitehaven Beach, where expansive, forest-fringed, snow-white sands stretch for 7km.

Daydream Island

Charter boat in the Whitsunday Passage

Whitsunday Cruising

Clear, turquoise waters and magnificent scenery make cruising the Whitsunday Passage an idyllic experience. A popular option is to hire a 'skipper-yourself' yacht, motor cruiser or catamaran (known as a 'bareboat') and crew it with friends. Some sailing experience is necessary, but you can recruit a guide for a couple of days to familiarise yourself with the vessel and local waters. Alternatively, you can opt for a crewed vessel—the choice ranges from a sleek maxi racing yacht to a traditional tallship—whose professional sailors will do all the sailing and prepare meals. You can even arrange for a seaplane to pick you up from your boat and take you on a scenic flight or to snorkel on the Outer Reef.

Most people take between 5 and 7 days to cruise the Whitsundays. Because the island chain is a sunken mountain range rather than a string of coral atolls, protected anchorages are plentiful. Camping permits are required if you plan to pitch a tent in a national park, but you do not need a permit to anchor off the islands.

A range of shorter trips is also available. High-speed motor vessels take visitors on daytrips to the Great Barrier Reef. Others, including maxi-yachts under full sail, air-conditioned ferries and rigid inflatables, make a more leisurely round of the main inner islands, beaches and fringing reefs. Between Jul and Sep, whalewatching tours bring visitors close to great humpbacks as they pass by on their mighty round trip from Antarctic to tropical waters.

Cazneaux Tree,
Flinders Ranges

South Australia

Encompassing almost 1 million km^2 and dramatic variations in landscape and climate, South Australia offers visitors a wide range of holiday experiences. The refined capital is renowned for its cultural treats, including the biennial Festival of Arts. To the east are the picturesque villages, parklands and fine eateries of the leafy Adelaide Hills, a popular daytrip destination. Also within easy reach of the capital are the state's famed wine regions, the Barossa Valley to the north, McLaren Vale to the south and Padthaway and Coonawarra a little further afield to the SE. A coastline studded with uncrowded beaches and seaside villages sweeps south and east from Adelaide past Kangaroo Island and the bird-rich wetlands of the Coorong; inland are caves, craters and soaring forests. To the north, the ancient Flinders Ranges shelter the unforgettable landscapes of Wilpena Pound. Across the state, quiet backroads and dedicated cycle paths cater to 2-wheeled touring, while a network of foot tracks takes walkers through some of the finest scenery. Visitors can also visit city and country restaurants to feast on exceptional local fare, ranging from delicious seafood to fresh produce from market gardens and orchards and specialist butchers and bakers.

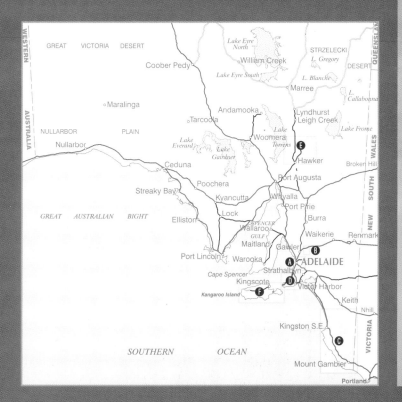

Adelaide

Best time to visit: Late summer for Festival of Arts (even numbered years) or Womadelaide (odd-numbered years); spring for roses and to see parks and gardens at their finest

Average daily temperatures: Jan 17–29°C, Apr 10–19°C, Jul 8–16°C, Oct 12–22°C

Getting there: Adelaide is linked by rail to Melbourne, by road to Melbourne (735km) and Sydney (1415km), and by air to all state capitals

Festivals and events:

Jan: Tour Down Under (international cycling race)

Feb: Womadelaide (World of Music, Arts and Dance; odd-numbered years only)

Mar: Adelaide Festival of Arts and Fringe Festival (even-numbered years only)

Apr: Clipsal 500 Adelaide V8 Supercar racing; Oakbank Easter Racing Carnival, Adelaide Hills; Hills Harvest Festival

May: Adelaide Cup

Aug–Sep: Royal Adelaide Show

Sep: Bay to Birdwood Run (pre-1949 cars)

Oct: Adelaide Rose Festival; Tasting Australia

(odd-numbered years); Bartercard Glenelg Jazz Festival; Royal Adelaide Wine Show; Classic Adelaide Rally (pre-1970 sports cars)

Oct–Nov: International Horse Trials

Nov: Christmas Pageant (street parade)

Dec: Lights of Lobethal; SA Day, banks of Torrens River

Activities: Arts and culture, wining and dining, visiting parks and gardens

Highlights: Adelaide Central Market; National Wine Centre of Australia; Adelaide Botanic Gardens; riding the 1920s tram from Victoria Square to waterfront Glenelg

Tip: For a quick and free introduction to the city centre, hop on one of the regular, brightly coloured, AdelaideFree buses.

Kids' stuff: South Australian Museum; Investigator Science and Technology Centre, Wayville, entry fee, Ph: (08) 8410 1123

Further information: South Australian Visitor and Travel Centre, 18 King William St, Adelaide, SA 5000, Ph: 1300 655 276, www.south australia.com

South Australia's capital is known for its sophisticated pleasures, including a wide variety of cultural offerings and fine foods and wines. Adelaide was planned in the 1830s by Colonel William Light to include a rectangular grid of city streets and a wide strip of encircling parkland that still occupies about 45% of the city's total area and separates it from the suburbs. The whole design can be viewed from the **Light's Vision** lookout on the summit of **Montefiore Hill**.

The CBD's orderly grid of wide, tree-lined streets makes it nearly impossible to get lost. Traffic-free **Rundle Mall**, the focal point for shoppers, is adjacent and parallel to gracious **North Terrace**, where many of Adelaide's most visited sights are located. These include the Art Gallery of South Australia and the South Australian Museum, which house the world's best collections of Aboriginal culture, and the nearby Tandanya Aboriginal Cultural Centre. Within easy walking distance, on the opposite side of the River Torrens in North Adelaide, the **Adelaide Oval** and nearby Montefiore Park Golf Course continue the rim of green.

Adelaide from the River Torrens

Places of Interest

Adelaide Botanic Gardens (1)
Adelaide Casino (2)
Adelaide Central Market (3)
Adelaide Festival Centre (4)
Adelaide Oval (5)
Adelaide Zoo (6)
Art Gallery of South Australia (7)
Migration Museum (8)
Montefiore Hill, Light's Vision (9)
National Wine Centre of Australia (10)
Parliament House (11)
South Australian Museum (12)
State Library of South Australia and Mortlock Library (13)
Tandanya Aboriginal Cultural Centre (14)

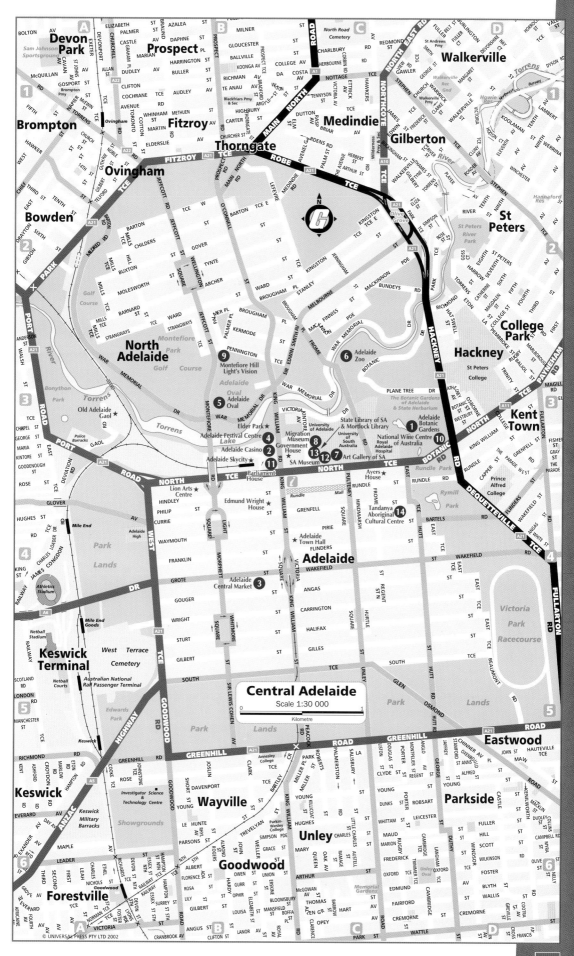

Central Adelaide
Scale 1:30 000

© UNIVERSAL PRESS PTY LTD 2002

City Sights

Established in 1855, the **Adelaide Botanic Gardens** are rich in subtropical and Mediterranean plants—some nurtured in enormous glasshouses—and known particularly for their collection of ornamental plants, palms and cycads; free guided walks are available. The Bicentennial Conservatory, which houses thousands of plants from Australia's tropical rainforests, and the International Rose Garden both require entry fees. A recent addition to this popular precinct is the **National Wine Centre of Australia**, which incorporates a fully operational 1ha vineyard and offers tastings from more than 50 Australian wine regions. Entry fee, Ph: (08) 8222 9222.

Adelaide **Central Market** dates from 1870 and is the oldest continuously operating market in Australia. A foodie's delight, it has arguably the finest range of fresh produce in the country. Mouthwatering offerings include salamis, wursts, cheeses, breads and seafood. A guided tasting tour takes visitors behind the scenes to sample the fare; fee, Ph: (08) 8336 8333, bookings essential.

Adelaide Zoo runs breeding programs for endangered Australian and exotic animal species. Among the former are orange-bellied parrots, regent honeyeaters, yellow-footed rock wallabies and

South Australian Museum

greater bilbies, some of which have been returned to the wild. Successes in the latter group include black-lion and golden-lion tamarinds and red pandas. Entry fee, Ph: (08) 8267 3255.

The **Art Gallery of South Australia** is one of several exhibition centres occupying substantial and splendidly restored Victorian buildings on North Terrace. Works by many well-known Australian artists, both indigenous and nonindigenous, hang here. Ph: (08) 8207 7000.

The **Migration Museum**, housed in the former Destitute Asylum, tells a multicultural story. Exhibits show why people from more than 100 nations chose to begin their new lives in South Australia, what they brought with them and what they hoped for. Entry by voluntary donation, Ph: (08) 8207 7580.

The 5 floors of the extensively redeveloped **South Australian Museum** house a diverse collection of South Australia's fossils, animals and minerals, as well as the Australian Aboriginal Cultures Gallery, the largest Aboriginal cultural display in the world; Ph: (08) 8207 7500.

The **Tandanya Aboriginal Cultural Centre**, just south of Rundle Mall, is a place of learning for both Aboriginal and nonAboriginal people. It holds regular performances and exhibitions, and offers Aboriginal art and artefacts for sale. Entry fee, Ph: (08) 8224 3222.

The **State Library of South Australia** in North Terrace incorporates the Mortlock Library, repository of important historical material; Ph: (08) 8207 7250. In the same complex, the **Bradman Collection** pays tribute to the world's most admired cricketer, immortalising 'The Don' through personal scrapbooks, cricket memorabilia, and audio and videotapes.

19th-century Palm House, Adelaide Botanic Gardens

The Adelaide Hills

Situated conveniently close to the city and dominated by the Mount Lofty Ranges, the Adelaide Hills combine thickly wooded valleys, undulating pastures and manicured parklands. The cool climate, acidic soils and high rainfall of the hills allowed settlers to create magnificent gardens and grow wine grapes, potatoes and strawberries and other temperate-zone fruits. Several local wineries offer cellar-door sales, while galleries and craft shops in the many charming 19th-century hill towns sell a wide variety of work by local artists. Bushwalkers can follow part of the scenic Heysen Trail (see p.167) which passes the home and studio of painter Sir Hans Heysen (in whose honour the trail was named) at Hahndorf as it winds through the Mt Lofty Ranges.

Belair NP, established in 1891, was South Australia's first national park. Recreational facilities include walking trails, unspoilt bush, free gas BBQs and tennis courts for hire; vehicle entry fee, Ph: (08) 8278 5477. Old Government House, in the heart of the park and once the governor's summer retreat, is open Sun and public holidays; 'gold'-coin entry, Ph: (08) 8278 8279.

Yellow-footed rock wallabies

Sightings of diverse native fauna are guaranteed at **Cleland Wildlife Park**; accompanying the daily feed-run or participating in koala-holding photo sessions ensures even closer encounters with the park's inhabitants which include rare yellow-footed rock wallabies; entry fee, Ph: (08) 8339 2444, www.cleland.sa.gov.au.

Mt Lofty Summit Visitor and Information Centre, with its café and stylish restaurant, is *the* place for panoramic views of city, coast and mountains. Several fine bushwalks begin at the Information Centre, where exhibits trace the region's history; Ph: (08) 8370 1054. The 7 intersecting valleys of **Mount Lofty Botanic Garden**, which opened in 1977, are stocked with introduced cool-climate plants such as rhododendrons, peonies and roses and are also a haven for native flora—Fern Gully is especially noteworthy. The popular, self-guided, 1-hour BankSA Nature Trail winds through the park's natural scrub, which is home to a prolific bird population. Parking fee, Ph: (08) 8222 9311.

Occupying a restored flour mill, the **National Motor Museum** at Birdwood displays more than 300 vintage cars and motorcycles. The collection includes Australia's oldest operational car, the 1899 Shearer Steam Carriage and the first Holden, produced in 1948. Visitors can play interactive games to test their road safety skills; entry fee, Ph: (08) 8568 5006.

Adelaide Festival

Every 2 years, the 3-week-long Adelaide Festival of Arts showcases art, music, drama, opera and dance. Since it began in 1960, its international reputation has grown steadily; it is now acknowledged as one of the world's great arts festivals. Performances are held in a range of venues across the city centre. Adelaide Writers' Week takes place during the first week and the main festival also overlaps with the Adelaide Fringe Festival, which features comedy, circus, cabaret and theatre, as well as contemporary music.

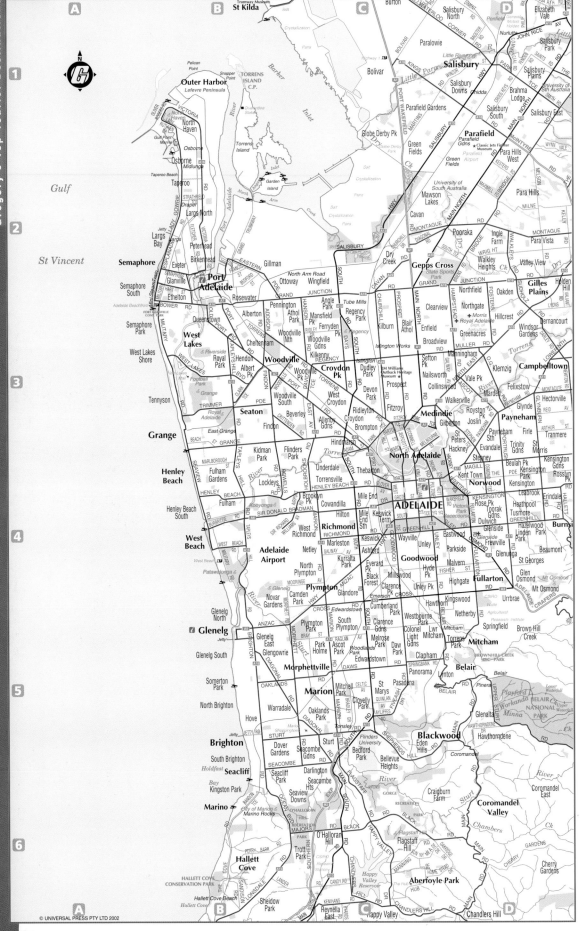

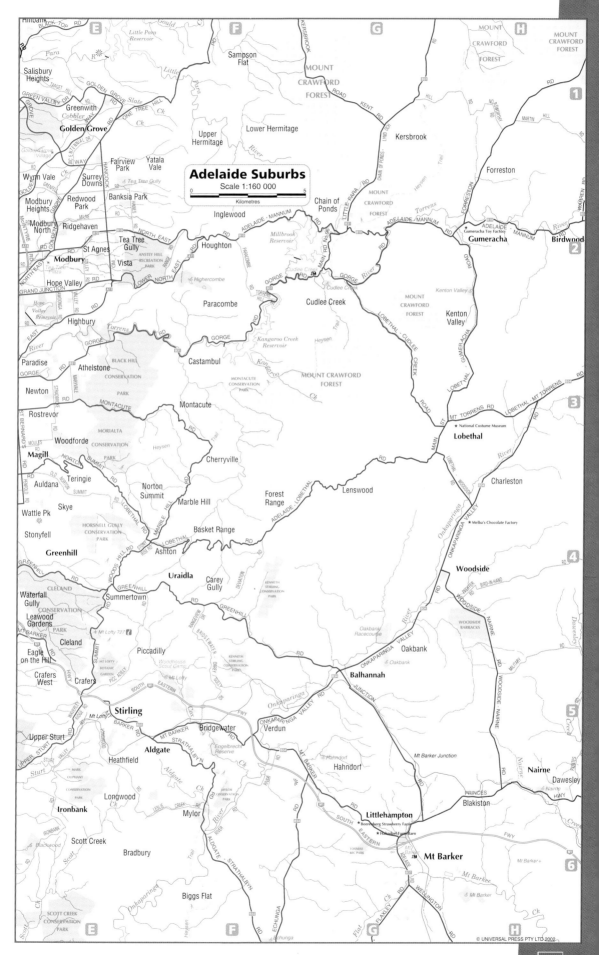

Adelaide Suburbs
Scale 1:160 000

0   5
Kilometres

The Barossa Valley

Best time to visit: Summer for stone fruits and alfresco dining; autumn for figs, pears and bushwalking; winter for cosy log fires; spring for wildflowers and orchard blossom

Average daily temperatures: Jan 14–29°C, Apr 9–21°C, Jul 4–13°C, Oct 8–20°C

Getting there: By road from Adelaide via A20 (Sturt Hwy) to Gawler, then B31 to Lyndoch; from the east via the Nuriootpa exit off the A20

Festivals and events:

Feb: Barossa Under the Stars (outdoor concerts)

Mar–Apr: Barossa Vintage Festival (odd-numbered years)

May: Barossa Balloon Regatta, Nuriootpa

Sep: Spring into the Barossa (food and wine events)

Oct: Barossa Music Festival

Nov: Tanunda's Para Rd Wine Path (new season wine releases); Lyndoch Lavender Festival

Activities: Wine-tasting, fine dining, browsing galleries and antique and craft shops, cycling, bushwalking (the Heysen Trail traverses the Barossa), hot-air ballooning

Highlights: Cellar-door tastings; local gourmet specialities including smoked meats, breads and quince paste; view from Mengler Hill Lookout, east of Tanunda; self-guided walking tours of Lyndoch, Bethany and Tanunda (brochures available from Barossa Wine and Visitor Information Centre, Tanunda); historic churches

Tip: Use the 'Butcher, Baker, Winemaker Trail' map (available free from the Barossa Wine and Visitor Information Centre) to plan your visit, or contact one of the specialist companies offering food and wine tours. Another option is to travel in style on the Barossa Wine Train from Adelaide to Tanunda then tour the valley and wineries by coach or limousine; fee, (08) 8212 7888.

Kids' stuff: Ask the tourist office about the Angaston Village Game, involving numerous local businesses.

Further information: Barossa Wine and Visitor Information Centre, Murray Street, Tanunda, SA 5352, Ph: (08) 8563 0600, www.barossa-region.org

The picturesque Barossa Valley is famed for its concentration of high-quality wineries, restaurants and German-influenced food culture. Its patchwork of gentle hills, neat vineyards and historic villages clustered around church spires lies just a pleasant 90min drive north of Adelaide. Settlement dates from the late 1830s, when wealthy English settlers began to occupy the eastern uplands at **Lyndoch**, **Angaston** and **Penrice** (its 1844 church is the valley's oldest-known building), and German-speaking religious refugees settled the valley floor at **Bethany** (which has a traditional Silesian village layout) and leafy **Tanunda**. The 30 or so stone churches scattered throughout the valley, mostly Lutheran, are famous for their pipe organs and stained-glass windows; most welcome visitors to their services.

Vineyards planted in the 1840s are still worked today and many of the growers are descendants of the original settlers. At **Seppeltsfield**, visitors can inspect an impressive complex of historic winery buildings or stroll through beautifully maintained gardens; Ph: (08) 8563 2626. **Nuriootpa** has several shops selling regional produce, and a scenic reserve on the banks of the North Para River. Accommodation options in the Barossa include self-catering in flower-fringed cottages and stately B&Bs.

Elderton Wines, near Nuriootpa, Barossa Valley

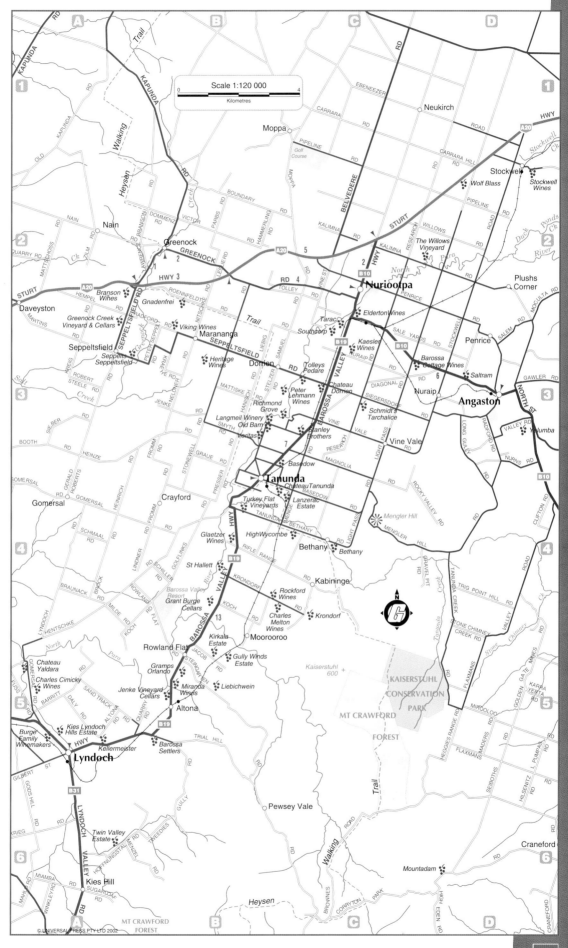

Scale 1:120 000
Kilometres

Coonawarra and the Limestone Coast

Best time to visit: Summer for beach and watersports; autumn for bushwalking and vintage; winter for wild seas; spring for wildflowers

Average daily temperatures: Jan 12–24°C, Apr 10–19°C, Jul 6–14°C, Oct 9–17°C

Getting there: By road from Adelaide via Princes Hwy to Robe (340km), Millicent (400km), Mt Gambier (450km); from Melbourne via Princes Hwy to Mt Gambier (430km)

Festivals and events:

Jan: Port MacDonnell Bayside Festival; Cape Jaffa Food and Wine Festival; Kingston Lions Fishing Competition

Feb: Mount Gambier Festival of Country Music

May: Penola Festival (arts, literature, wine and food)

Jun: McLaren Vale Sea and Vines Festival

Oct: McLaren Vale Wine Bushing Festival; Coonawarra Cabernet Celebration

Nov: Robe Village Fair

Activities: Wine-tasting, surfing, swimming, snorkelling, diving, fishing, boating, canoeing, kayaking, windsurfing, sailing, water-skiing, birdwatching, cycling, bushwalking, caving

Highlights: Coorong NP; Naracoorte Caves; river cruise to Princess Margaret Rose Caves, fee, Glenelg River Cruises, Ph: (08) 8738 4191, separate fee for entry to caves, Ph: (08) 8738 4171; Blue Lake at Mt Gambier

Tip: Paddle your own canoe up the mirror-surfaced Glenelg River past Nelson's rustic boatsheds into Lower Glenelg NP.

Kids' stuff: Wonambi Fossil Centre, Naracoorte Caves; calm waters of Lacepede Bay for swimming; fishing near boat ramp at Kingston SE

Further information: Millicent Visitor Centre, 1 Mount Gambier Rd, Millicent, SA 5280, Ph: (08) 8733 3205; Lady Nelson Visitor and Discovery Centre, Jubilee Hwy East, Mt Gambier, SA 5290, Ph: (08) 8724 9750, **www.mountgambier tourism.com.au**; Sheep's Back Museum, McDonnell St, Naracoorte, SA 5271, Ph: (08) 8762 1518; Robe Visitor Information Centre, Robe Library, Mundy Terrace, Robe, SA 5276, Ph: (08) 8768 2465

An immense layer of cave-riddled limestone underpins this entire region and forms many of its most distinctive features. Laid down as marine sediments over millions of years, it was ocean floor until the sea retreated at the end of the last ice age. Today, the coastline's beaches, bays, coastal lakes and historic ports—now mainly holiday resorts and lobster-fishing centres—attract large numbers of visitors, especially in summer.

Kingston S.E. offers safe swimming and dolphin sightings in the waters of wide **Lacepede Bay**. **Robe**, with its popular Long Beach and pretty harbour, was a landing point for thousands of Chinese prospectors bound for the Victorian gold-rush; restaurants, galleries, craft shops and B&Bs are scattered through its heritage streets. The former whaling port of **Beachport**, on Rivoli Bay, is now a busy holiday village with an impressive wharf.

The regional centre of **Mt Gambier** is built on the continent's most recently active volcano; its startling, 70m-deep **Blue Lake** fills an ancient crater, and from the high rim there are excellent views south to the distinctive bulk of volcanic **Mt Schank**. Visitors can join a tour to the lake via an old mine shaft; fee, Aquifer Tours, Ph: (08) 8723 1199.

Charming 19th-century buildings in **Penola**, the region's oldest town, include the 1867 schoolhouse where Australia's first saint, Mary MacKillop, once taught; paving stones in the main street carry a surprisingly long list of other well-known former residents. At **Coonawarra**, where a fabled strip of 'terra-rossa' soil produces rich red wines, more than 20 wineries open their cellar doors for tastings and sales. Further north, the World Heritage-listed **Naracoorte Caves** include Fossil Cave, famed for its spectacular limestone formations and fossil beds; entry fee, Ph: (08) 8762 3412.

The region has a wide range of accommodation. Many restaurants specialise in superb local foods and wines.

Coastal scenery near Robe

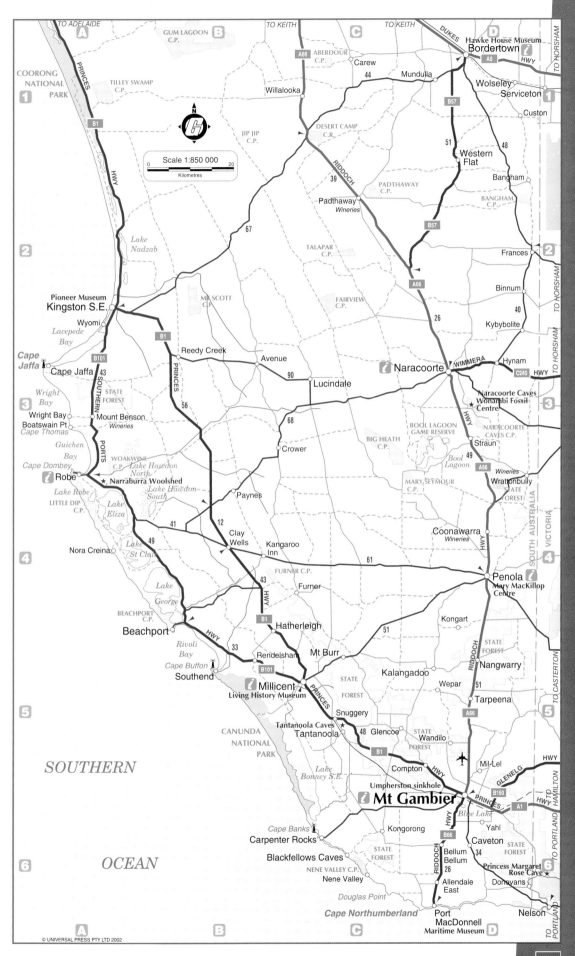

Scale 1:850 000

Kilometres

© UNIVERSAL PRESS PTY LTD 2002

The Fleurieu Peninsula

Best time to visit: Summer for beach activities and berry picking; autumn for bushwalking; winter for whales; late winter for almond blossoms; spring for wildflowers; year-round for wine-tasting

Average daily temperatures: Jan 16–28°C, Apr 12–22°C, Jul 7–15°C, Oct 11–21°C

Getting there: By road from Adelaide via Southern Expressway then well-signposted Fleurieu Way to Cape Jervis (110km); alternatively, cross the peninsula on A13 to Victor Harbor (85km) or B37 to Goolwa (85km)

Festivals and events:

Jan: Fleurieu Food, Wine and Cockle Festival, Goolwa; Goolwa to Milang Beach Yacht Race

Feb: Multicultural Festival, Aldinga Beach; Mt Compass Cow Race

Mar: Wooden Boat Festival, Goolwa (odd years); Steam and Machinery Rally, Goolwa (even years)

Apr: Town Crier's Competition, Victor Harbor

Jun: Whale season launch, Victor Harbor

Jul–Aug: Willunga Almond Blossom Festival

Sep–Oct: Victor Harbor State Folk Festival (long weekend)

Nov: Cocklefest, Goolwa

Activities: Surfing, swimming, snorkelling, diving, fishing, boating, canoeing, kayaking, windsurfing, sailing, whalewatching, birdwatching, cycling, bush-walking, golf, browsing galleries and craft markets, cellar-door wine-tasting, sampling local cuisine

Highlights: Cockle steam train from Victor Harbor to Goolwa, Sun only, fee, Ph: (08) 8231 4366; Granite Island Horse Tram (pulled by Clydesdales), fee, Ph: (08) 8552 1777; Granite Island Penguin Discovery Tour, fee, Ph: (08) 8552 7555 for bookings; Deep Creek Conservation Park

Tip: Join a cruise from Goolwa into Coorong NP to view the mouth of the Murray River, pelican breeding colonies and waterfowl wetlands (take your binoculars for birdwatching); Goolwa Cruises, Ph: (08) 8555 2203, or Coorong Experience, Ph: (08) 8555 1133.

Kids' stuff: Greenhills Adventure Park, Ph: 1300 365 599; Wild Rose Miniature Village, entry fee, Ph: (08) 8554 6513; Urimbirra Wildlife Park, entry fee, Ph: (08) 8554 6554; all in Victor Harbor

Further information: McLaren Vale and Fleurieu Visitor Centre, Main Road, McLaren Vale, SA 5171, Ph: (08) 8323 9944, www.fleurieu peninsula.com.au; Signal Point Visitor Information Centre, The Wharf, Goolwa, SA 5214, Ph: (08) 8555 1144, www.alexandrina. sa.gov.au; Victor Harbor Visitor Information Centre, The Causeway, Victor Harbor, SA 5211, Ph: (08) 8552 5738, www.tourismvictor harbor.com.au; Whale Information Line, Ph: 1900 931 223

The Fleurieu Peninsula's long coastline, tranquil rural hinterland, Mediterranean climate and proximity to Adelaide have made it a popular daytrip and weekend destination. Sandy beaches, fishing towns and holiday resorts line the western side of the peninsula. Inland, lofty lookouts provide panoramic views over the wilder southern shores, and scenic roads meander through vineyards and farmland. Other attractions include nearly 20 conservation parks, an extensive network of marked walking trails, and heritage towns with galleries, antique shops and craft markets. Visitors can feast on superb cuisine in the region's many fine eateries or fill a hamper with local produce, such as almonds, olives, berries, cheeses, seafood and wine, for a seafront or bushland picnic. An excellent range of accommodation is also available.

The long, wide beaches of **Aldinga**, on Adelaide's outer fringes, are popular year-round; divers can explore a marine trail here featuring a spectacular underwater cliff. Inland, picturesque **Willunga** combines 19th-century streetscapes and slate footpaths and gutters with rose nurseries and almond groves; in late winter the groves are snowy with blossom. **Cape Jervis**, at the tip of the peninsula, is the departure point for ferries to Kangaroo Island (visible across the waters; see p.170) and is also the southern terminus of the **Heysen Trail** (see opposite). Norfolk Island pines line **Victor Harbor**'s busy beachfront; a

Granite Island Horse Tram, Victor Harbor

The Heysen Trail

One of Australia's longest bushwalking tracks, the Heysen Trail passes through some of the most scenic parts of the state on its 1500km route from Cape Jervis to the Flinders Ranges. Serious walkers tackling its entire length can make use of the numerous huts and hostels along the way, and there are many access points for day ramblers. Some sections are closed in summer because of bushfire danger. Detailed maps and notes are available from visitor centres, the Friends of the Heysen Trail Shop, 10 Pitt St, Adelaide, SA 5000, Ph: (08) 8212 6299, and the Office for Recreation and Sport, www.recsport.sa.gov.au/trails/heysen.htm.

horse-drawn tram hauls visitors across a 1km wooden causeway to **Granite Island**, location of a 1000-strong fairy penguin colony. To the east along the seafront is **Port Elliot**, with its heritage buildings and elegant Strand, and Boomer surf beach.

The fashionably refurbished historic river port of **Goolwa**, near the mouth of the Murray River, once hummed with river trade; even now there are likely to be more boats than cars here. Visitors can admire the paddlesteamer *Oscar W* moored at the wharf, watch wooden boat-building displays, take in the views from the huge barrages that separate the fresh Murray waters from the salty sea, or stroll along the dune boardwalk behind the surf beach. A bridge, built after a decade of controversy and protests from the Ngarrindjeri Aboriginal people, now links the town to Hindmarsh Island.

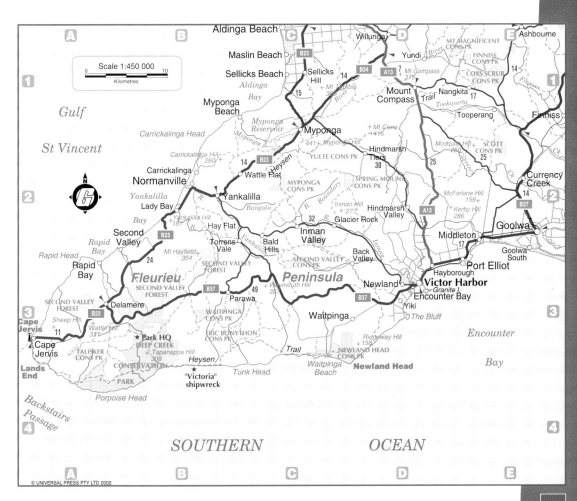

The Flinders Ranges

Best time to visit: Spring for bushwalking, wildflowers and wildlife; summer is very hot

Average daily temperatures: Jan 26–38°C, Apr 12–25°C, Jul 8–18°C, Oct 12–25°C

Getting there: By road from Adelaide on A1, then via Wilmington and Quorn to Wilpena Pound (450km), Blinman (500km)

Festivals and events:

Apr: Flinders Ranges NP Autumn Events

May: Hawker Races

Jun: Quorn Races

Sep: Beltana Picnic Races; Hawker Art Exhibition

Oct: Flinders Ranges NP Spring Events

Activities: Bushwalking, birdwatching, 4WD touring, artist and photography workshops at Wilpena Pound Resort, stargazing, camel rides

Highlights: Views at sunset east to bluffs of Wilpena Pound from Moralana Scenic Drive and at sunrise west from Stokes Hill Lookout; views of Heysen Range from road to Brachina Gorge; scenic flight over ranges, Wilpena Pound and glistening salt bed of Lake Torrens; raw beauty of Parachilna Gorge; Aboriginal rock art; wildlife

Tip: Conventional vehicles should manage roads as far north as Blinman. Weather conditions in the ranges are notoriously changeable, and particular care is needed when driving on unsealed roads after rain.

Kids' stuff: Before heading inland, visit the Tunnel of Time display at Wadlata Outback Centre, Port Augusta, a multimedia exhibit describing the geology, flora and fauna of the Flinders Ranges.

Further information: Wadlata Outback Centre, Flinders Tce, Port Augusta, SA 5700, Ph: (08) 8642 4511, www.flinders.outback.on.net; Flinders Ranges Information Centre, Seventh St, Quorn, SA 5433, Ph: (08) 8648 6419; Flinders Ranges NP, Elder St, Hawker, SA 5434, Ph: (08) 8648 4244

Formed more than 500 million years ago, the Flinders Ranges are among the most ancient landscapes on Earth. Over the eons, wind and water have fashioned majestic red bluffs and carved out deep, spectacular gorges. A place of dramatic beauty, the Flinders offer some of the best bushwalking in the state (ranging from gentle strolls to demanding treks), adventurous 4WD touring, Aboriginal history, clean air, numerous opportunities to encounter its plentiful wildlife, and the wonder of the changing light on craggy peaks. Aside from a few motels, accommodation is mainly in self-catering units and at campsites.

The saw-toothed peaks encircling **Wilpena Pound**, the most distinctive feature of **Flinders Ranges NP** (vehicle entry fee; permits required for camping) rise from the arid plains like a stone-walled island. Within is a vast natural amphitheatre where abundant wildlife, including emus, kangaroos and wallabies, grazes a grassy basin. This has long been an important area for Aboriginal people, who named it *wilpena*, meaning 'cupped hand' or 'bent fingers'; evidence of their long habitation includes 5000-year-old ochre and charcoal paintings at **Arkaroo Rock**, just south of the park entrance. In the 1850s, when pioneer European cat-

The walls of Wilpena Pound, Flinders Ranges NP

tlemen used this readymade enclosure for stock, they added 'pound' to the Aboriginal name.

Walking trails crisscross the Pound; maps are available from the national park headquarters at **Wilpena**; Ph: (08) 8648 0049. Solar-powered Wilpena Pound Resort, on gum-tree-lined Wilpena Creek, caters to all budgets, with motel units, a caravan park and 400 campsites set among native pines; 4WD tours and scenic flights can be booked from here; Ph: (08) 8648 0004. An easy walk away is the old Hill Homestead, from where a steep track climbs to Wangara Lookout and its panoramic views of the Pound. Only fit and experienced walkers should tackle the challenging 8hr climb from the resort to the summit of **St Mary Peak**, the highest point in the ranges (1189m). A lookout at **Stokes Hill**, just outside the park, offers views over the Pound's eastern scarps, displays explaining local Aboriginal culture and history, and a scale model of the Pound with geological information.

To the north, **Parachilna** township

is home of the historic Prairie Hotel, famous for its roo burgers and other fine 'feral food' offerings; Ph: (08) 8648 4895. Ruggedly beautiful **Parachilna Gorge** is the northern end of the 1500km Heysen Trail (see p.167), which passes through the ranges on its way south. **Angorichina Tourist Village**, established in the late 1920s as a sanatorium for WWI veterans, has caravan and camping sites, cabins and units, and is the starting point for the walking trail to the crystal waters of Blinman Pools; Ph: (08) 8648 4842.

Wildflowers in the Flinders Ranges

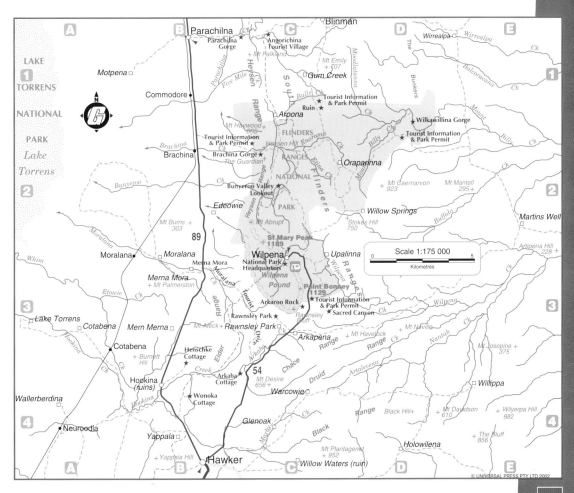

Kangaroo Island

Best time to visit: Spring and summer to enjoy the colourful blooms of the island's diverse flora and for beach activities and watersports; autumn and winter for bushwalking, whalewatching and fairy penguin sightings

Average daily temperatures: Jan 15–28°C, Apr 12–22°C, Jul 7–16°C, Oct 10–21°C

Getting there: Vehicle ferry from Cape Jervis, 110km by road south of Adelaide, Sealink, Ph: (08) 8202 8688; or by air from Adelaide (35min)

Festivals and events:

Mar: Anglers Fishing Championships (locations throughout the island), Game Fishing Tournament, American River

Apr: Kangaroo Island Easter Fair, Parndana

Sep: Kangaroo Island Sailing Regatta, Kingscote

Oct: Kingscote Agricultural Show; Blessing of the Fleet, Kingscote

Nov: Parndana Agricultural Show

Activities: Nature tours, bushwalking, fishing, sailing, diving, snorkelling, surfing, kayaking, windsurfing, swimming, cycling, horseriding, caving, 4WD touring, birdwatching, golf

Highlights: Walking among sea lions at Seal Bay; fairy penguin tour, Kingscote, fee, Ph: (08) 8553 2381; sampling island produce—Clifford's Honey Farm, Ph: (08) 8553 8295, Island Pure Sheep Dairy, Ph: (08) 8553 9110, Gum Creek Marron Farm, Ph: (08) 8553 5255; Remarkable Rocks; Kelly Hill Caves

Tip: Sea lions breed and give birth over a 6-month period every 18 months; you can therefore plan your visit using this following guide to breeding seasons: Feb–Jul 2003, Aug–Jan 2004, no breeding season in 2005, Feb–Jul 2006

Kids' stuff: A Maze 'n' Fun (fun park), Nepean Bay, entry fee, Ph: (08) 8553 9012; Parndana Wildlife Park, entry fee, Ph: (08) 8559 6050; Paul's Place, Stokes Bay (native and farm animals) entry fee, Ph: (08) 8559 2232

Further information: Gateway Visitor Information Centre, Howard Dr, Penneshaw, Kangaroo Island, SA 5222, Ph: (08) 8553 1185, www.tourkangarooisland.com.au; Flinders Chase NP, PMB 246, Kingscote, SA 5223, Ph: (08) 8559 7220 (general enquiries) and (08) 8559 7235 (accommodation manager, for lighthouse cottage bookings).

Unspoilt and uncrowded Kangaroo Island is a nature-lovers' paradise. Free from the ravages of foxes and rabbits and with 30% of its area protected by national park or conservation park, it has become a virtual ark, packed with plants and animals, some seldom seen or now extinct on the mainland. Added bonuses include the dramatic coastal scenery and excellent food. Indeed, the island is a gourmet's delight, producing a wide range of seafood, including crayfish (lobster) and its freshwater cousins marron and yabby, cow and sheep cheeses, honey from a unique strain of Italian bee, free-range poultry and quality wines.

You can take your own car by vehicle ferry or hire a car or bicycle on the island. If self-driving, it is worth purchasing an Islands Parks Pass, which is valid for 12 months and gives access to the parks, historic lighthouses and most ranger-guided tours, including those at Seal Bay. Those without transport can join a wide range of sightseeing tours, ranging from coach tours to personalised 4WD packages. Visitors should keep in mind that this is a big island (more than 150km long) and really needs several days to do it justice. The island's wide range of accommodation includes historic homestead B&Bs and secluded lighthouse-keepers' cottages.

Dusk is the best time to see wildlife: grey kangaroos, wallabies and koalas (introduced and now numbering thousands) are frequently seen, and in winter several thousand fairy penguins nest in burrows along the eastern shore. But the island's greatest attraction is the colony of sea lions at **Seal Bay**. The sea lions raise their young on a wide, dune-backed beach; visitors can either observe from the 400m-long boardwalk or join a ranger-guided stroll on the white sands; fee for boardwalk access and tour, Ph: (08) 8559 4207. Nearby **Murray Lagoon**,

Australian sea lion, Seal Bay

the island's largest lake, is crowded with birdlife, including black swans, ducks, stilts and sandpipers.

Flinders Chase NP, at the island's western end, is home to a colony of fur seals (near **Cape du Couedic**), the location of huge, wind-sculpted boulders known as the **Remarkable Rocks**, and provides patient observers with sightings of introduced platypuses from a viewing walkway at **Rocky River**. To the east, in **Kelly Hill Conservation Park**, lies a system of 140 000-year-old caves with intricate limestone formations; fee for ranger-guided tours, Ph: (08) 8559 7231.

Anglers can pull in prized fish such as King George whiting from jetties and rocky outcrops, or charter a boat for deep-sea fishing and unforgettable views of pristine coast. Scuba divers can investigate the island's undersea Maritime Heritage Trail, which includes more than 50 shipwrecks, some situated relatively close to shore. The waves of **Vivonne Bay** and **Pennington Bay** attract surfing enthusiasts, while Harriet River, with its shallow lagoon, offers safe swimming.

Historic Hope Cottage, Kingscote

Kingscote was South Australia's first official settlement, predating Adelaide by 5 months; its 19th-century buildings include Hope Cottage, one of 3—Faith, Hope and Charity—built of local stone in 1859, and now home to local history displays. In **Penneshaw** an excellent maritime museum brings alive stories of shipwrecks, lighthouses and sea trade. Both towns have fairy-penguin rookeries and tours are available. The town of **American River**, situated on a sheltered tidal estuary, has fine fishing and abundant birdlife; skippered charter yachts operating from here offer day and overnight cruises.

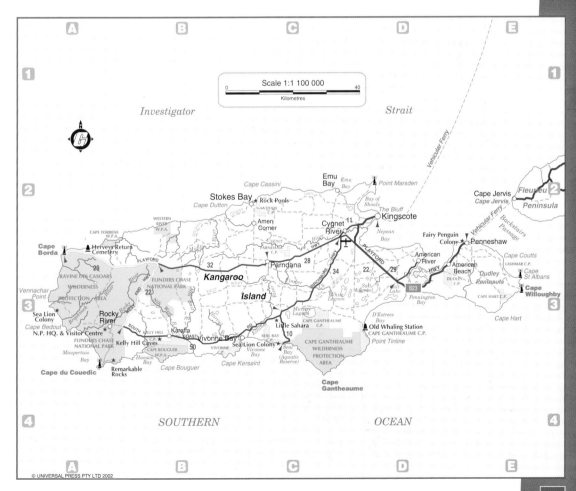

Clifftop overlooking the Murchison River, Kalbarri NP

Western Australia

Western Australia covers one-third of the continent and is Australia's largest state, although it has the country's smallest population. Cut off for millennia by barriers of ocean and desert, SW Western Australia has become one of the most botanically rich regions in the world, its extraordinarily numerous and diverse plant species—many unique to the region—flourishing in its protective isolation. The towering karri forests and spectacular springtime wildflower displays here are major attractions. In the far SW, the Margaret River district is known for its fine wines, gourmet treats, exceptional surf beaches and dramatic coastal scenery. Sunny, friendly Perth, the capital, superbly positioned between the broad Swan River and the pristine beaches of the Indian Ocean coast, offers a wide range of cultural and recreational activities. To the north is fascinating Monkey Mia, where wild dolphins mingle with humans in the crystal waters of Shark Bay, and the tropical outpost and pearling centre of Broome, on the edge of the rust-red Kimberley.

Tourist Information

i **Western Australian Visitor Centre**
cnr Forrest Pl and
Wellington St
Perth
WA 6000
Ph: 1300 361 351
www.westernaustralia.net

Top Tourist Destinations

Ⓐ Perth
Ⓑ Broome
Ⓒ Margaret River
Ⓓ Shark Bay
Ⓔ The Stirling Range and Albany

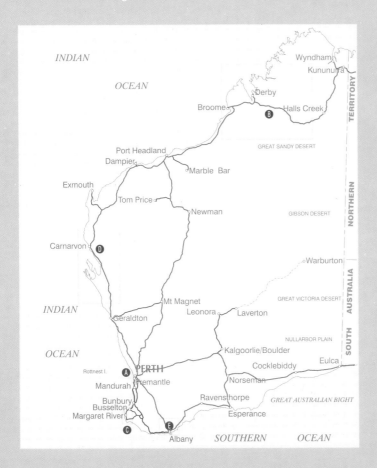

Perth

Best time to visit: Year-round; spring for
wildflowers; summer for beaches; autumn for
vineyard harvests

Average daily temperatures: Jan 17–30°C,
Apr 13–25°C, Jul 8–17°C, Oct 11–22°C

Getting there: By road from Adelaide via Great
Eastern Hwy and Eyre Hwy (2730km); direct flights
from all mainland states; by rail from Sydney,
Melbourne and Adelaide (regular passenger and
car-carrying services)

Festivals and events:

Jan: Fremantle Sardine Festival; Australia Day
fireworks display, Swan River

Feb: Rottnest Channel Swim (19km swim from
Cottesloe Beach to Rottnest Island)

Mar: Festival of Perth (international and local theatre,
dance, film and visual arts); International Sailing
Regatta Australia Cup, Royal Perth Yacht Club;
Festa di Rottnest (Italian festival with live music,
food and street performers)

May: Wine Harvest Festival, Bickley and Carmel
Valleys, Perth Hills

Sep: Royal Perth Show; Wildflower Festival, Kings
Park; Artrage, alternative festival of arts

Oct: Spring in the Valley (celebration of food, wine,
art and music in Swan Valley wineries)

Nov: AWESOME arts festival for young people

Dec: Perth International Tattoo

Activities: Wining and dining, shopping, visiting
museums and galleries, browsing art and craft
shops, sailing, canoeing, kayaking, fishing,
swimming, windsurfing, snorkelling, diving,
parasailing, whitewater rafting, bushwalking,
horseriding, wine-tasting

Highlights: Kings Park; Swan River cruise; Swan
Bells tower; swimming at Crawley and Peppermint
Grove; windsurfing and sailing at Cottesloe and
Scarborough; snorkelling at Marmion Marine Park;
WA Maritime Museum, Fremantle; historic
Fremantle Markets and the cafe strip of South Tce;
car-free Rottnest Island

Tip: Get to know inner Perth by using the Perth
Central Area Transit (CAT) System, a frequent, free
bus service that operates in the city centre and
takes in many of the main tourist destinations. A
separate 'cat', also free, operates in Fremantle.

Kids' stuff: WACA cricket museum, entry fee, Ph:
(08) 9265 7222; Scitech Discovery Centre, entry
fee, Ph: (08) 9481 5789; Perth Zoo, South Perth,
entry fee, Ph: (08) 9474 3551; Aquarium of WA
(with underwater, walk-through glass tunnel),
Hillary's Boat Harbour, entry fee, Ph: (08) 9447
7500; Adventure World (funpark, with rides,
waterslides and picnic area), Bibra Lake, entry fee,
Ph: (08) 9417 9666; cycling in Kings Park and on
Rottnest Island

Further information: Perth Visitor Centre, cnr
Forrest Pl and Wellington St, Perth, WA 6000,
Ph: 1300 361 351, www.westernaustralia.net;
Fremantle Tourist Bureau, Fremantle Town Hall,
cnr William and Adelaide Sts, Fremantle, WA 6160,
Ph: (08) 9431 7878; Rottnest Visitor Information,
Thomson Bay, Rottnest Island, WA 6161, Ph:
(08) 9372 9752, www.rottnest.wa.gov.au

The gleaming riverside city of Perth has both a magnificent position and a great climate. It is known for its relaxed, alfresco lifestyle, with long hours of sunshine allowing watersports and other outdoor activities to be enjoyed year-round. The compact CBD, contained between Wellington St and St Georges Tce, is an excellent holiday base, providing easy access to shopping, theatres, museums, restaurants, park-fringed riverfront and the bushlands and spring wildflowers of Kings Park. Cosmopolitan Fremantle, Perth's historic port, straddles the Swan River mouth just south of the city and is known for its concentration of fine heritage buildings, chic eateries, galleries, proud maritime tradition and lively entertainment scene. Rottnest Island, with its quokkas (small wallabies), clear waters and great dive sites, is an easy day trip from either Perth or Fremantle. Running north of the city along the coast is a string of pristine beaches, and offshore lie several islands providing opportunities for both fishing and diving. Inland is the lush Swan River Valley, with its wineries, rolling farmlands and picturesque townships.

Places of Interest

Art Gallery of Western Australia (1)
Barracks Archway (2)
Cloisters (3)
His Majesty's Theatre (4)
London Court (5)
Old Mill (6)
Parliament House (7)
Perth Mint (8)
Perth Town Hall (9)
Perth Zoo (10)
Queens Gardens (11)
Scitech Discovery Centre (12)
St Georges Anglican Cathedral (13)
St Marys Catholic Cathedral (14)
Stirling Gardens (15)
Supreme Court Gardens (16)
Swan Bells (17)
Western Australian Museum (18)

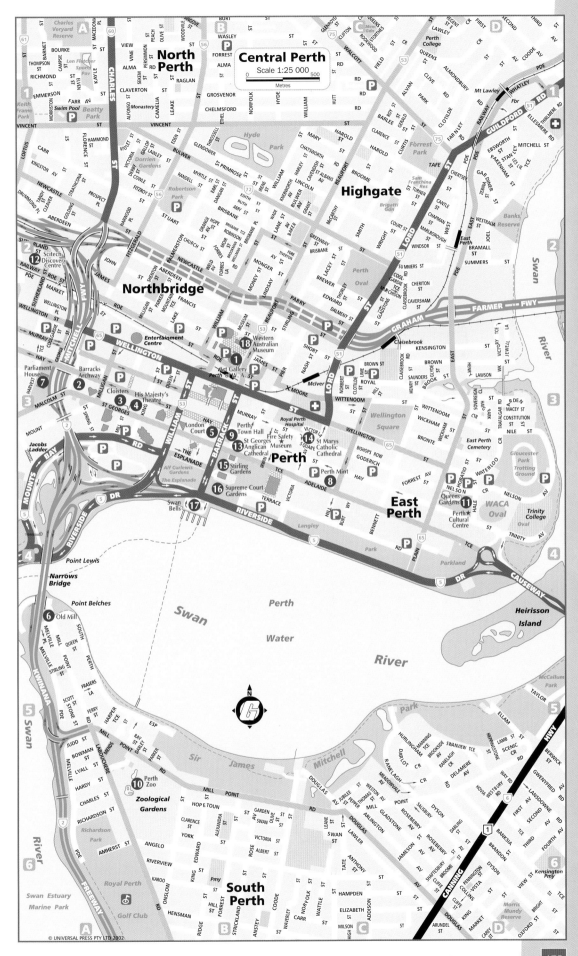

Central Perth

In the 1960s and 1970s Perth was transformed when many colonial buildings were replaced by sleek skyscrapers; today the city is a pleasant mixture of old and new. Dating from 1867, **Perth Town Hall** is sited on the city's highest point, and for many decades its Gothic-style clock tower was Perth's most prominent feature. Visitors to the 1899 **Perth Mint**, the oldest operating mint in the country, can inspect Australia's largest collection of gold nuggets, then watch ingots being poured; entry fee, Ph: (08) 9421 7223.

The opulent **His Majesty's Theatre** is Australia's only remaining Edwardian venue for live entertainment; the building is also home to the Museum of Performing Arts, which has constantly changing exhibitions of memorabilia and costumes; free tours of the building, museum admission by gold coin, Ph: (08) 9265 0900. The **Cloisters**, dating from 1858 and originally a school, is now part of an office complex, while **Barracks Archway** is all that remains of the large, 1860s, convict-built military barracks demolished in 1966 to make way for the freeway. Across Narrows Bridge is the 4-bladed, 1835 **Old Mill**, a Perth landmark and one of its oldest buildings; both the

mill and the adjacent miller's cottage are furnished with relics of pioneer days; entry fee, Ph: (08) 9367 5788.

The **Western Australian Museum** has an extensive range of cultural-history and natural-science exhibitions (including an impressive collection of meteorites); the complex includes the 1856 Old Gaol and an early settler's cottage; entry fee for special exhibitions, Ph: (08) 9427 2700. Adjacent is the modern **Art Gallery of Western Australia**, with its splendid collection of Australian, European and Asian-Pacific art; entry fee for special exhibitions, Ph: (08) 9492 6622.

The city's main shopping area is concentrated around Hay and Murray Sts, and the malls between them, and nearby **London Court**, a shopping arcade with mock-Tudor architecture and a scaled-down version of London's Big Ben. Nearby, the restored 1890s warehouses of cobblestoned King St house gourmet eateries, galleries (with an extensive collection of Aboriginal art on offer) and fashion shops. **Northbridge**, on the edge of the CBD, is *the* place to eat at, its concentration of restaurants and cafes offering a wide range of cuisines. Inner-west **Subiaco** has classy boutiques, antique shops, bookshops, restaurants and 2 colourful weekend markets.

Statue of gold miners outside Perth Mint

Perth's CBD viewed from Kings Park

Parks and Gardens

Stirling Gardens, in the heart of the CBD and Perth's oldest public garden, is characterised by mature shade trees and well-tended flower beds; land set aside here in 1829 was originally intended for botanical gardens, and this was where Perth's first grapes and other imported fruits were grown. Nearby **Supreme Court Gardens** is a popular place to eat lunch and, in summer, the venue for events such as Opera in the Park. **Queens Gardens**, to the east, was originally a claypit, and supplied the bricks for many of Perth's colonial buildings; today it is a serene park, with lakes filling the old claypits, massed flower displays and a replica of the Peter Pan statue in London's Kensington Gardens.

Magnificent 400ha **Kings Park** covers the slopes and heights of riverside Mount Eliza and provides sweeping panoramas east over the city and Swan River to the Darling Ranges. More than half of the park is natural bushland, in spring ablaze with colourful wildflowers (celebrated with a wildflower festival); the rest includes the landscaped Botanic Garden, lakes, fountains, picnic areas and playgrounds. Visitors can explore the park's numerous paths on foot or bicycle (bicycles are available for hire near the restaurant in Fraser Ave), or join the Perth Tram Company's bus tour, fee, Ph: (08) 9322 2006. The park is the venue for a number of outdoor events in summer, including the Sunset Cinema, which screens near the Lakeside Picnic Area, entry fee, Ph: (08) 9385 5400. The steep steps of Jacobs Ladder link the park with the riverfront. Kings Park Information kiosk, Ph: (08) 9480 3600.

Swan Bells of St Martin

A gift to Perth from London, the Swan Bells include 12 historic bells dating from the early 1700s which formerly hung in St Martin-in-the-Fields Church in London and are referred to in the nursery rhyme 'Oranges and Lemons' ('... you owe me 5 farthings say the bells of St Martins ...'). With an additional 6  modern bells, they now hang in a glass-and-steel riverfront tower, purpose-built to take their massive weight, and together make up the largest set of change-ringing bells in the world. They are rung daily by volunteer members of the Australian and New Zealand Association of Bellringers. Visitors can watch both the swinging bells and the bellringers from an observation platform in the tower. Barrack Sq, entry fee, Ph: 9218 8183.

On the Water

Perth's scenic coastal and river waters are popular venues for a range of watersports, from yacht racing to surfing and diving. The long, wide Indian Ocean beaches are renowned for their white sands and spectacular sunsets. Most offer safe swimming, but strong winds (common in the afternoon) can make some dangerous for children and inexperienced swimmers. The safest are busy **Cottesloe**, known also for its street cafes and boutiques, uncrowded **City Beach** and, to the north, **Sorrento**. **Swanbourne** is Perth's nude beach. The best surf beaches include **Scarborough**, for both board and body surfing, and **Trigg** (however, both can be unsafe for inexperienced swimmers when the surf is rough). Scarborough has the added attraction of the weekend Scarborough Fair Market.

The waters of **Marmion Marine Park**, which extend north from Trigg to Burns Beach and offshore for 5km, are warmed by the Leeuwin Current (which also washes by Rottnest Island) and are home to sizeable colonies of seals and dolphins. Marmion's chain of inshore reefs is a diver's paradise, its caves and ledges teeming with myriads of colourful marine life; the park also includes sheltered and shallow Mettam's Pool, a safe swimming spot ideal for introducing children to snorkelling.

Diver exploring the chain of inshore reefs in Marmion Marine Park

Popular **Swan River** beaches include **Crawley** and **Peppermint Grove**. On weekends, the river comes alive with armadas of pleasure launches and colourful sailing craft. Cruise boats operating out of Barrack St Jetty offer half-day excursions downriver and to Fremantle, city dinner cruises, and full day cruises upstream to the heart of the Swan Valley wine- and olive-growing region. There is excellent fishing in the Swan estuary, off the beaches, and around Fremantle.

Cottlesloe Beach

Cellar-door entrance at Houghtons Winery, Swan Valley

The Swan Valley

The Swan Valley is a rewarding daytrip by road or cruise boat. **Guildford** was established beside the Swan in 1829 as a port and market town; many of its oldest buildings remain, including the Rose and Crown Hotel (which has operated as an inn since 1841), and the town is also known for its antique shops, cafes and restaurants. Further east are small farms and vineyards. Grapes thrive in the deep, loamy soil here and wine has been produced in the valley since the 1830s. Today, the region is home to 2 of Western Australia's largest winemaking companies (Houghton and Sandalford) and a number of small family wineries, and is known especially for chardonnay, shiraz and chenin blanc. All the wineries offer tastings and cellar-door sales; some also have restaurants. Cruise tours of the Swan Valley usually include lunch and wine-tastings. The area is also home to a number of artists' studios and galleries.

Sprawling **John Forrest NP** provides magnificent vistas back towards Perth across the Swan coastal plain and contains numerous walking trails that thread through rugged wilderness and lead to quiet pools and spectacular waterfalls. One of the park's more unusual attractions is the John Forrest Heritage Trail, a walk along a disused railway line, which passes through the 340m-long Swan View Tunnel. It was completed in 1895 and is the only railway tunnel ever constructed in the state.

In its upper reaches, the Swan is known as the Avon, the result of the river being discovered and named in widely separated places. In winter and spring, churning rapids formed as the Swan/Avon descends through the Darling Range attract whitewater canoeists.

Entrance to Swan View Tunnel, John Forrest NP

179

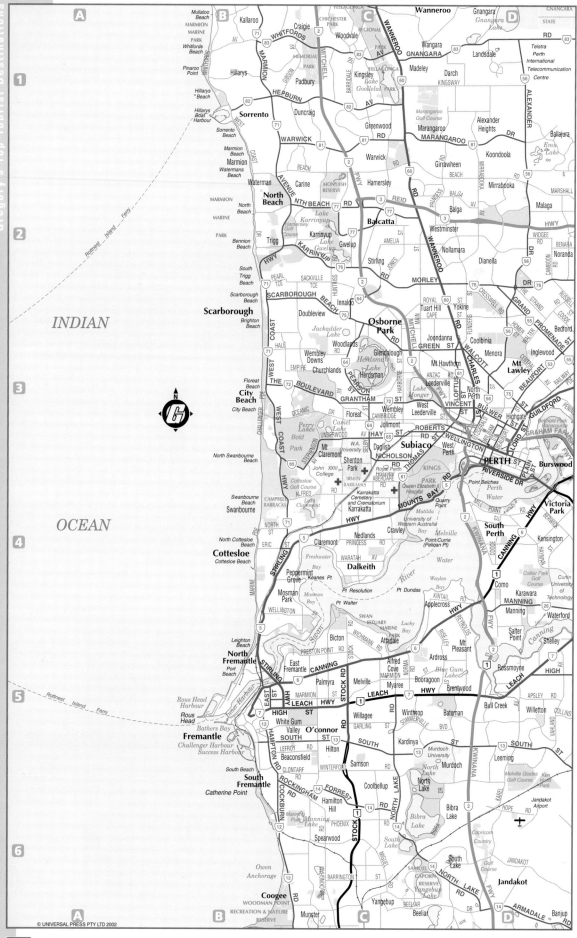

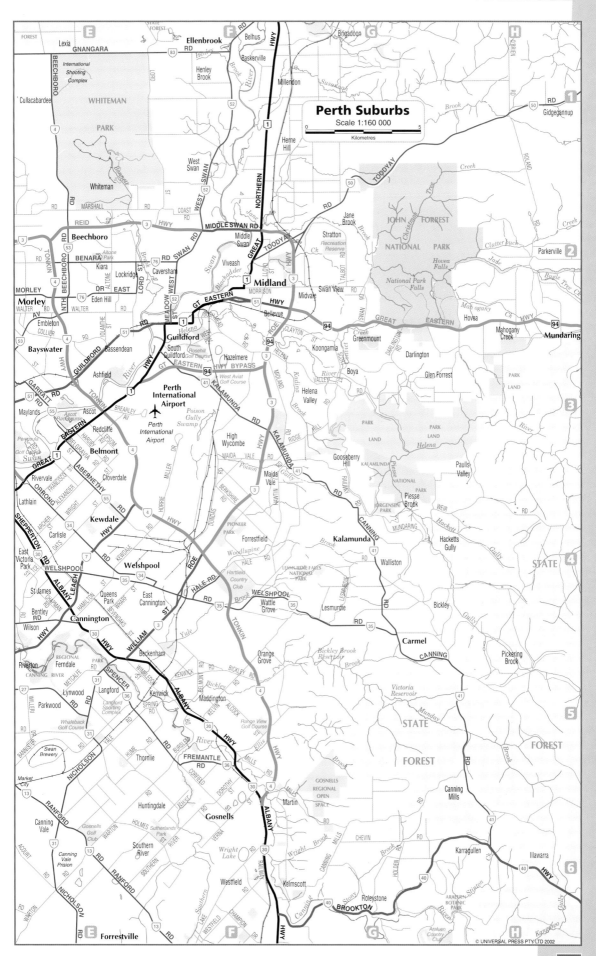

Perth Suburbs
Scale 1:160 000

0 _____ 5
Kilometres

Fremantle

Dynamic Fremantle, Perth's port, is reached by train or a 30min drive from the CBD. Here, historic streetscapes and docks busy with commercial, fishing and pleasure-craft form a backdrop to a thriving cultural and alternative arts scene and vibrant nightlife. Restored heritage buildings house galleries (some specialising in Aboriginal artworks), boutiques, bookshops, antique shops, pubs and a multicultural mix of fine eateries. The many attractions here include the **Fremantle Markets**, where more than 150 stalls sell goods ranging from fresh produce to opals; the **E Shed Markets**, which offer speciality shops and live entertainment; alfresco dining beside the **Fishing Boat Harbour**; and the 'cappuccino strip' of **South Tce**.

Convict-built **Fremantle Prison**, in use until 1991, is now open to the public; entry fee, Ph: (08) 9430 7177. The waterfront **Western Australian Maritime Museum** houses the reconstructed remains of the Dutch ship *Batavia*, lost off the NW coast in 1629; free entry, Ph: (08) 9431 8444. The associated New Maritime Museum, on Victoria Quay, is home to *Australia II*, winner of the 1983 America's Cup (Fremantle hosted the unsuccessful defence of the Cup 4 years later).

Fremantle Markets

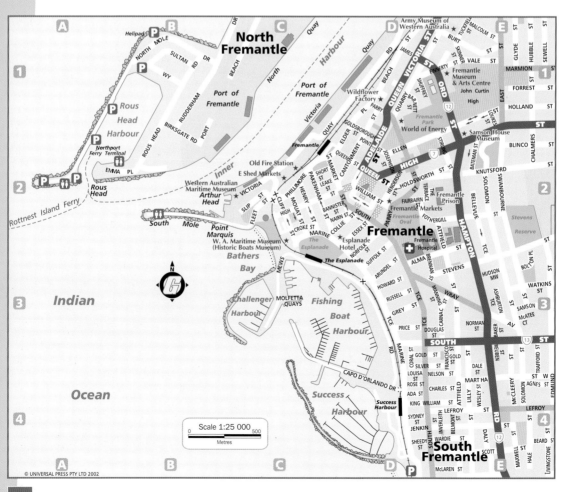

Rottnest Island

Lying 18km west of Fremantle and reached by regular ferry services from Fremantle, Perth and Hillary's Boat Harbour, Rottnest is ideal for either a daytrip or a relaxing longer break. It offers pristine beaches for swimming and surfing; sparkling bays for windsurfing, sea-kayaking and boating; great fishing; and coastal walks and cycle paths leading through stunning scenery.

The crystal-clear waters are perfect for snorkelling and diving; for just offshore are some of the world's southernmost coral reefs. Home to myriad marine life including sponges and a wide variety of hard and soft corals, these reefs are washed by the warm Leeuwin Current, which carries tropical waters southward along the continental shelf. Oct–Jun is the prime diving season.

Plaques on land and underwater mark the locations of a number of wrecks; the wrecks themselves are best viewed by snorkelling over them or from the glass-bottomed *Underwater Explorer* tour

boat, fee, Ph: (08) 9292 5161. Bicycles, available for hire on the island, are the main mode of transport, and children especially revel in the freedom of riding on car-free roads. Alternatively, you can take a ride on the historic **Oliver Hill** light railway, fee, Ph: (08) 9372 9752.

Rottnest was named in 1696 by Dutch explorer Willem de Vlamingh; he and his men mistook the small, solidly built wallabies (quokkas) here for a type of large rat and so called the island 'rat's nest' in Dutch. Today, the friendly quokka population (estimated at about 10 000) is one of Rottnest's main attractions: unworried by holidaymakers, the creatures spend most of the day resting in the shade then emerge in the late afternoon to browse on low shrubs, grasses and succulent plants.

Accommodation on Rottnest includes the historic Rottnest Hotel, Ph: (08) 9292 5011, and the Rottnest Lodge Resort, Ph: (08) 9292 5161, both at **Thomson Bay**, and a range of villas (some with ocean views), cottages, cabins, and campsites managed by the Rottnest Island Authority, Ph: (08) 9432 9111.

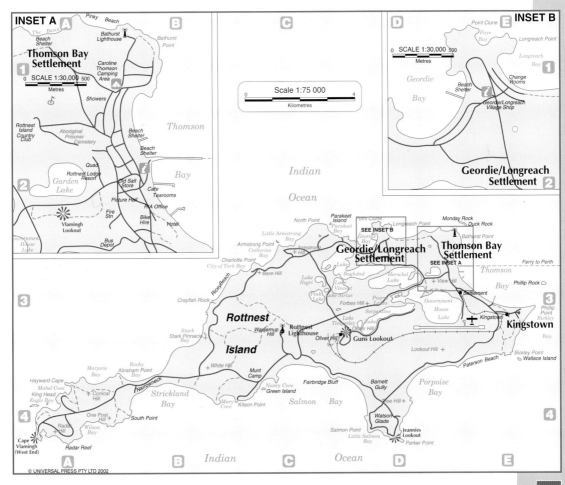

Broome

A long-established pearling post with a remarkably cosmopolitan atmosphere, Broome has been transformed in recent years by up-market tourist developments into one of the country's top holiday destinations. The town's exotic multicultural mix is a legacy of its pearling heyday, when Aboriginal, Japanese, Malay and Pacific-Islander sailors worked on the luggers. Historic Chinatown, Broome's original commercial centre, is now home to some of the world's finest pearl showrooms as well as an impressive array of eateries. Accommodation ranges from exclusive resorts to beachfront campsites.

The long white curve of **Cable Beach** offers safe swimming in clear waters and is a particularly popular place to watch the sun set over the Indian Ocean. Extremely low tides between Mar and Oct combine with a full moon to produce another Broome attraction, the 'Staircase to the Moon'; this optical illusion occurs when the night sky is reflected in the gleaming, exposed mudflats of **Roebuck Bay**. Evening markets are held at Town Beach on the first and second nights of the 'Staircase'.

Broome is also a top birdwatching spot; more than 300 species, including migratory shorebirds from Siberia, have been sighted from **Broome Bird Observatory**, fee for tours, Ph: (08) 9193 5600. Offshore, charter and tour vessels cruise the wild coast, the Buccaneer Archipelago, and the coral reefs of Rowley Shoals (280km to the west).

Japanese cemetery in Broome

Fitzroy Crossing lies in the heart of the ancient, rust-red lands and brilliant blue skies of the Kimberley, where deep-cut gorges shelter magnificent galleries of Aboriginal rock art. In Devonian times, 350 million years ago, these lands lay beneath a tropical sea; the massive limestone ridge of the Napier Range is actually an ancient barrier reef, and in places marine fossils stud gorge walls. In **Windjana Gorge NP**, the Lennard River runs through a 3.5km-long canyon hung with rock figs and clumps of spinifex; **Tunnel Creek NP** protects a 750m-long cavern, home to both bats and freshwater crocodiles. Aboriginal cultural tours visit both gorges; book through the Fitzroy Crossing Tourist Bureau.

The deep canyon of **Geikie Gorge NP** was carved out by the Fitzroy River. Cruise boats, including the Darngku Heritage Cruise (book through the Fitzroy Crossing Tourist Bureau) glide by the yellow, orange and grey walls; freshwater crocodiles, sawfish and stingrays are sometimes seen. A 4WD vehicle is required to reach all the gorges; tours available through several Broome-based companies include camping equipment and food as well as transport.

Tunnel Creek NP

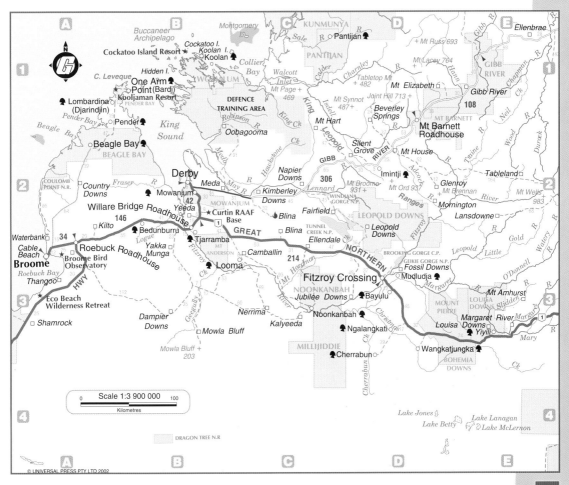

Margaret River

Best time to visit: Year-round; spring (Sep–Nov) for wildflowers; winter and spring Jun–Dec) for whalewatching; summer (Nov–Mar) for beach activites and watersports; autumn (Apr–May) for wine harvest

Average daily temperatures: Jan 15–25°C, Apr 13–21°C, Jul 10–16°C, Oct 11–18°C

Getting there: By road from Perth via Bussell Hwy to Busselton (230km), Margaret River (290km) and Augusta (320km); charter flights from Perth to Busselton and Margaret River

Festivals and events:

Jan: Leeuwin Estate Family Concert (Australia Day); Busselton Beach Festival; GWN Festival of Busselton

Feb: Leeuwin Estate Concert; Amberley Estate Winery Semillon and Seafood; Busselton Jetty Swim

Mar: Augusta River Festival, Augusta

Apr: Salomon Margaret River Masters surfing competition

May: Busselton Triathlon

Sep: Margaret River–Augusta Orchid Show; Busselton Wildflower Exhibition

Oct: Augusta and District Spring Garden Show

Nov: Margaret River Wine Region Festival (food, wine and art); Margaret River Agricultural Show; Busselton Agricultural Show; Margaret River Classic surfing competition; Wineries to Waves Fun Run

Dec: Yallingup Malibu Surfing Classic

Activities: Visiting wineries, swimming, surfing, diving, snorkelling, windsurfing, fishing, caving, climbing, abseiling, bushwalking, canoeing, sea-kayaking, horseriding, whalewatching, browsing art galleries and craft shops, scenic drives

Highlights: Wining and dining; coastal and forest walking trails; cycle track (40min) from Margaret River to Prevelly Beach; Lake Cave guided tour; spectacular scenic drives through coastal limestone country, karri forest and rural hinterland; Cape Naturaliste Lighthouse walk; whalewatching in season; canoeing up the Margaret River to Aboriginal sites, fee, Ph: (08) 9797 1084; *Swan* wreck dive—Cape Dive, Ph: (08) 9756 8778, offer guided dive trips, including equipment; view from top of Cape Leeuwin Lighthouse

Tip: Treat yourself to a gourmet vineyard lunch and sample local treats such as marron, seafood or game matched with Margaret River wines.

Kids' stuff: Yoganup Playground, Busselton foreshore; birds-of-prey flight displays, Eagle's Heritage, Margaret River, entry fee, Ph: (08) 9757 2960; camel rides on Smiths Beach, Yallingup, fee, Ph: (08) 9755 1118; CaveWorks Interpretive Centre (displays on geology of area, cave tours), Margaret River, Ph: (08) 9757 7411

Further information: Busselton Tourist Bureau, cnr Peel Tce and Causeway Rd, Busselton, WA 6280, Ph: (08) 9752 1288; Dunsborough Tourist Bureau, Dunsborough Park Shopping Centre, Dunsborough, WA 6281, Ph: (08) 9755 3299; Margaret River Tourist Bureau, cnr Bussell Hwy and Tunbridge Rd, Margaret River, WA 6285, Ph: (08) 9757 2911

Stretching from Cape Naturaliste south to Cape Leeuwin, the Margaret River region offers visitors an outstanding list of attractions including award-winning wines and gourmet food, magnificent forest scenery, fascinating cave systems, and a stunning coastline with great surfing beaches, sheltered swimming spots, excellent fishing and famed dive locations. Dining options range from upmarket restaurants to waterfront cafes and fish-and-chip shops. Accommodation in the wine district includes chalets and lodges (there are no high-rise resorts), many with spa baths and other luxury touches; along the coast are family-orientated holiday parks, beach houses and apartments, and bush cottages.

Sugarloaf Rock, Leeuwin–Naturaliste NP

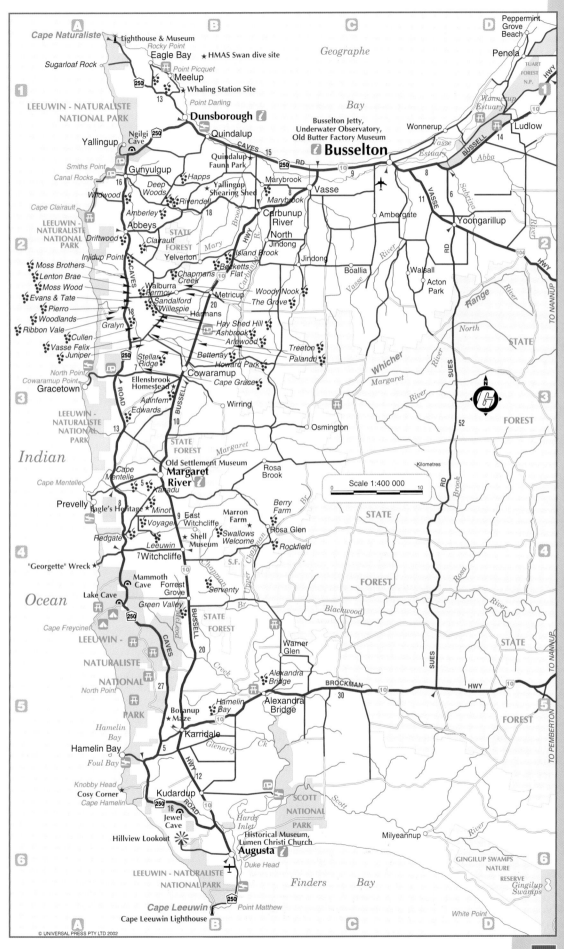

© UNIVERSAL PRESS PTY LTD 2002

Cooked marron, a local speciality

Food and Wine

The thriving Margaret River wine industry dates from the mid 1960s, when a group of doctors took note of a report

Margaret River wine and grapes

suggesting that the climate and conditions here were ideal for winegrowing. Today, more than 75 wineries produce some of the country's best wines, with the local chardonnay and cabernet sauvignon being particularly highly regarded. Leading wineries include Leeuwin Estate, the location of an enormously successful annual outdoor concert, Ph: (08) 9759 0000; Cape Mentelle, which has a history of prize-winning red wines, Ph: (08) 9757 3266; Cullen Wines, a boutique winery renowned for its outstanding cabernet merlot, Ph: (08) 9755 5277; and Amberley Estate Winery, host of the annual Semillon and Seafood event, Ph: (08) 9755 2288. Most wineries offer cellar-door sales and many have restaurants—perfect for a long lunch overlooking the vines. And if you are more partial to beer, the lakeside Bootleg Brewery, near Dunsborough, Ph: (08) 9755 6300, produces a range of award-winning boutique beers.

Gourmet foods on offer include marron (freshwater crayfish with large tails packed with sweet, tender meat)—for close encounters call in at the Margaret River Marron Farm, Ph: (08) 9757 6279— seafood, game, olives and olive oils, asparagus, berries, cheeses, and jams, fudges, honey and condiments. You can even visit a chocolate factory (and taste the merchandise): Margaret River Chocolate Company, Ph: (08) 9755 6555.

Coast and Caves

Bounded by water on 3 sides, the region has a wealth of bays, beaches and jutting capes. Most of the rugged western shore is protected in the 120km-long strip of **Leeuwin–Naturaliste NP**, Ph: (08) 9752 1677. A bushwalker's delight, it has an extensive network of tracks including the demanding but spectacularly scenic Cape to Cape Trail, which winds for 140km along the entire coast but can be sampled in separate sections. Many shorter bushwalks, such as the Cape Naturaliste Track (3.2km), lead to dramatic lookouts bordering the wild ocean.

The great swells of the Indian Ocean roll year-round onto the beaches and reefs, where some of the country's best surfing action is found—top spots include **Margaret River**, **Yallingup**, **Smiths Beach** and **Prevelly**. In the north, white sandy beaches and sheltered waters make the shores of **Geographe Bay** ideal for family holidays; popular destinations here include **Busselton** and **Dunsborough**. Whalewatching tours operate out of Dunsborough from Sep–Dec; fee, Ph: (08) 9755 2276.

The area is also renowned for its excellent dive sites. Two of the best are the wreck of the *Swan*, which lies off **Eagle Bay** and now harbours an entire reef ecosystem, and the far end of the 1.8km-long Busselton Jetty, where almost every pylon is encased in marine life and schools of fish of all shapes, colours and sizes swirl by almost constantly.

Augusta, in the south of the region and once the haunt of whalers, is now a favoured whalewatching spot, with both humpback and southern right whales visiting from Jun–Dec; charters operate Jun–end Aug, fee, Ph: (08) 9755 2276. The waters here also offer superb fishing. Cape Leeuwin Lighthouse stands on the extreme SW corner of the continent, where the Indian and the cool Southern oceans meet; there are fine views from the top; entry fee, Ph: (08) 9758 1920.

A soft limestone ridge running the length of the coast between **Cape Naturaliste** and **Cape Leeuwin** is honeycombed with one of the most extensive limestone cave systems in the world. Caves open for inspection include **Ngilgi Cave**, near Yallingup, which has impressive red-and-orange shawl formations, entry fee, Ph: (08) 9755 2155; and **Mammoth Cave**, which is rich in ancient fossils, and **Lake Cave**, which contains delicate formations and a mirror-surfaced pool, both near Margaret River, entry fee for each, Ph: (08) 9757 7411. The hi-tech Caveworks Interpretive Centre, directly above Lake Cave, has fascinating displays on how the caves were formed. Further south, near Augusta, is the lofty, stalactite-encrusted cavern of **Jewel Cave**; entry fee, Ph: (08) 9757 7411.

Stalactites and stalagmites in Lake Cave

Shark Bay

Best time to visit: Year-round, but best Apr–Oct, when winds are generally lightest and temperature is mild; winter (Jun–Sep) offers best chance to see visiting dolphins; late winter to spring (Aug–Nov) for wildflowers; late winter (Jul–Sep) for whalewatching; summer can be extremely hot.

Average daily temperatures: Jan 21–30°C, Apr 19–28°C, Jul 13–21°C, Oct 16–25°C

Getting there: By road from Perth via Brand and North West Coastal Hwy to Denham (830km) and Carnarvon (900km); by air from Perth to Denham

Festivals and events:

Aug: Carnarvon Festival; Shark Bay Fishing Fiesta

Nov: Blessing of the Fleet, Kalbarri

Activities: Interaction with dolphins, swimming, windsurfing, canoeing, snorkelling, diving, fishing, sailing, 4WD touring, bushwalking, birdwatching, wildlife tours, whalewatching, viewing spring wildflower display

Highlights: Wild bottlenose dolphins of Monkey Mia; glass-bottomed boats at Monkey Mia, fee, Ph: (08) 9948 1274; scenic and wildlife cruises on *Shotover*, fee, Ph: (08) 9948 1481, or catamaran *Aristocat*, fee, Ph: (08) 9948 1446, both departing from jetty at Monkey Mia; Shell Beach; Eagle Bluff for shark and osprey sightings; Shark Bay Scenic Air Charters, fee, Ph: (08) 9948 1773; stromatolites at Hamelin Pool Nature Reserve; sunsets

Tip: Dolphins visiting Monkey Mia do not arrive at a set time. They are more likely to come in the morning, usually from about 8.00am on, but be prepared to spend most of the day waiting. The dolphins rarely miss a day.

Kids' stuff: Dolphin-feeding at Monkey Mia (rangers often involve children in the activity)

Further information: Shark Bay Tourist Bureau, Knight Tce, Denham, WA 6537, Ph: (08) 9948 1253; CALM (Conservation and Land Management) District Office, Knight Tce, Denham, WA 6537, Ph: (08) 9948 1208

The combination of friendly dolphins, magnificent coastal scenery, pristine beaches, prolific and diverse wildlife (including ancient life forms called stromatolites), spectacular wildflowers and important historic sites makes Shark Bay one of Australia's most fascinating tourist destinations. So impressive are the region's natural attractions that in 1991 it was declared a World Heritage Area, and was one of the few sites in the world to meet all 4 natural criteria for listing.

Shark Bay was the site of some of the earliest visits to Australia by European navigators. **Dirk Hartog Island**, off the western side of the bay, is named after the first recorded European visitor, a Dutch mariner who landed on the island in 1616. In 1699, Englishman William Dampier spent 7 days in the broad inlet he christened Shark Bay. Many other natural features carry the names of 19th-century French captains and their ships.

There is camping and limited accommodation at Monkey Mia; a wider range of options, including B&Bs, farmstays and waterfront cottages, is available at Denham (Australia's most westerly town) and Carnarvon. A number of whale-watching, diving and fishing cruises, scenic coach tours and 4WD nature-based tours operate from both centres and can be arranged and booked through the Shark Bay Tourist Bureau.

Green sea turtle in the waters of Shark Bay

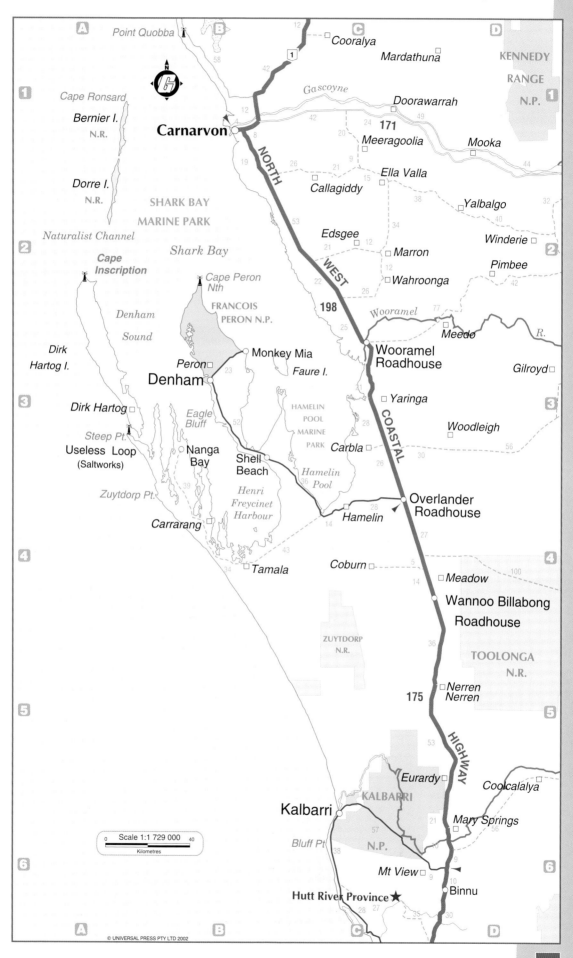

© UNIVERSAL PRESS PTY LTD 2002

Tourists and dolphins at Monkey Mia

The Dolphins of Monkey Mia

Interacting with wild bottlenose dolphins is a daily ritual in the clear, shallow waters of Monkey Mia. The animals began visiting in the 1960s, encouraged by a local woman who tossed fish to a group of dolphins that regularly followed her husband's fishing boat to shore. Since the 1980s, CALM (the department of Conservation and Land Management) has managed the viewing and feeding in such a way that the dolphins do not become dependent on handouts.

Feeding times are deliberately irregular and the amount of food provided is strictly controlled—only freshly caught local fish are used and each dolphin is offered no more than one-third of its daily food requirement. Young dolphins are not provided with food until park rangers are sure that their natural hunting skills are fully developed.

Seven dolphins are regular visitors to Monkey Mia, another 12 or so appear occasionally, and more than 120 live in the waters offshore. The dolphins come in up to 3 times a day, although sometimes they are not fed. Visitors can walk and swim among them, and touch and feed them under the supervision of rangers. The dolphin feeding area is part of **Monkey Mia Reserve**; entry fee, Ph: (08) 9948 1366 (fees help fund the management and care of the dolphins).

Encounter with a bottlenose dolphin, Monkey Mia

Coastal Treasures

Shark Bay lies in a transition zone between warm and cold ocean currents, resulting in a rich array of marine life such as dolphins, marine turtles (including a large colony of loggerheads), manta rays, sea snakes, sharks and visiting humpback whales. Vast seagrass meadows here, the most extensive in the world, are home to the largest dugong population on Earth. The region is also renowned for its rich fishing grounds, with pink snapper, tailor, mackerel and whiting the main catches. **Steep Point**, a rocky headland jutting into the Indian Ocean south of Dirk Hartog Island, is one of Australia's most impressive (and rewarding) fishing spots. For divers and snorkellers, there are colonies of colourful corals (staghorn, brain and plate) and sponges in the bay and, in shallow waters off **Cape Peron**, the wreck of the *Gudrun* which sank in 1901 and is the largest intact and undisturbed wooden wreck off the coast of Western Australia.

Red cliffs at Cape Peron

Hamelin Pool is home to a stunted forest of rock-like, spongy domes called stromatolites, the work of possibly the oldest life forms on Earth, cyanobacteria. These micro-organisms are thought to have been around for 3.5 billion years, and the stromatolites at Hamelin—formed from sediments bound by cyanobacteria mucus—may be 3500 years old. A sandbar limiting the tidal flushing of the pool, combined with a high rate of evaporation, means the waters here are twice as salty as normal seawater; this hypersalination deters fish and most other forms of marine life that would otherwise feed on the stromatolites. A 200m boardwalk leads over the best examples. Nearby is the Hamelin Pool Historic Telegraph Office, now a museum with tearooms, Ph: (08) 9942 5905.

Shell Beach is made entirely of tiny white cockle shells, which are up to 10m deep in places. Like the stromatolites, the cockles thrive in the highly saline waters, and the shell deposits have accumulated over several thousand years. The boardwalk at the edge of **Eagle Bluff** (home to ospreys) provides an excellent vantage point for observing sharks, and sometimes dugongs feeding far below on seagrass beds close to the shore.

The Shark Bay region has approximately 700 species of wildflowers and Western Australia's longest flowering period. In season, the rolling shrublands of **Francois Peron NP** (fee, 4WD only north of Peron Homestead) are bright with wattles, hakea and the purple Shark Bay daisy. To the south, the heathlands, gorges and coastal clifftops of **Kalbarri NP** are renowned for their spectacular displays of gold and orange banksias; grevilleas in white, yellow and red; green and red kangaroo paws; featherflowers; orchids; and river gums.

Ancient stromatolites at Hamelin Pool

The Stirling Range and Albany

Best time to visit: Spring and early summer (Sep–Dec) for wildflowers; summer for swimming and birdwatching; Jul–Aug for whalewatching and year-round for birdwatching

Average daily temperatures: Jan 15–22°C, Apr 12–20°C, Jul 8–15°C, Oct 10–18°C

Getting there: By road from Perth via Albany Hwy to Albany (410km); by air from Perth to Albany

Festivals and events:

Jan: Wignalls Vintage Blues and Jazz Festival, Albany; summer craft markets

Mar: Porongurup Wine Festival and Markets; Highland Gathering and Games, Albany

Apr: Albany Festival; Albany Art Prize

Jun: Albany Classic Car Event

Sep: Cranbrook Wildflower Display; Albany Wildflower Display; Mt Barker Wildflower Exhibition; Kojonup Wildflower Display

Oct: Porongurup Wildflower Display; Great Southern Wine Festival

Nov: Albany Agricultural Show

Activities: Viewing wildflowers, fishing, swimming, boating, windsurfing, canoeing, rockclimbing, abseiling, birdwatching, whalewatching (in season), wine-tasting, scenic drives

Highlights: Princess Royal Harbour and King George Sound; scenic drives and coastal formations of Torndirrup NP; local oysters and mussels; spring wildflower displays of Porongurup NP and Stirling Range NP; winery tours

Tip: Visit the oyster and mussel hatchery at Emu Point, Albany, and buy a bag of the produce for a beachfront feast. Winter and spring visitors to Stirling Range NP should be prepared with warm and waterproof clothing, even for short walks.

Kids' stuff: Whaleworld, Albany, entry fee, Ph: (08) 9844 4021; good swimming at Middleton Beach (with playground and BBQ facilities), Goode Beach or in the calm waters at Emu Point; replica of brig *Amity* on Albany foreshore, entry fee; Albany Bird Park, entry fee, Ph: (08) 9842 5363; Deer-o-dome, Albany, entry fee, Ph: (08) 9841 7436; Willowie Wildlife Park and Horseriding, Albany, entry fee, Ph: (08) 9846 4365

Further information: Albany Visitor Centre, Proudlove Pde, Albany, WA 6332, Ph: (08) 9841 1088; Mt Barker Tourist Bureau, Albany Hwy, Mt Barker, WA 6324, Ph: (08) 9851 1163; Denmark Tourist Bureau, Strickland St, Denmark, WA 6333, Ph: (08) 9848 2055

Southern Western Australia is home to a range of spectacular and diverse attractions. Stretching south from the **Stirling Range**—scenic showcase for the state's famed spring wildflower displays—it takes in towering karri forest, vineyards and wineries (between **Denmark**, **Mt Barker** and **Porongurup**), and rolling farmlands, as well as the ocean-battered cliffs and pristine swimming coves of the rugged coastline. Accommodation in the region includes beachfront caravan parks, holiday units, farmstays, B&Bs and charming country cottages.

The regional centre of **Albany**, which overlooks the sheltered waters of magnificent **Princess Royal Harbour**, was Western Australia's first European settlement, being founded in 1827, 2 years before Perth. In the 1890s, it was the landing place for thousands of prospectors heading to the Kalgoorlie goldfields. Albany has many historic buildings; a number of heritage walking trails visit significant sites in the town and environs.

Until 1978, Australia's last whaling station operated on the southern shores of **King George Sound**; the complex is now

Bluff Knoll in the Stirling Range

home to the **Whale World** museum of whaling history, which includes a beached and restored whalechaser. In a remarkably short time, whales (hump-backs and southern rights) have returned to calve in nearby sheltered bays. The dramatic shoreline of neighbouring **Torndirrup NP** includes the huge ocean-carved granite span of the **Natural Bridge**, and the **Blowholes**, holes and cracks in the coastal cliffs which snort air and spray when the seas are high.

Inland, the granite bulk of **Stirling Range NP**, which rises island-like from the surrounding plains, is known for the staggering concentration, variety and beauty of its wildflowers. Over 1500 species grow here (more than in the entire British Isles), nearly 90 of which are found nowhere else; the flowers are at their best in late spring and early summer (Oct–Dec). The Stirling Range peaks are often shrouded in mist; **Bluff Knoll**, within the park, is the highest point in the state's SW, at 1073m, and the only place in Western Australia where winter snow is likely.

The **Cranbrook** area, just to the north, is particularly rich in orchids. To the south, the karri forests and granite domes protected in **Porongurup NP** are home to 800 plant species, including 5 unique to the region. Scenic drives provide magnificent views of the Porongorup Range and the surrounding countryside.

Restored whalechaser at the Whale World museum near Albany

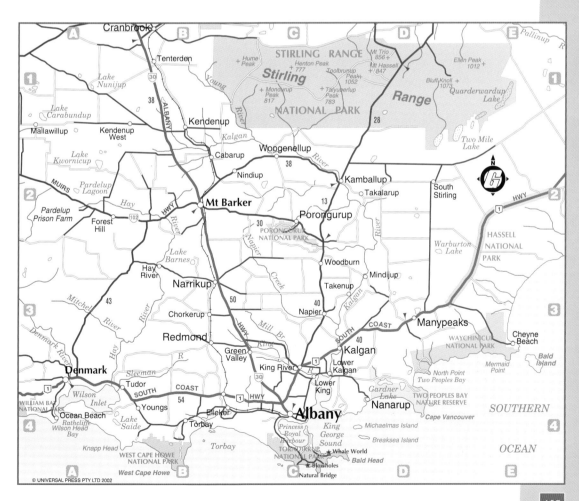

Red Centre landscape with
Uluru (Ayers Rock)
in the distance

Northern Territory

The vast and sparsely populated Northern Territory stretches from the steamy tropics to the arid interior. It offers sensational scenery, a long and rich Aboriginal heritage, and diverse and prolific flora and fauna. Within its borders lie some of Australia's best-known natural treasures, including the great landmarks of Uluru (Ayers Rock) and Kata Tjuṯa (the Olgas) in the Red Centre, and the wetlands and wildlife of Kakadu NP in the Top End. Visitors can cruise beside crocodiles, fish for famously large barramundi, marvel at ancient rock-art galleries, ride camels across red sands, and cool off in sparkling inland waterholes. The capital, Darwin, is known for its exciting cultural mix, Asian-style food markets and stunning harbour. In the south, at the heart of the continent, is the legendary Outback town of Alice Springs. Fly-drive holidays are a popular way to explore the Northern Territory, with many car-rental outlets offering a range of campervans, motorhomes and camping gear, as well as 4WD and conventional vehicles.

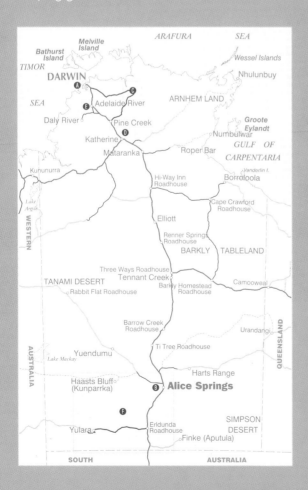

Tourist Information

 Tourism Northern Territory
1st Floor,
22 Cavenagh St
Darwin
NT 0801
Ph: (08) 8941 1824
www.northernterritory.com

Top Tourist Destinations

Ⓐ Darwin
Ⓑ Alice Springs
Ⓒ Kakadu National Park
Ⓓ Katherine Gorge
Ⓔ Litchfield National Park
Ⓕ The Red Centre

Darwin

Best time to visit: Winter, the dry season (May–Oct), offers balmy days and clear nights; summer, the wet season (Nov–Apr), is characterised by lush vegetation, spectacular lightning storms and the presence of stinger jellyfish along the coast

Average daily temperatures: Jan 25–32°C, Apr 24–33°C, Jul 20–31°C, Oct 25–34°C

Getting there: Darwin is linked by air to all mainland capitals and to several Asian cities; by road from Alice Springs via Stuart Hwy (1495km), from Broome via Great Northern Hwy and Victoria Hwy (1865km), and from Cairns via Bruce Hwy, Barkly Hwy and Stuart Hwy (2755km)

Festivals and events:

Mar: Irish Festival

Apr: Darwin Sailing Club Open Day and Commodore's Challenge

May: Arafura Games (Asia–Pacific sporting competition, odd years only, various locations); V8 Supercar Championships, Hidden Valley Raceway

Jun: Round the Islands Yacht Race; Chinese Dragon Boat Festival; City to Surf Run; NT Orchid Spectacular; Marrara Indoor Stadium

Jul: Darwin Cup Carnival (8-day horse-racing carnival); Royal Darwin Show

Aug: Fringe Festival; Beer Can Regatta, Mindil Beach; Festival of Darwin

Nov: Darwin to Adelaide World Solar Car Challenge

Dec: Aboriginal and Torres Strait Islander Art Award Show; New Year's Eve fireworks on Darwin Wharf

Activities: Browsing galleries for Aboriginal artworks, exploring multicultural markets, sunset harbour cruises, boating, fishing, visiting parks and gardens, crocodile-spotting cruises

Highlights: Tropical sunsets, exotic food-and-craft street markets; harbour cruises; Darwin Wharf Precinct, with its outdoor eating and live music; East Point Reserve; Charles Darwin NP

Tip: Visit East Point Reserve at dusk for spectacular sunset views across Fannie Bay to the city; this is also when the reserve's large colony of agile wallabies emerges to feed.

Kids' stuff: Aquascene (daily hand-feeding of hundreds of fish at Doctors Gully; times vary with tides), entry fee, Ph: (08) 8981 7837; Crocodylus Park (crocodiles, emus, cassowaries, sea turtles and more), entry fee, Ph: (08) 8922 4500; Indo Pacific Marine aquarium

Further information: Tourism Top End, Beagle House, cnr Knuckey and Mitchell Sts, Darwin, NT 0800, Ph: (08) 8936 2499, www.tourism topend.com.au; Tourism Northern Territory, 1st Floor, 22 Cavenagh St, Darwin, NT 0801, Ph: (08) 8941 1824 www.northern territory.com

Closer to several Asian cities than to most other Australian capitals, Darwin is renowned for its fascinating blend of cultures, its relaxed lifestyle and its exotic street markets. The city is superbly sited on a peninsula fringed by inlets, bays and beaches, with the compact CBD, including the main shopping precinct of **Smith St Mall**, concentrated in a few blocks in the SE. Residential areas are located mainly in the north and in the satellite community of Palmerston. Darwin's distinctively modern architecture, featuring innovative, cyclone-resistant buildings, is the result of a massive reconstruction program initiated after the devastation wrought by Cyclone Tracy in Dec 1974.

Accommodation includes caravan parks (on the edge of town), hostels, holiday flats and up-market hotels. Asian food features strongly in the city's eateries. Like the rest of the Top End, Darwin experiences 2 seasons—the Wet (summer), with rain most days, and the Dry (winter), when temperatures and humidity are lower and most tourists visit.

Smith St Mall

Places of Interest

Cenotaph (1)
Chinese Temple (2)
Darwin Entertainment Centre (3)
Darwin Wharf Precinct (4)
Doctors Gully (5)
Fannie Bay Gaol Museum (6)
Government House (7)
Mindil Beach Lookout (8)
Museum and Art Gallery of the Northern Territory (9)
Old Court House (10)
Northern Territory Parliament House (11)
Smith St Mall (12)

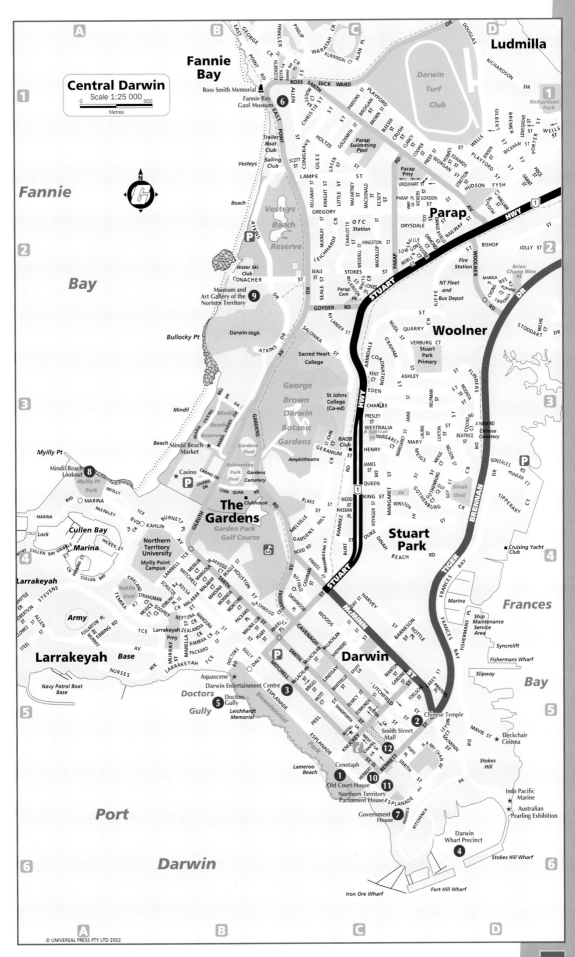

Central Darwin
Scale 1:25 000
0   500
Metres

Ludmilla

Fannie Bay

Fannie

Bay

Parap

Woolner

Larrakeyah

The Gardens

Stuart Park

Cullen Bay

Larrakeyah

Doctors Gully

Darwin

Frances

Bay

Port

Darwin

Tropical Capital

Following Cyclone Tracy, Darwin was completely remodelled; its new layout was characterised by tree-lined streets, modern public buildings and large areas of landscaped open space. Notable post-Tracy buildings include the **Northern Territory Parliament House**, with its grand granite-and-timber interior, and the nearby Supreme Court; both are open to the public and have impressive collections of Aboriginal art on display.

The **Chinese Temple** was rebuilt on the site of the 1887 original and houses a museum highlighting Chinese history in the Territory. The **Darwin Wharf Precinct**, now revamped as a tourist area, includes the **Australian Pearling Exhibition**, a historical overview of pearling in northern Australia, entry fee, Ph: (08) 8941 2177; the **Indo Pacific Marine** aquarium, entry fee, Ph: (08) 8981 1294; and WWII oil-storage tunnels carved out of solid rock, tours available, entry fee, Ph: (08) 8985 4779. Former cells in **Fannie Bay Gaol Museum** house grim displays from the days when this was Darwin's main gaol (1883–1979).

The city's wealth of parks includes the **George Brown Darwin Botanic Gardens**,

Chinese Temple interior

which has tropical-plant displays and a self-guided Aboriginal Plant-Use walk, Ph: (08) 8981 1958, and the 200ha **East Point Reserve**, which features natural forest and mangroves, open parkland, picnic areas and safe swimming in **Lake Alexander** and is also the site of the East Point Military Museum, entry fee, ph: (08) 8981 9702. Walkers and cyclists can explore a network of tracks through the internationally important wetlands of **Charles Darwin NP**; there are sweeping harbour views from the lookout beside the picnic area, Ph: (08) 8947 2305.

Exhibit at East Point Military Museum, East Point Reserve

Nightcliff Beach and the Timor Sea

Pleasure-craft, fishing boats and cruise vessels ply the sheltered waters of Darwin's extensive shoreline. Most of the popular sunset harbour cruises leave from the marina at **Cullen Bay**; the range of craft on offer includes an old pearling lugger, a luxury catamaran and a ferry. The city beaches of **Mindil** (also the site of the famed sunset markets) and Vesteys are popular during the dry season, but unsafe for swimming in the Wet due to the presence of deadly stinger jellyfish. A stinger net protects part of **Nightcliff Beach** in north Darwin; further north, a section of **Casuarina Beach** is officially designated for nude bathing.

Multicultural Markets

Darwin's rich mix of cultures is best experienced at its colourful street markets. The most famous is the Asian-style Mindil Beach Sunset Market in Gilruth Ave, Mindil Beach; its street entertainment and stalls selling food (Thai, Indian, Chinese, Greek and more), tropical fruits and vegetables, and crafts attract a crowd of up to 15 000 every Thur and Sun night (dry season only). Darwin's oldest market, at Rapid Creek, in the north of the city, operates every Sun morning year-round, selling locally grown fruit and vegetables, exotic plants and palms, and tempting meals and snacks. The Nightcliff Market, in the shopping centre at Nightcliff, is *the* place for Sun breakfast, offering a wide choice of food stalls and a mouth-watering array of fresh tropical fruits and live music. The popular and stylish Parap Village Market opens for business every Sat morning in the Shopping Village at Parap, selling Asian fare, seafood, organically grown vegetables, flowers, plants and local crafts. A visit to the Palmerston and Rural Weekly Markets, held on Fri evening (dry season only) at the Francis Mall Palmerston Shopping Centre, is a great family night out. About 130 stalls sell traditional foods from around the world as well as crafts, plants and local produce; there is also a children's play area.

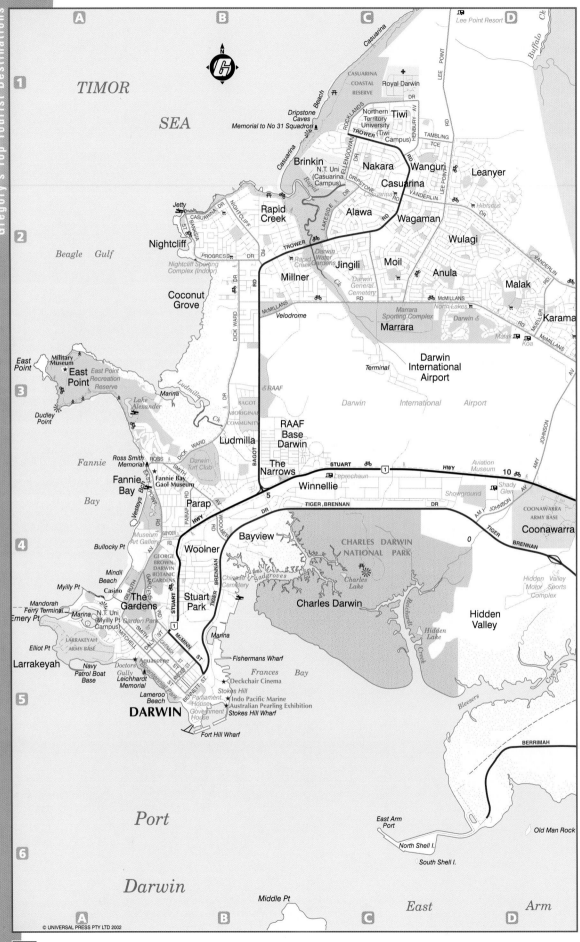

TIMOR

SEA

Beagle Gulf

Dripstone Caves
Memorial to No 31 Squadron

CASUARINA
COASTAL
RESERVE

Royal Darwin

Northern
Territory
University
(Tiwi
Campus)

Tiwi

Brinkin

N.T. Uni
(Casuarina
Campus)

Nakara

Wanguri

Leanyer

Casuarina

Nightcliff

Rapid
Creek

Alawa

Wagaman

Wulagi

Nightcliff Sporting
Complex (Indoor)

Darwin
Water
Gardens

Jingili

Moil

Anula

Coconut
Grove

Millner

Rapid
Creek Ck

Darwin
General
Cemetery
RD

Malak

Karama

Velodrome

McMILLANS

Marrara
Sporting
Complex

Darwin

North Lakes

Malak

Koa

Marrara

Darwin
International
Airport

East
Point

Military
Museum

East
Point

East Point
Recreation
Reserve

Lake
Alexander

Marina

Darwin

International

Airport

Terminal

Aviation
Museum

Dudley
Point

Ludmilling

BAGOT
ABORIGINAL
COMMUNITY

RAAF

RAAF
Base
Darwin

Fannie

Ross Smith
Memorial

Darwin
Turf Club

Ludmilla

The
Narrows

STUART

Leprechaun

10

HWY

Fannie
Bay

Fannie Bay
Gaol Museum

Winnellie

Showground

Shady
Glen

Bay

Bullocky Pt

Museum
Art Gallery

Parap

5

TIGER, BRENNAN

DR

COONAWARRA
ARMY BASE

Mindil
Beach

GEORGE
BROWN
DARWIN
BOTANIC
GARDENS

Woolner

Bayview

CHARLES DARWIN
NATIONAL PARK

0

Coonawarra

Casino

Chinese
Cemetery

Sadgroves

Charles
Lake

Hidden Valley
Motor Sports
Complex

Myilly Pt

Mandorah
Ferry Terminal

Marina

N.T. Uni
(Myilly Pt
Campus)

The
Gardens

Garden Park

Stuart
Park

Charles Darwin

Hidden
Valley

Emery Pt

Elliot Pt

LARRAKEYAH
ARMY BASE

Marina

Hidden
Lake

Larrakeyah

Navy
Patrol Boat
Base

Doctors
Gully
Leichhardt
Memorial

Aquascene

Fishermans Wharf

Deckchair Cinema

Frances Bay

Bleesers

Lameroo
Beach

Parliament
House

Stokes Hill

Indo Pacific Marine

DARWIN

Government
House

Australian Pearling Exhibition
Stokes Hill Wharf

BERRIMAH

Fort Hill Wharf

Port

East Arm
Port

North Shell I.

Old Man Rock

Darwin

South Shell I.

Middle Pt

East

Arm

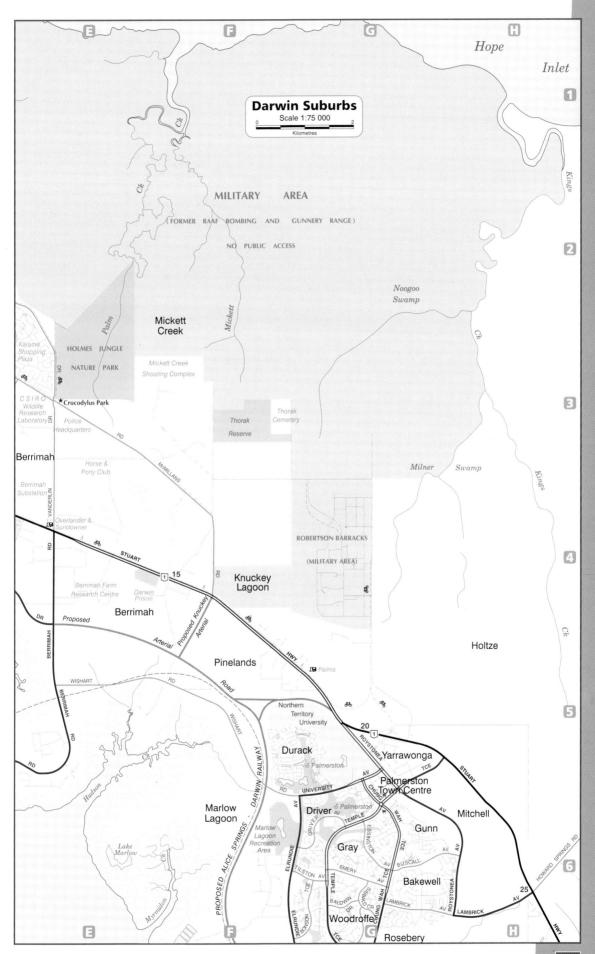

Darwin Suburbs
Scale 1:75 000
0   2
Kilometres

Hope

Inlet

E   F   G   H

1

MILITARY   AREA

(FORMER RAAF BOMBING AND GUNNERY RANGE)

NO PUBLIC ACCESS

2

Noogoo Swamp

Mickett Creek

HOLMES JUNGLE

NATURE PARK

Mickett Creek Shooting Complex

Karama Shopping Plaza

C S I R O Wildlife Research Laboratory

★Crocodylus Park

Police Headquarters

Thorak Reserve

Thorak Cemetery

3

Berrimah

Berrimah Substation

Horse & Pony Club

Milner   *Swamp*

McMILLANS

RD

ROBERTSON BARRACKS

(MILITARY AREA)

Overlander & Sundowner

STUART

1 15

Berrimah Farm Research Centre

Darwin Prison

Knuckey Lagoon

Holtze

4

Berrimah

Proposed

Arterial

Proposed Knuckey Arterial

HWY

WISHART

Pinelands

Road

Palms

Northern Territory University

20 1

5

BERRIMAH RD

WISHART RD

Durack

ROYSTONEA

Yarrawonga

TCE

STUART

Palmerston

Hudson

PROPOSED ALICE SPRINGS — DARWIN RAILWAY

RD

UNIVERSITY

Palmerston Town Centre

Mitchell

Marlow Lagoon

Marlow Lagoon Recreation Area

Driver

Palmerston

TEMPLE

CHUNG WAH

ESSINGTON

Gunn

AV

HOWARD SPRINGS RD

6

Lake Marlow

Ck

Gray

EMERY

BUSCALL

Bakewell

25

ELRUNDIE

TILSTON TCE

TEMPLE

BALDWIN

MORSON DR

BIBIS CR

CHUNG WAH

LAMBRICK

ROYSTONEA AV

LAMBRICK AV

HWY

Myrmidon

Woodroffe

Rosebery

E   F   G   H

203

Alice Springs

Best time to visit: Year-round, but most comfortable autumn to spring (Apr–Oct); winter nights can drop below freezing

Average daily temperatures: Jan 21–35°C, Apr 11–27°C, Jul 4–20°C, Oct 14–30°C

Getting there: By road from Adelaide via Stuart Hwy (1554 km), and from Darwin via Stuart Hwy (1934km); by rail on the Ghan from Adelaide (you can also put your car on the train); by air from mainland capitals

Festivals and events:

Apr: Heritage Week

Apr–May: Alice Springs Cup Carnival

May: Bangtail Muster (parade and sports events)

Jun: Finke Desert Race (460km-return desert race for motorcycles and other vehicles)

Jul: Alice Springs Show; Camel Cup Carnival (camel races)

Aug: Old Timers' Annual Fete; Alice Springs Rodeo; Australian Safari Off-Road Challenge (Alice–Darwin)

Sep: Henley-on-Todd Regatta (bottomless 'boats' raced on dry riverbed)

Nov: Corkwood Festival (arts, craft, food and entertainment)

Activities: Learning from local indigenous people about Aboriginal culture, browsing galleries and craft shops, bushwalking, horseriding, camel riding, hot-air ballooning

Highlights: Numerous galleries selling Aboriginal paintings, arts and crafts; didgeridoo lessons at the Aboriginal Art and Culture Centre, tour fee applies, Ph: (08) 8952 3408; Alice Springs Desert Park, an introduction to the region's habitats, animals and plants, entry fee, Ph: (08) 8951 8788; Alice Springs Telegraph Station Historical Reserve,

Tip: The Alice Wanderer bus does a loop around several of the major sights in town; passengers can get on and off wherever they like; fee, Ph: 1800 669 111

Kids' stuff: Camel rides at Frontier Camel Farm, fee, Ph: (08) 8953 0444; Alice Springs Reptile Centre (feed and touch some of the large collection), entry fee, Ph: (08) 8952 8900; School of the Air (hear broadcast lessons on school days), entry fee, Ph: (08) 8951 6834

Further information: Central Australian Tourism Industry Association, Gregory Tce, Alice Springs, NT 0870, Ph: (08) 8952 5800 or 1800 645 199, www.centralaustraliantourism.com

Alice Springs Telegraph Station Historical Reserve

Nestled in the foothills of the time-worn and starkly beautiful MacDonnell Ranges, the legendary Outback town of Alice Springs is packed with Aboriginal culture and European pioneer history. It came into being in 1870 as a station on the Overland Telegraph Line. The original station buildings, situated beside the spring that gave the town its name, have been restored and are open for inspection. They now form part of **Alice Springs Telegraph Station Historical Reserve**; entry fee, Ph; (08) 8952 3993.

Other sites of interest include Alice Springs Cultural Precinct, which incorporates the **Araluen Centre for Arts and Entertainment** and the **Aviation Museum**, entry fee, Ph: (08) 8951 1122; the **Royal Flying Doctor Service Base**, which has audiovisual presentations and interactive displays, entry fee, Ph: (08) 8952 1129; **Olive Pink Botanic Garden**, featuring over 300 species of arid-zone plants, entry by donation, Ph: (08) 8952 2154; and **Anzac Hill**, in the north of the town, which provides stunning views over Alice Springs to the MacDonnells (especially at sunset). The region is also famed for its Aboriginal artworks.

For information on the MacDonnell Ranges and the Larapinta Trail, see p.214.

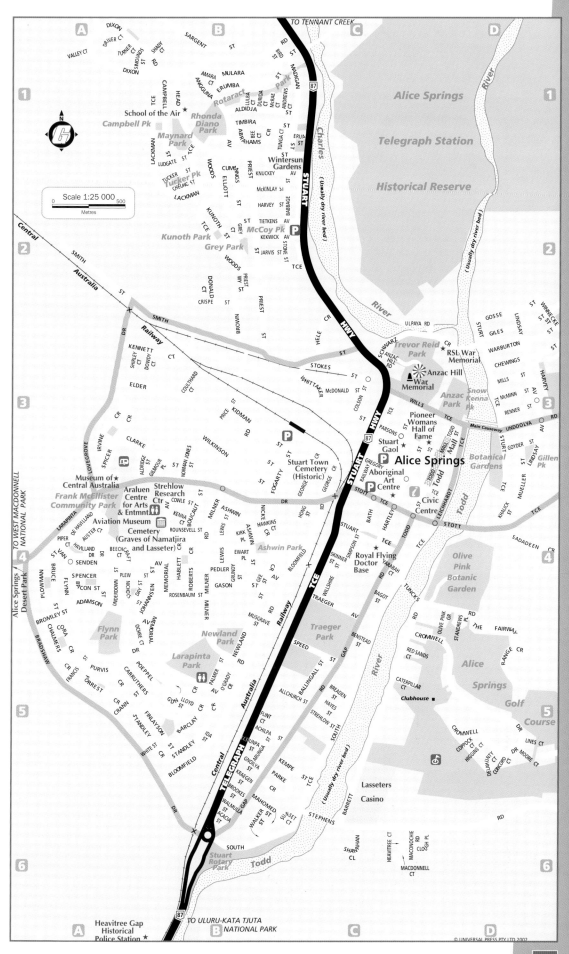

© UNIVERSAL PRESS PTY LTD 2002

Kakadu National Park

Best time to visit: Year-round, but most comfortable from late Jul–Sep when humidity is lowest; ranger-guided walks are available Jun–Sep. The Wet (or 'green') season, Nov–Apr, is best for waterfalls, lightning and waterway cruising but can be very hot. The end of the Wet (Mar–May) is the peak time for barramundi fishing. The build-up to the Wet (Oct–Dec) can be uncomfortably humid.

Average daily temperatures: Jan 24–33°C, Apr 23–34°C, Jul 19–31°C, Oct 24–37°C

Getting there: By road from Darwin via Arnhem Hwy (260km); by charter plane from Darwin to Jabiru

Festivals and events:

Mar: Kakadu Klash (barramundi fishing) Competition, South Alligator River

Apr: Kakadu Biathlon (fishing and golf)

Aug: Oenpelli Open Day (only day when visitors can enter Arnhem Land, without permit; festival of food, crafts and sports)

Sep: Jabiru Wind Festival; NT Freshwater Fly-Fishing Tournament, Corroborree Billabong

Activities: Birdwatching and wildlife observation, bushwalking, Aboriginal art sites and cultural tours, scenic cruises, boating, fishing, scenic flights, photography

Highlights: Yellow Water Wetland dawn and sunset tours and cruises, Yellow Water Cruises, Ph: (08) 8979 0145; scenic flights, Jabiru Tourist Centre, Ph: (08) 8979 2548; Mamukala wetlands; Ubirr art site (dry season only); Warradjan Aboriginal Cultural Centre displays, Ph: (08) 8979 0051; Guluyambi cultural cruise, Ph: (08) 8979 2411; Nourlangie Rock art site

Tip: Kakadu can be very hot, so always carry water and walk at cooler times of the day. Tropical-strength insect repellent, is essential (mosquitoes here carry the Ross River virus). A long-sleeved shirt and sunhat will protect you from sunburn.

Kids' stuff: Boardwalk at Yellow Water; displays and videos, Bowali Visitor Centre; Warradjan Aboriginal Cultural Centre; safe swimming at shaded pools in most hotels and lodges, and at public swimming pool in Jabiru

Further information: Jabiru Tourist Centre, Shop 6, Tasman Plaza, Jabiru, NT 0886, Ph: (08) 8979 2548; Bowali Visitor Centre, Kakadu Hwy, Kakadu, NT 0886; Ph: (08) 8938 1120; Tourism Top End, Beagle House, cnr Knuckey and Mitchell Sts, Darwin, NT 0800, Ph: (08) 8936 2499, www.tourismtopend.com.au; NT Holiday Centre, Ph: 13 30 68, www.ntholidays.com.au

World Heritage-listed Kakadu NP protects a magical ecological and cultural treasure trove including pristine ecosystems rich in wildlife, spectacular scenery and magnificent galleries of Aboriginal rock art. The park also offers top-class fishing in waters ranging from coastal estuaries to barramundi-rich rivers and billabongs (regulations apply, check with park management).

Accommodation includes up-market resorts, backpacker lodges and camping areas. Friendly **Jabiru** township, in the centre of Kakadu, provides services for park visitors, the local Aboriginal community and the adjacent Ranger uranium mine. Good sealed roads provide access to much of the park for conventional vehicles, though some may be closed during the Wet. The informative displays at the **Bowali Visitor Centre** are an excellent introduction to the region and its environments. Kakadu NP is managed jointly by its Aboriginal traditional owners and the Commonwealth government. An entry fee applies.

Great egret amid water lilies

Kakadu NP is vast—nearly 20 000km^2—and encompasses most habitats of the tropical north. Mangrove-lined coasts, floodplains, rivers, waterlily-covered billabongs and tropical woodlands dominate the north of the park; gorges and eroded rock stacks characterise the drier south. Kakadu's prolific wildlife includes an estimated 10 000 insect species, more than 1700 plant species, nearly 280 bird species (about one-third of the total number of bird species found in Australia), more than 100 reptile species (including crocodiles) about 60 mammal species, 25 frog species and 55 fish species.

Saltwater crocodile prowling near the shoreline at Yellow Water Billabong

Tranquil **Yellow Water**, part of the South Alligator River floodplain, is known for its teeming birdlife in the Dry. An early morning cruise here, an unforgettable experience at any time of year, is particularly spectacular in the dry season, when waters have receded from the floodplain and waterbirds—including brolgas, egrets, jabirus and whistling ducks—crowd onto this permanent waterway; you're also likely to spot saltwater crocodiles. From the early dry season onwards, Yellow Water's wildlife can also be observed from a boardwalk bordering the billabong.

The **Mamukala** wetlands, off the Arnhem Hwy, to the north, provide further birdwatching opportunities, and again are most dramatic late in the dry season, when thousands of magpie geese congregate here to feed.

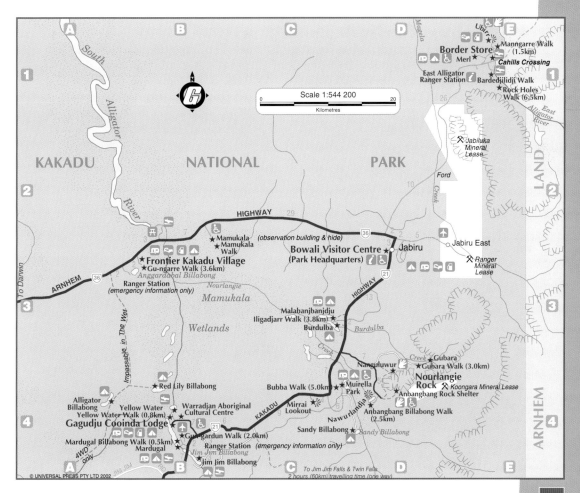

Nourlangie Rock, viewed from the Anbangbang Water Billabong

On the Rocks

One of the park's great drawcards, **Jim Jim Falls**, which plummets from 200m-high cliffs into a deep pool, is accessible only during the dry season via a 60km (2hr) each way, 4WD trip from Kakadu Hwy. Camping facilities allow visitors to stay overnight and enjoy nearby **Twin Falls** the next day. Reached via a drive along a bumpy 10km track, followed by a short inflatable-mattress ride through a gorge, Twin Falls drops a sheer 70m into a clear pool fringed by boulders and white sands. During the Wet, visitors can view these falls only on a scenic flight, but are then presented with the truly memorable spectacle of both cascades flowing at furious full volume.

Aboriginal people have lived in these lands continuously for at least 50 000 years. Scattered throughout Kakadu is evidence of their occupation, including shelters, stone tools, grindstones, camp-sites and, concealed in the stone country of the escarpment and gorges, one of the world's greatest concentrations of rock art, including at least 7000 sites. This represents one of the longest historical records of any group of people on Earth.

Standing 230m above the surrounding plain and easily accessible by road, **Nourlangie Rock** is the site of the ancient **Anbangbang Rock Shelter**, a wet-season

The Many Seasons of Kakadu

The Aboriginal people of Kakadu recognise 6 distinct seasons. *Gunumeleng* (Oct–Dec) is a pre-monsoon period of hot and increasingly humid weather. *Gudjeuk* (Jan–Mar) is a time of violent thunderstorms, heavy rain and flooding, with heat and humidity generating an explosion of plant and animal life. By Banggereng (Mar) waters are receding, plants are fruiting and animals caring for their young. *Yekke* (Apr–May) is a season of morning mists and drying winds, when wetlands and billabongs are carpeted with waterlilies. During *Wurrgeng* (Jun–Jul) humidity and temperatures are at their lowest (temperatures can drop to 17°C at night), and well-fed magpie geese, whistling ducks and other waterfowl crowd the shrinking waterways. *Gurrung* (Aug–Sep) is windless and hot, with thunderheads building gradually as the cycle of seasons begins all over again.

Depictions of warriors and long-necked turtle, Ubirr

retreat in regular use over at least 20 000 years, and several rock walls bearing layers of paintings laid down over thousands of years. Distinct styles associated with particular periods include ancient stick-like figures and more recent and complex X-ray paintings. Information boards on the 1.5km circuit walk (partly wheelchair accessible, about 1hr) tell the stories of the paintings, and during the dry season rangers give talks several times a day. A moderately steep walk to the rock's summit, best undertaken in the late afternoon, rewards with an impressive vista over the escarpment. Nearby, to the SW, **Anbangbang Billabong Walk** (2.5km, dry season only) skirts a lily-covered billabong and provides views back to Nourlangie Rock. North of the rock, **Gubara Walk** (3km, 2hr one way) winds past sandstone cliffs to pools shaded by monsoon forest.

Ubirr, close to the food-rich waters and floodplains of the **East Alligator River**, was also used as a campsite for thousands of years. Its rock-art galleries are reached by a 1km circuit walk (partly wheelchair accessible) and include stick figures and X-ray paintings, depictions of animals hunted for food (such as barra-

mundi, turtles, possums and wallabies) and a painting of a thylacine (extinct on the mainland for thousands of years). Rangers give talks on the rock art during the dry season. The 360° panorama of the surrounding country from the lookout on the top of Ubirr is especially impressive at sunset. Yet more about the area and its long human heritage can be learned during one of the Guluyambi cultural cruises on the East Alligator River, led by Aboriginal guides.

Aboriginal boy fishing in the East Alligator River

Katherine Gorge

Best time to visit: Year-round; the dry season (May–Sep) is more comfortable and better for canoeing and bushwalking; the Wet (Nov–Mar) is better for spectacular waterfalls and water-lily displays (but note that some roads may be closed)

Average daily temperatures: Jan 24–35°C, Apr 20–34°C, Jul 13–30°C, Oct 23–37°C

Getting there: By road from Darwin via Stuart Hwy to Katherine (325km); daily air services to Katherine from Alice Springs and Darwin

Festivals and events:

May: Katherine Country Music Muster; Pine Creek Gold Rush Festival

Jun: Katherine Show, Rodeo and Campdraft; Pine Creek Cup Races

Aug–Sep: Katherine Flying Fox Festival

Activities: Canoeing, kayaking, cruising, scenic flights, river fishing, swimming in waterholes, camping, bushwalking, cycling, horseriding, 4WD safaris, fossicking, stargazing, birdwatching and wildlife observation, Aboriginal cultural tours, browsing galleries for Aboriginal artworks

Highlights: Boat cruise or canoe trip on Katherine Gorge; scenic helicopter flight, North Australian Helicopters, Katherine, Ph: (08) 8972 3150; Edith Falls; Katherine Hot Springs; Aboriginal art

Tip: Fitness levels permitting, exploring Katherine Gorge by canoe (rather than on a tourist cruise) is an unforgettable experience. Single and double canoes are available for hire for half-day, full-day and overnight trips. Book in advance, as limited numbers of canoes are permitted in the gorge; contact the Visitor Information Centre.

Kids' stuff: Katherine School of the Air, Gorge Rd, Katherine, NT 0851, entry fee, Ph: (08) 8972 1833; swimming in rockholes, Katherine Swimming Pool and Katherine Hot Springs

Further information: Katherine Visitor Information Centre, cnr Stuart Hwy and Lindsay St, Katherine, NT 0850, Ph: (08) 8972 2650; Nitmiluk Visitor Information Centre, Gorge Rd, Nitmiluk NP, NT 0851, Ph: (08) 8972 1886; Parks and Wildlife Commission of the Northern Territory, PO Box 344, Katherine, NT 0851, Ph: (08) 8973 8888

Katherine Gorge lies in the semiarid tropics, where the red of the Outback meets the green of the tropical north. Now protected by Nitmiluk NP, its centrepiece is a series of 13 magnificent, red-walled, sandstone gorges carved over millions of years by the Katherine River.

During the dry season, the river ceases to flow in some sections, whereas in the Wet floodwaters surge through the gorge. Gorge cruises range from 2–9hr (at the end of the dry season, the longer cruises involve a certain amount of walking between gorges) and take in Aboriginal rock paintings, waterfalls and plant life; scenic flights are also available. There are no saltwater crocodiles here, but the smaller and less dangerous freshwater variety may be glimpsed basking on rocks. Accommodation in the region includes camping and caravan sites, homestays, backpacker lodges, budget cabins, motels and hotels.

The more than 100km of marked bushwalking trails in the national park range from easy riverside strolls to more challenging overnight excursions such as the 4hr (each way) Smitt Rock Walk, a diffi-

Katherine Gorge

Swimming hole at Edith Falls

cult trek that rewards with some of the most impressive vistas in the region.

Edith Falls, in the western section of the park and accessed off the Stuart Hwy, is a series of pretty cascades that runs all year into a forest-fringed swimming hole (the swimming is safe, although you may see small freshwater crocodiles here); there's also a free campsite with showers, toilets and BBQ facilities.

Outside the park, the limestone **Cutta Cutta Caves** are home to the rare orange horseshoe bat; entry fee, guided tours,

Ph: (08) 8972 1940. Attractions in the regional centre of **Katherine** include **Katherine Hot Springs**, a shaded, spring-fed thermal creek on the edge of the **Katherine River**, and **Historic Springvale Homestead**, built in 1878 by Alfred Giles and surrounded by the enormous Indian raintrees he planted for each of his children; free tours May–Oct, Ph: (08) 8972 1355. **Pine Creek**, to the north, was the site of a goldrush in the 1870s; some interesting old iron and timber buildings from that period remain.

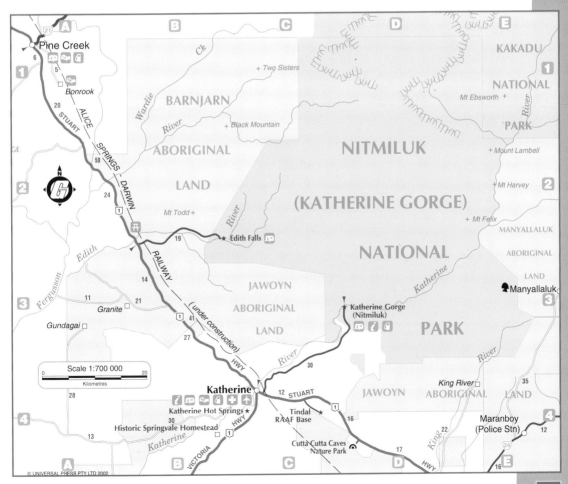

Litchfield National Park

Best time to visit: Generally accessible year-round, although during the Wet (Nov–Apr) heavy rains can cause road closures and make swimming holes dangerous; spring-fed waterfalls flow year-round.

Average daily temperatures: Jan 24–35°C, Apr 20–34°C, Jul 13–30°C, Oct 23–37°C

Getting there: By road from Darwin via Stuart Hwy (130km)

Festivals and events:

Apr: Adelaide River War Cemetery Anzac Day Service

Jun: Top End Tour, Darwin Cycling Club, Batchelor; NT Country Music Talent Quest, Adelaide River

Jul: Adelaide River Show, Rodeo, Campdraft and Gymkhana

Aug: Adelaide River Country Race Meeting

Oct: Parachute Display, Batchelor

Activities: Bushwalking, camping, swimming in waterholes, birdwatching and wildlife observation, fishing, Aboriginal cultural tours

Highlights: Swimming in spring-fed waterholes; waterfalls and plateau vistas; rainforest walks; Magnetic Termite Mounds boardwalk

Tip: Swim only in waterholes such as Wangi Falls, Florence Falls and Buley Rockhole; the Finniss and Reynolds Rivers are home to saltwater crocodiles and unsafe for swimming.

Kids' stuff: Batchelor Butterfly Farm (tropical garden, play area); entry fee, Ph: (08) 8976 0199

Further information: Tourism Top End, Beagle House, cnr Knuckey and Mitchell Sts, Darwin, NT 0800, Ph: (08) 8936 2499; Parks and Wildlife Commission, Darwin Region, Goyder Centre, 25 Chung Wah Tce, Palmerston, NT 0830, Ph: (08) 8999 5511

Only 2hr by road from Darwin, Litchfield NP's rainforests, termite mounds, weathered sandstone escarpments, waterfalls and cool, clear pools can be enjoyed on a daytrip from the capital, although you could easily spend several days here. Accommodation is available at campsites in the park (fees apply), hotels in **Batchelor** (a former WWII airfield and US training centre) and **Adelaide River** (a historic Overland Telegraph Line town and the site of Australia's largest war cemetery) and, to the NE, bungalows and apartments at Lake Bennett Wilderness Resort. Litchfield's main attractions— **Buley Rockhole**, a series of waterfalls and spa-like swimming holes; **Wangi Falls**, a popular swimming spot with a rainforest walking track; **Tolmer Falls**; the double cascade of **Florence Falls;** and the **Magnetic Termite Mounds** boardwalk— are linked by sealed roads and easily accessed by conventional vehicles. If you are travelling in a 4WD, you can also visit the intriguing sandstone pillars and block formations of the **Lost City**.

Florence Falls

Temperature controlled Highrise

Towering up to 2m or more above the plains, each of the thin, slab-like termite mounds scattered across the Northern Territory's wet grasslands houses a vast colony of soldiers and workers headed by a king and queen. Each 'castle' is a work of ingenious engineering, built by sightless worker termites using a mixture of saliva, excreta and mud, which dries rock hard and weatherproof. The intricate architecture of the interior includes arches, tunnels, air vents, nursery chambers and larders—the termites feed on dead grass harvested at night by the workers and chewed into fine pellets for storage. Mounds may be in use for a century or more.

The identical alignment of the mounds, with the thin edges pointing to the North and South magnetic poles and the broad sides facing east and west, minimises their exposure to the sun—at noon only the thin top catches its full force—and maintains an even temperature within. Magnetic alignment of mounds is found only in tropical Australia. In other parts of the tropics, termites avoid heat by retreating into the cooler earth, but here they must stay in the mound in summer to keep dry. Temperature control is therefore a vital local adaptation.

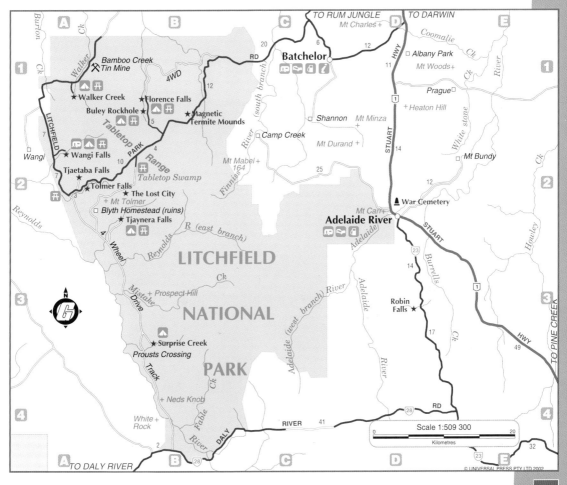

The Red Centre

Best time to visit: Late autumn to spring (Jun–Sep), when days are warm, clear and dry, although winter nights can drop below freezing; summer can be uncomfortably hot

Average daily temperatures: Jan 21–37°C, Apr 13–28°C, Jul 3–20°C, Oct 13–31°C

Getting there: By road from Alice Springs via Stuart Hwy and Lassetter Hwy to Yulara (445 km), and from Darwin to Yulara (1935km); by air from Alice Springs, Cairns, Perth and Sydney to Connellan Airport, 7km from Yulara

Festivals and events:

Sep: Great Pram Battle (pram relay race, market stalls, entertainment), Yulara

Nov: Starmaker Night, Yulara (celebration of astronomy and the night sky)

Activities: Aboriginal cultural tours, bushwalking, birdwatching, wildlife observation, swimming, camel-riding, 4WD safaris, stargazing, photography

Highlights: Sunrise and sunset over the Rock (tours available at these times, including one by camel); walks around Uluru; Aboriginal-led Anangu Uluru Tours (including sunrise, walking, bush-food and cultural tours), fee, Ph: (08) 8956 2123; Sounds of Silence desert dinner under the stars, including lecture on night sky from astronomer, fee, Ph: (08) 8947 3988; Valley of the Winds and Olga Gorge walking trails, Kata Tjuta

Tip: Make your first stop the excellent Uluru–Kata Tjuta Cultural Centre, where you can learn about the region's cultural heritage from the Anangu, its traditional owners. The desert sun, even in winter, is very strong, so wear a broad-brimmed hat and always carry water.

Kids' stuff: Displays and videos at the Uluru–Kata Tjuta Cultural Centre; learning about Aboriginal culture, bush foods, spear-throwing on Anangu tours; playgrounds and childrens' facilities at Yulara resorts

Further information: Central Australian Tourism Visitor Information Centre, Gregory Terrace, Alice Springs, NT 0870, Ph: (08) 8952 5800, www. centralaustraliantourism.com; Uluru–Kata Tjuta Cultural Centre, Uluru, NT 0872, Ph: (08) 8956 3138; Uluru–Kata Tjuta Visitors Centre, Yulara Dr, Yulara, NT 0872, Ph: (08) 8957 7377

The extraordinary rockscapes of **Uluru** (Ayers Rock), Australia's most famous landmark, and nearby **Kata Tjuta** (the Olgas), and the rich Aboriginal heritage associated with both, make the Red Centre one of the country's top tourist destinations. Lesser-known but equally impressive attractions in this region include **Kings Canyon** in **Watarrka NP**, which offers sweeping views from the canyon rim; **Palm Valley** in **Finke Gorge NP**, which is renowned for its red cabbage palms; and the dramatic gaps and gorges of **West MacDonnell NP**.

Permanent waterholes at all these sites provide refuge for desert creatures. Birdlife includes finches, budgerigars, honeyeaters, crested pigeons and wedge-tailed eagles; you may also see lizards, rock wallabies and dingoes, though most mammals here are nocturnal.

Accommodation at Ayers Rock Resort, **Yulara**, ranges from campsites and budget cabins to a 5-star hotel; the 3.5–4.5-star Kings Canyon Resort is the only accommodation in Watarrka NP.

Kata Tjuta (the Olgas) at sunset, Uluru-Kata Tjuta NP

Kings Canyon in Watarrka NP

Aboriginal Land

Visitors travelling in Aboriginal land (shaded brown on the map below) must carry a permit. If you are on an organised tour, this will have been arranged for you; if you are travelling on your own, you need to apply to the Central Land Council, 33 Stuart Hwy, PO Box 3321, Alice Springs, NT 0871, Ph: (08) 8951 6211. Processing can take up to 6 weeks. Permits for the Mereenie Loop Rd must be purchased in person. You can do this at the Central Australian Tourism Visitor Information Centre (see address opposite) or at Glen Helen Resort, Namatjira Dr, Ph: (08) 8956 7489; Hermannsburg Petrol Station, Ph: (08) 8956 7480; or Kings Canyon Resort, Watarrka NP, Ph: (08) 8956 7442.

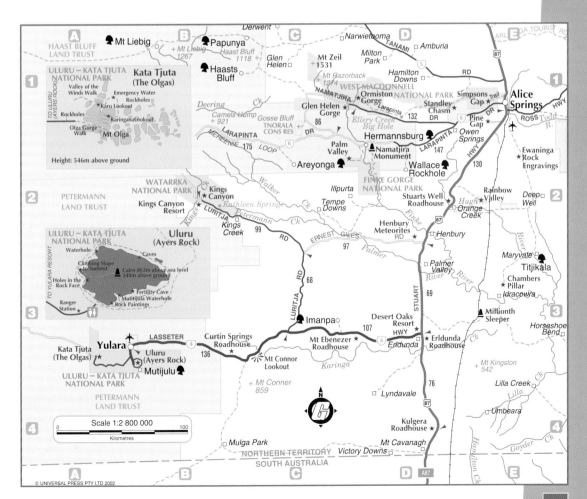

© UNIVERSAL PRESS PTY LTD 2002

Ormiston Gorge, West MacDonnell NP

Touring the Centre

Sealed roads allow conventional vehicles to reach the principal attractions. The unsealed **Mereenie Loop Rd**, which takes in many of the region's highlights, can be negotiated in a conventional vehicle but is best driven in a 4WD. Because it trav-erses Aboriginal land, travellers must obtain an entry permit before setting off.

The section of the MacDonnell Ranges to the west of Alice Springs is protected by **West MacDonnell NP**. The ancient mountains here are known for their dazzling hues, which change from pink and mauve to fiery ochre, depending on the time of day, and for their cool, hidden gorges and chasms, most of which can be accessed by vehicle from Namatjira Dr. **Standley Chasm** should be visited at midday, when the overhead sun sets the sheer walls blazing with colour. The deep waterholes at **Ormiston Gorge** and **Glen Helen Gorge** provide welcome swimming spots on a hot day.

You can also access the gorges from the 220km **Larapinta Trail**, a walking track with spectacular ridgetop views, which begins just north of the Old Telegraph Station in Alice Springs and winds west through the park. Each of the trail's 12 sections starts and ends at a vehicle-accessible trailhead; sections vary in length, allowing walkers a wide range of options ranging from a day walk to a 2-week camping adventure. Several sections are designed for those with limited bushwalking experience; Section 1, for example, which runs from the Telegraph Station to **Simpsons Gap** (23km, an overnight hike), follows a wide graded path also suitable for cycling. The cooler months are best for walking.

Standley Chasm, West MacDonnell NP

Uluṟu–Kata Tjuṯa NP

Uluṟu–Kata Tjuṯa NP is World Heritage listed for both its natural phenomena and its cultural significance. The immense monolith of **Uluṟu**, which rises abruptly from the red, sandy plains to a height of 348m, is an unforgettable sight from a distance; up close, the overwhelming aura of power and mystery makes it easy to understand why it plays such a significant role in the culture of its traditional owners, the Aṉangu.

The Base Walk, a 9.4km, 3–4hr circuit, takes in caves, waterholes and rock art, and offers ever-changing perspectives on Uluṟu's furrowed and pitted flanks. It can be undertaken as a self-guided tour or in the company of an Aṉangu guide, who will explain the cultural significance of the various features and share long-held knowledge of bush tucker and the medicinal properties of plants (book at the Cultural Centre). One of this region's great experiences is watching the changing colours of Uluṟu at dawn and dusk. There are observation areas at the best viewpoints; you can either join a tour or make your own way there.

Kata Tjuṯa, 50km to the west, towers 500m above the plains. It consists of a tight cluster of 36 red domes separated by a maze of steep-walled valleys. Like Uluṟu, it is of great spiritual significance to the Aṉangu people. The **Valley of the Winds Walk** (7.5km, 3hr) takes you around several domes before making the sharp climb to **Karingana Lookout**. The shorter **Olga Gorge Walk** leads into the shaded gorge formed by the massive walls of Kata Tjuṯa's 2 highest domes.

The park is managed jointly by the Aṉangu and the Commonwealth Government. An entry fee applies.

Olga Gorge walk, Uluṟu–Kata Tjuṯa NP

To Climb or Not to Climb?

The traditional owners of Uluṟu would prefer that visitors do not climb the Rock—for safety reasons and out of respect for Aṉangu culture. The designated route follows the traditional path taken by ancestral beings on their arrival at Uluṟu and is of great spiritual significance. If you choose to climb, be aware that the route is steep and physically demanding, and requires a high degree of fitness. Plaques bearing the names of people who died attempting to reach the top can be seen near the base. If you choose not to climb, you can take the equally rewarding Base Walk, then celebrate your decision by purchasing a certificate (available in visitor centres and shops) proclaiming 'I didn't climb Uluṟu'.

Sleepy Bay,
Freycinet NP

Tasmania

Tasmania crams a wealth of tempting tourist destinations into its compact landmass. Travelling distances are usually short and there is a good network of roads. Pristine beaches, rolling farmlands, historic villages, wild rivers, temperate rainforest and mountain wilderness are all less than a half-day's drive from either of the beautiful cities of Hobart and Launceston. Clean waters and rich soil produce a cornucopia of exceptional fare—salmon, tuna, crayfish and shellfish fresh from cold seas; wild trout, seasonal fruits, elegant cool-climate wines and acclaimed cheeses. In the central highlands and SW, spectacularly scenic, World Heritage-listed wilderness areas lure walkers from around the world. European settlement in Tasmania dates from 1804, and much of the island's colonial heritage, ranging from grand Georgian houses to chilling convict gaols, is well preserved and open to the public. Accommodation includes a network of charming B&Bs and boutique hotels (many in meticulously restored historic buildings), luxury wilderness lodges, secluded self-catering cottages and backpacker hostels.

Tourist Information

i **Tasmanian Travel & Information Centre**
cnr Davey and Elizabeth Sts
Hobart
Tas 7000
Ph: (03) 6230 8233
www.discovertasmania.com

Top Tourist Destinations

Ⓐ Hobart
Ⓑ Cradle Mountain–Lake St Clair National Park
Ⓒ The Freycinet Peninsula
Ⓓ Launceston and the Tamar Valley
Ⓔ The South-West
Ⓕ The Tasman Peninsula

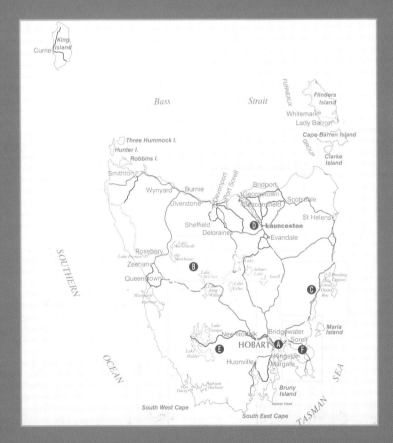

Hobart

Best time to visit: Summer for food and festival activities; spring to autumn for inland fishing (licence required)

Average daily temperatures: Jan 12–22°C, Apr 9–18°C, Jul 4–12°C, Oct 7–17°C

Getting there: By road from Launceston via Midland Hwy (200km); direct air services from Melbourne and Sydney

Festivals and events:

Jan: Taste of Tasmania; Hobart Summer Festival; Sandy Bay Regatta

Jan–Feb: Clarence by the Water Jazz Festival

Feb: Hobart Summer Festival; Royal Hobart Regatta; Australian Wooden Boat Festival (odd years)

Mar: Estia Greek Festival (food, music and craft)

Apr: Targa Tasmania motor rally

May: Chrysanthemum Show, Hobart Town Hall

Sep: Tulip Festival; Daffodil and Camellia Show; Blooming Tasmania (statewide, runs to May)

Oct: Royal Hobart Show

Nov: Point to Pinnacle Fun Run (Wrest Point to Mt Wellington summit); Spring in the Valley, Derwent Valley; Rose and Iris Show

Dec: Arrival of Sydney–Hobart Yacht Race fleet; arrival of Melbourne–Hobart Yacht Race fleet; Hobart Summer Festival

Activities: Strolling among historic buildings, browsing art and craft galleries, river cruising, sailing, swimming, watersports, diving, fishing, rockclimbing, abseiling, cycling, mountain biking, horseriding, golf

Highlights: Views from Mt Wellington; Salamanca Pl and market; Battery Pt; Derwent River cruise; dockside eateries with amazingly fresh seafood and stunning views; half-day scenic flights over south-western wilderness

Tip: Plan your visit to coincide with the Salamanca Markets, held each Sat, 9am–3pm; hundreds of stalls offer fresh local produce, uniquely Tasmanian clothing (you can pick up a warm hat and scarf here) and crafts.

Kid's stuff: Antarctic Adventure (activities and interactive exhibits), Salamanca Pl, entry fee, Ph: (03) 6220 8220; Cadbury Chocolate factory

Further information: Tasmanian Travel & Information Centre, cnr Davey and Elizabeth Sts, Hobart, Tas 7000, Ph: (03) 6230 8233, www.discovertasmania.com

The relaxed city of Hobart lies between the sparkling Derwent River and the majestic bulk of Mt Wellington. Its compact centre is a lively mix of past and present, where convict, colonial and seafaring heritage sits easily alongside art and craft galleries, innovative eateries and the bustle of a busy port. Founded in 1804, Hobart is Australia's second-oldest state capital and its smallest. Well-preserved bushland reaches close to its heart and white-sand beaches fringe its southern shores. Commercial fishing boats, pleasure-craft and larger vessels (including the Antarctic ice-breaker *Aurora Australis*, with its distinctive, bright orange hull) ply the river. Restaurants and food outlets are concentrated in North Hobart.

Places of Interest

Anglesea Barracks ①
Arthur Circus ②
Constitution Dock ③
Derwent River Cruise ④
Federation Concert Hall ⑤
Government House ⑥
Maritime Museum of Tasmania ⑦
Narryna Heritage Museum ⑧
Parliament House ⑨
Penitentiary Chapel and Criminal Courts ⑩
Princes Park ⑪
St Davids Park ⑫
Salamanca Place ⑬
Tasmanian Museum and Art Gallery ⑭
Town Hall ⑮
Victoria Dock ⑯

Victoria Dock, Hobart

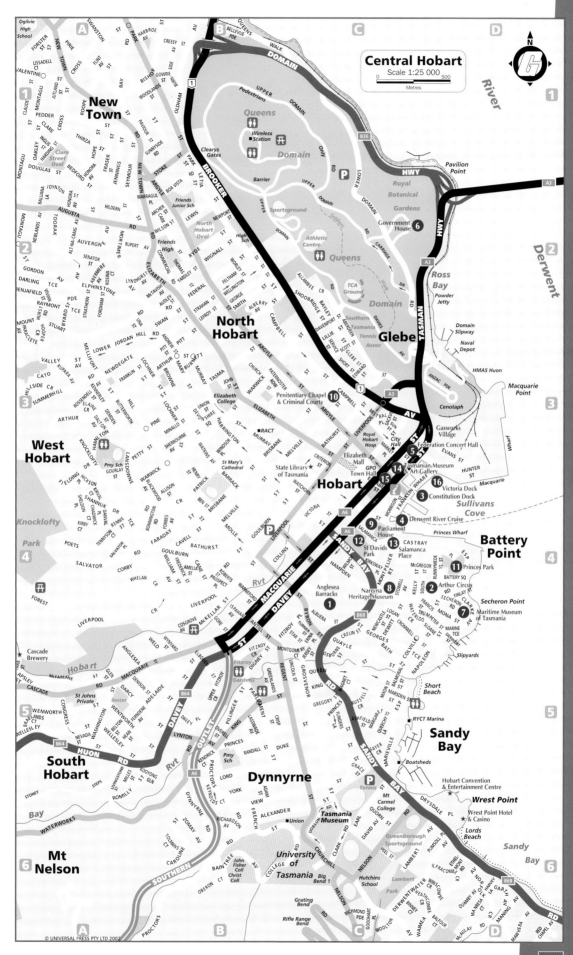

Central Hobart
Scale 1:25 000
0   500
Metres

New Town

West Hobart

North Hobart

Glebe

Hobart

Battery Point

South Hobart

Dynnyrne

Mt Nelson

Sandy Bay

© UNIVERSAL PRESS PTY LTD 2002

City Sights

Anglesea Barracks is the oldest military establishment still in use in Australia. The convict-built officer's quarters and mess date from 1814, the hospital with its colonial veranda from 1818, and the military goal (which now houses the museum) from the 1840s. The magnificent avenue of linden trees was planted in 1860. Open to the public.

Battery Point, which takes its name from the gun battery that once stood on this point, was formerly a mariners' village. Its charming streets include **Arthur Circus**, site of the city's oldest houses, 15 cottages that originally faced a village green. The National Trust conducts a weekly (Sat) walking tour of the area; fee, Ph: (03) 6223 7570.

Narryna, a classic 1830s Georgian sandstone-and-brick gentleman's residence with a walled and flagstoned courtyard and a coach-house, is now home to an impressive social history museum. Colonial treasures on display include toys, kitchen equipment, silverware, clothing and pieces of embroidery. You can also stroll through the old-world garden. Entry fee, Ph: (03) 6234 2791.

The **Penitentiary Chapel** and **Criminal Courts** complex dates from 1831 and was in use until 1983. Now restored, it is headquarters of the Southern Regional Office of the National Trust, which conducts daily tours of the cells, underground passages and execution yard. Entry fee, Ph: (03) 6231 0911.

Japanese Garden, Royal Tasmanian Botanical Gardens

Founded in 1878, the **Royal Tasmanian Botanical Gardens** feature a subantarctic plant house, an ornamental Japanese garden and an extensive collection of conifers; the lower slopes of the adjacent Queen's Domain protect the last of Hobart's original bushland.

Salamanca Place, with its stylishly restored sandstone terrace of Georgian warehouses, is best known for its splendid Sat art and craft market.

Wrest Point Casino, Australia's first hotel-casino, rises beside the river in the exclusive waterfront suburb of Sandy Bay; a regular ferry service links it to the city and Battery Point.

Victoria Dock dates from the whaling days of the 1830s and now shelters a fishing fleet. Along with adjoining **Constitution Dock**—finishing point for the gruelling Sydney–Hobart Yacht race—it is home to a range of seafood outlets, including floating 'fish punts'.

Arthur Circus, Battery Point

View over Hobart from Mt Wellington in winter

Around Hobart

Mt Wellington rises sharply on Hobart's south-western fringes and, at 1270m, is one of the highest peaks on the island. A drive to the summit is a must for an eagle's-eye view of the city, wide river and distant sea (to the east) and of expansive wilderness (to the west). The summit can sometimes be shrouded in cloud, and it snows frequently in winter. Hire a bicycle for an unforgettable ride down the mountain; Brake Out Cycling Tours, Ph: (03) 6239 1080.

The handsome **Cascade Brewery** complex, in the lee of the mountain beside Hobart Rivulet, was constructed in the 1820s. Tours of its workings include tastings but also involve a fair amount of walking and climbing. Fee, bookings essential, Ph: (03) 6221 8300.

Highly recommended is the scenic circuit drive up the western side of the Derwent, across either **Bowen Bridge** (40km round trip) or **Bridgewater Causeway** (80km round trip), and down the eastern side of the river to the **Tasman Bridge**, which leads back to the city.

Just north of the city centre is gracious **Runnymede**, built in the 1830s for outspoken local lawyer Robert Pitcairn and in later years home to the island's first Anglican archbishop. Set in grounds overlooking **New Town Bay**, the house has been restored and furnished by the National Trust in the style of an 1850s gentleman's residence; entry fee, Ph: (03) 6278 1269. In the same direction is the **Cadbury Chocolate Factory**, which offers guided tours of its manufacturing plant; entry fee (includes samples), bookings essential, Ph: (03) 6249 0333.

The earliest European settlement in Tasmania was the short-lived 1803–04 encampment across the waters at Risdon Cove; virtually untouched since its abandonment, the area is now protected by the **Risdon Cove Historic Site**; entry fee, Ph: (03) 6233 8399. **Bellerive Oval**, to the south, is the home of Tasmanian cricket and has views over the Derwent to Hobart and adjacent wooded slopes.

Taste of Tasmania

Advertised as the largest open-air restaurant in the Southern Hemisphere, the week-long Taste of Tasmania festival is held annually on Hobart's waterfront to coincide with the arrival of the Sydney–Hobart Yacht Race fleet. Top restaurants and producers of Tasmania's finest food and beverages tempt the crowds with samples of their fare; the range varies from year to year. Admission is free; you then find a table and buy the treats of your choice.

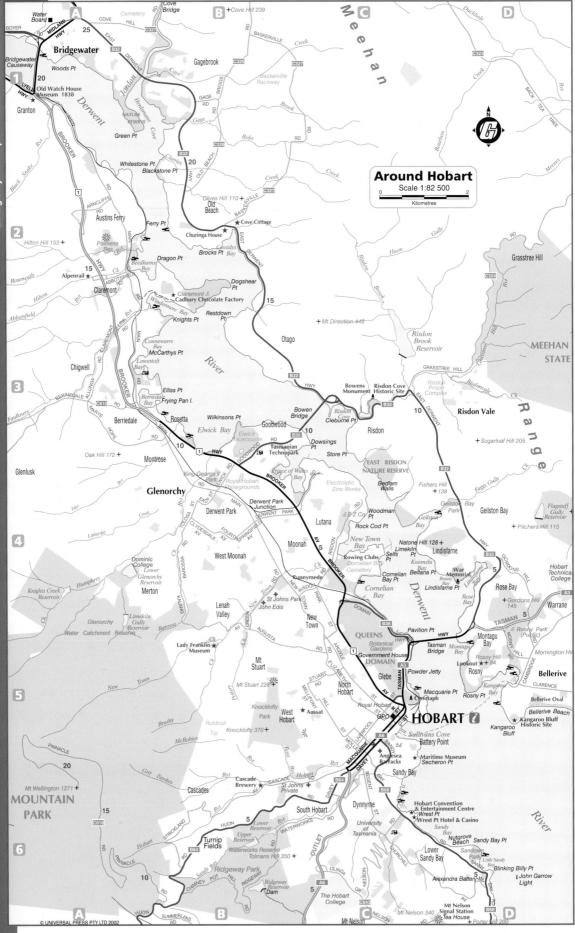

Around Hobart
Scale 1:82 500

0   2
Kilometres

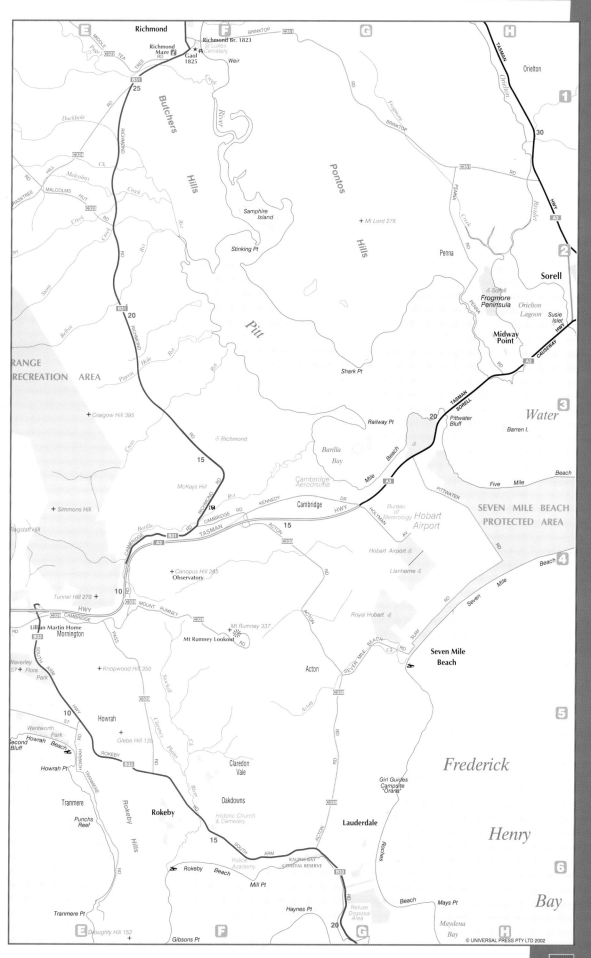

Cradle Mountain–Lake St Clair National Park

Best time to visit: Summer for bushwalking, wildflowers, clear days; Oct–Apr for trout-fishing season; winter for cross-country skiing

Average daily temperatures: Jan 6–17°C, Apr 4–11°C, Jul 0–5°C, Oct 2–10°C

Getting there: By road from Hobart via Lyell Hwy (A10) to Derwent Bridge (173km); from Launceston via Bass Hwy (A1) to Cradle Mountain Visitor Centre (145km); from Devonport to Cradle Mountain Visitor Centre (85km)

Festivals and events:

Feb: Cradle Mountain Run (ultra-marathon on the Overland Track)

Apr: Tasmanian Heritage Festival (statewide)

Jun: Tastings @ the Top, Cradle Mountain Lodge

Activities: Bushwalking, horseriding, trout-fishing (in season, licence required), windsurfing and canoeing, cross-country skiing

Highlights: Dove Lake circuit walk; wildlife sightings (wallabies, wombats, Tasmanian devils, possums); boat ride across Lake St Clair

Tip: There is a park entry fee, but if you plan to visit several parks buy a National Parks Pass, Ph: (03) 6233 6191. As in all high country, the weather can be unpredictable; be prepared with warm and waterproof clothing at all times, even for short walks in high summer.

Kids' stuff: At dusk, possums and Tasmanian devils come to be fed at Cradle Mountain Lodge.

Further information: Parks and Wildlife Service, Cradle Mountain Visitor Centre, PO Box 20, Sheffield, Tas 7306, Ph: (03) 6492 1110; Parks and Wildlife Service, 134 Macquarie St, Hobart, Tas 7000, Ph: (03) 6233 6191; Tasmanian Travel & Information Centre, cnr Davey and Elizabeth Sts, Hobart, Tas 7000; Ph: (03) 6230 8233; www.discovertasmania.com

One of the most popular natural attractions on the island, spectacular **Cradle Mountain–Lake St Clair NP** protects a dramatic glacier-carved landscape of soaring peaks, mirror-surfaced lakes, waterfalls, chilly rainforest and button-grass plains. In the northern section, there is vehicle access as far as **Dove Lake**. Several short walks in this area lead through sensational scenery, including the 10min, wheelchair-accessible Rainforest Walk, which runs from the visitor centre just inside the park entrance to Pencil Pines Falls, and the highly recommended, 2hr Dove Lake Loop Track, which follows the lake shore beneath Cradle Mountain.

Waldheim Chalet is a replica of the home and guest chalet that was built here in 1912 by naturalist and conservationist Gustav Weindorfer and destroyed by fire in 1976; it was rebuilt in King Billy pine using traditional bush carpentry techniques and now houses displays on the history of the park.

The legendary **Overland Track** is a 7-day, 80km trek across the highest region of Tasmania. Most walkers start at the northern end; tents must be carried as hiker's huts are often full. Much of the track runs along boardwalks and over bridges designed to minimise damage to the delicate environment.

Accommodation in the north includes Cradle Mountain Lodge, Ph: (03) 6492 1303, and Cradle Mountain Wilderness Village, Ph: (03) 6492 1018, just outside the park, and the self-catering Waldheim Cabins, Ph: (03) 6492 1110, within.

Vehicle access to the southern edge of the park is through the isolated settlement of **Derwent Bridge**; accommodation is available nearby. Gouged out by glaciers, **Lake St Clair** is the deepest lake in Australia. Day visitors can enjoy cruises across the lake and a choice of short walks. There are picnic facilities at both ends of the park.

Dove Lake and Cradle Mountain

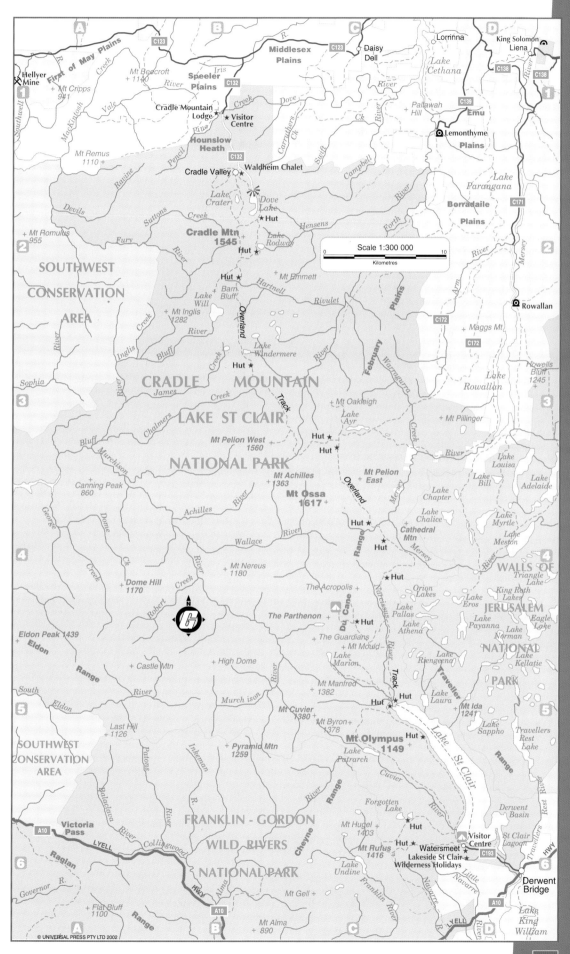

The Freycinet Peninsula

Best time to visit: Summer for swimming and berries; spring for heathland wildflowers; spring to autumn for all outdoor activities; winter can be very cold with chilling winds

Average daily temperatures: Jan 12–21°C, Apr 10–19°C, Jul 6–14°C, Oct 8–18°C

Getting there: By road from Hobart on Tasman Hwy (A3) to Swansea (140km); from Launceston via Tasman Hwy (A3) and C302 (140km)

Festivals and events:

Feb: Bicheno Festival Weekend

Mar: Coles Bay Classic (game-fishing)

Apr: Tasmanian Heritage Festival (statewide); Freycinet Vineyard Easter Jazz Concert

Sep: Swansea Show; Blooming Tasmania (statewide, runs to May)

Nov: Swansea Fun Fish

Activities: Swimming, sailing, sea-kayaking, snorkelling, diving, fishing, offshore cruising, bushwalking, climbing, abseiling, birdwatching

Highlights: Wineglass Bay lookout and beach; Freycinet Lodge; sea-kayaking; sea cruises; Swansea's heritage buildings; Kate's Berry Farm; Freycinet Marine Farm

Tip: The views from the Wineglass Bay lookout are absolutely stunning and amply reward the 30min winding climb from the car park. During the summer school holidays, the lookout can get very crowded, so visit at sunrise, or in less busy periods, if you want to savour the panorama in relative solitude.

Kids' stuff: During summer, park rangers offer a variety of activities for children, including walks, talks and slide shows.

Further information: Tasmanian Travel & Information Centre, cnr Davey and Elizabeth Sts, Hobart, Tas 7000, Ph: (03) 6230 8233, www.discovertasmania.com; Parks and Wildlife Service, Park Office, Freycinet National Park, Ph: (03) 6257 0107

Sheltered white-sand beaches, dramatic wilderness and a mild, maritime climate make the Freycinet Peninsula one of the island's most popular destinations. There's something here for everyone— gentle walks and safe swimming for families, adventure sports for travellers seeking a challenge, and luxurious short breaks for those in need of pampering. Also on offer is an abundance of high- quality local produce.

European settlement at historic **Swansea** dates from 1840, and many of the town's early buildings, including elegant Georgian houses and quaint cottages, are now used as holiday accom- modation. Seafood is a highlight here, with local restaurants serving fish, crayfish and oysters. Nearby boutique wineries produce classic cool-climate whites, and visitors to Kate's Berry Farm, Ph: (03) 6257 8428, can buy fresh fruit,

The Hazards on Freycinet Peninsula

jams and berry ice-cream. **Coles Bay**, the only township on the peninsula, is the site of the Freycinet Marine Farm, which grows oysters and mussels and offers tours with tastings; entry fee, bookings essential, Ph: (03) 6257 0140.

Accommodation on the Freycinet Peninsula ranges from camping grounds, backpacker dorms, B&Bs and self-contained cottages to the eco-friendly Freycinet Lodge, Ph: (03) 6257 0101, which lies within Freycinet NP.

Freycinet is a strip of unspoilt wilderness of extraordinary beauty, and fortunately more than 10 000ha of it is protected by **Freycinet NP**. Visitors can explore the park via an excellent network of bushwalking tracks. The most popular destination is **Wineglass Bay**. Forming a perfect crescent shape, it is rimmed with dazzling white sand, bounded by clear, turquoise waters and almost completely encircled by steep, wooded slopes. It can be reached via a short walk from Coles Bay or on a popular 11km scenic circuit walk which first climbs to a lookout atop the red granite ridge of the **Hazards** and

also takes in **Hazards Beach** and the base of **Mt Mayson**. Other local attractions include **Sleepy Bay**, where boulders are coloured bright orange by lichen, and the expansive sands of **Friendly Beaches**.

Freycinet NP is home to a wide range of marsupials, including wombats, ring-tail possums, spotted quolls, Tasmanian devils and Bennett's wallabies. Birdlife is equally prolific, with yellow-tailed black cockatoos, green rosellas, sea eagles and yellow-throated honeyeaters among the most conspicuous species.

Freycinet Sea Charters, Ph: (03) 6357 0355, offers full- and half-day cruises around the far reaches of the park, including rocky Schouten Island. Seals, dolphins, fairy penguins and pilot whales are frequently sighted . **Moulting Lagoon**, situated just outside the park and usually speckled with hundreds of black swans, is a waterfowl-breeding wetland of international importance.

Camping in the park is so popular over the Christmas and New Year period that sites are allocated by a ballot drawn on 1 October; a fee is charged.

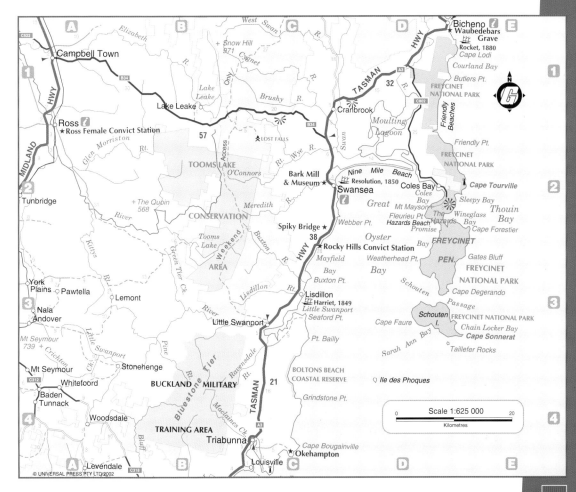

Launceston and the Tamar Valley

Elegant **Launceston**, the state's second-oldest city, is beautifully sited at the confluence of the North and South Esk rivers, which flow on as the Tamar to Bass Strait. Georgian and Victorian buildings and formal parks and gardens grace the compact city centre. A 10min walk away is granite-walled **Cataract Gorge** and the landscaped reserve of First Basin, with its gardens, picnic spots, swimming pools, chairlift and eateries. Historic National Trust properties on the city's edge include 1838 Franklin House, the stately 1838 mansion Clarendon (one of the most significant buildings in the state), and 1819 Entally House in Hadspen; all are open to the public.

Devonport is the entry and exit point for large numbers of visitors to Tasmania. Its Tiagarra Aboriginal Centre, situated on scenic **Mersey Bluff**, protects more than 250 rare Aboriginal rock engravings, 11 of which can be seen on a 1km circuit walk; fee, Ph: (03) 6424 8250.

The rich agricultural lands to the south and east of Devonport are dotted with historic settlements. These include the National Trust-classified towns of **Deloraine**, where beautifully maintained 1840s buildings are occupied by galleries and restaurants, and **Westbury**, where the 1841 White House, a restored Georgian corner shop and residence,

Lady Stelfox *river cruise, Launceston*

is open for inspection; fee, Ph: (03) 6393 1171. The Tamar Valley is Tasmania's premier wine-growing region; its rich soil and temperate weather are especially suited to cool-climate wines. The Wine Route, which runs from **Rowella** east to **Pipers Brook** and is marked by signposts bearing a distinctive yellow-and-blue logo, links 15 vineyards, many of them with restaurants.

Ben Lomond NP is the island's main ski resort, offering both downhill and cross-country skiing and, in summer, alpine walks, rockclimbing and abseiling.

The Heritage Highway

Running between Launceston and Hobart, and for more than a century known simply as the Main Road, the Midland Hwy is one of the oldest routes in the nation. Convict chain gangs began shaping it in 1811, reducing the 8-day overland trek to a 15hr coach journey (horses were changed every 15km at regular staging posts). Convict labour also built solid stone townships along the way, including Evandale, Campbell Town, Ross and Oatlands, some of which are now classified by the National Trust.

Ski school, Ben Lomond NP

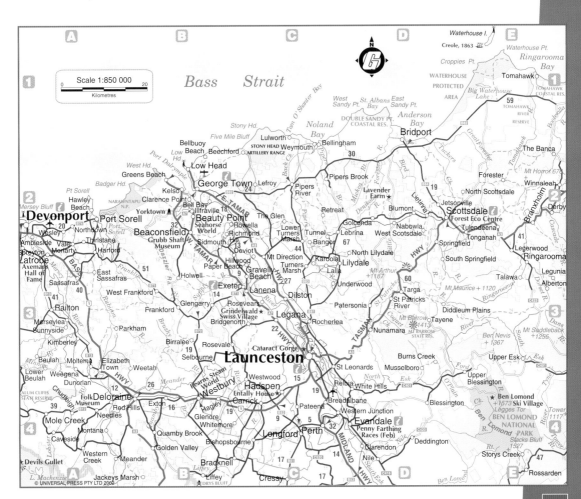

The South-West

Best time to visit: Summer for bushwalking; spring, summer and autumn for fly-fishing; winter for alpine skiing

Average daily temperatures: Jan 9–19°C, Apr 7–14°C, Jul 3–9°C, Oct 5–13°C

Getting there: By road from Hobart via Huon Hwy (A6) to Geeveston (60km) and Southport (100km), via Lyell Hwy (A10) and Gordon River Rd to Mt Field NP (80km) and Strathgordon (160km), and via Lyell Hwy to Franklin–Gordon Wild Rivers NP (180 km); by light plane to Southwest NP—TasAir, Ph: (03) 6248 5088, or Par Avion, Ph: (03) 6248 5390; by sea to Port Davey and Bathurst Harbour; or on foot—Tassielink, Ph: (03) 6344 4437 or 1300 300 520, takes walkers to and from Cockle Creek, Scotts Peak and Frenchmans Cap

Festivals and events:

Mar: Taste of the Huon, Huon Valley; Piners Festival, Strachan (celebration of timber industry)

Apr: Tasmanian Heritage Festival (statewide)

Sep: Blooming Tasmania (statewide, runs to May)

Oct: The Great Bronte Tie-In (trout expo)

Activities: Bushwalking, birdwatching, whitewater rafting, trout-fishing (licence required), sea-kayaking, alpine skiing

Highlights: Flight into Melaleuca; Russell Falls; drive to Strathgordon; Tahune Forest AirWalk canopy walkway (wheelchair accessible), Geeveston, fee, Ph: (03) 6297 0017; historic streets of New Norfolk and Bothwell; Snowy Range Trout Fishery, Ph: (03) 6266 0243

Tip: Be aware that you share the mountain roads with heavily laden logging trucks. In season, buy fresh-picked berries and Huon Valley apples from roadside stalls.

Kids' stuff: Walk the Creepy Crawly Nature Trail off the Scotts Peak Rd.

Further information: Parks and Wildlife Service, 134 Macquarie St, Hobart, Tas 7000, Ph: (03) 6233 6191; Tasmanian Travel & Information Centre, cnr Davey and Elizabeth Sts, Hobart, Tas 7000, Ph: (03) 6230 8233, www.discovertasmania.com

A drive of less than 2hr from Hobart to the north, NW or SW takes you to the edge of a vast, World Heritage-listed wilderness, a bushwalkers' paradise of mountains, moorland, tall forest, wild rivers, gorges and ravines.

Walking trails in **Mt Field NP** include the 10min, wheelchair-accessible circuit via the 7-stepped cascade of Russell Falls, and half- and full-day return walks through towering trees and past icy tarns. Downhill skiers can enjoy gentle runs served by 4 lifts.

Franklin–Gordon Wild Rivers NP offers an outstanding 4-day hike via stunning wilderness to the quartzite peak of **Frenchmans Cap**, and thrilling white-water rafting on the Franklin River.

Southwest NP has no facilities and no road access; the only settlement, at remote **Melaleuca**, consists of an airstrip, an occasionally staffed ranger's hut, a simple cabin and a bird observatory (where you may catch sight of the rare orange-bellied parrot). To reach Melaleuca, visitors must take a light-plane flight to the airstrip, arrive by sea, or walk. Some specialist tour operators combine scenic flights with multiday cruises. There are 2 principal walking routes. The often-muddy but spectacular **South Coast Track** is an inspirational 6- to 8-day, 85km trek from the fishing village of **Cockle Creek** (at the end of Australia's most southerly road). The 5-day, 75km **Port Davey Track** runs south from **Lake Pedder** through the **Arthur Range**. Walkers generally trek in via one of these tracks then fly out, or vice versa.

Strathgordon, once a settlement for dam workers, has the most convenient accommodation for visitors to Southwest NP; the road in has breathtaking views over lakes Pedder and Gordon, and meets Lake Pedder at **Teds Beach**.

Russell Falls, Mt Field NP

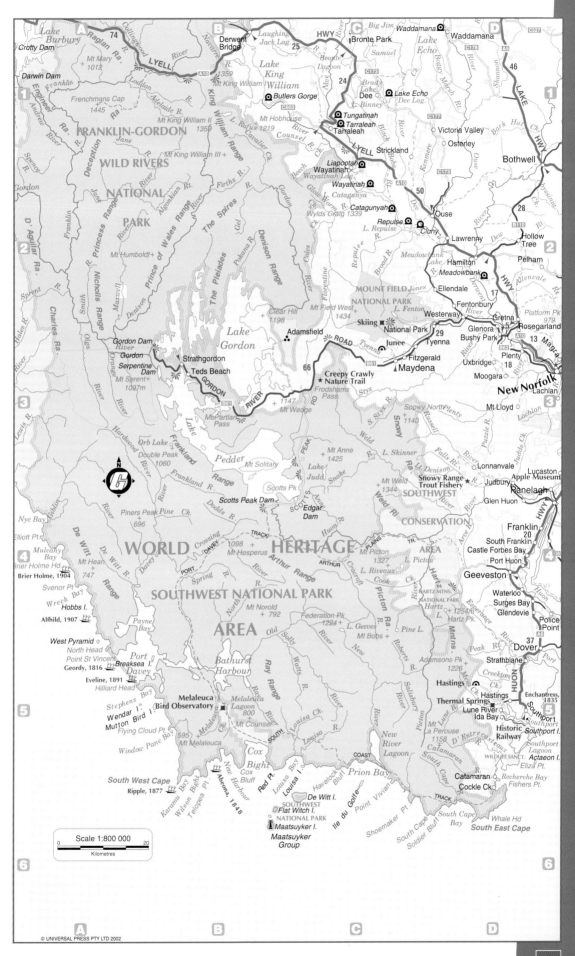

Scale 1:800 000
Kilometres

The Tasman Peninsula

Best time to visit: Spring, summer and winter; Port Arthur scenic flights and harbour cruise not available Jul–Aug

Average daily temperatures: Jan 12–22°C, Apr 9–18°C, Jul 4–12°C, Oct 7–17°C

Getting there: By road from Hobart via Tasman Hwy (A3) to Sorell, then Arthur Hwy (A9) to Port Arthur (95km)

Festivals and events:

Jan: Spring Bay Festival, Triabunna

Apr: Tasmanian Heritage Festival (statewide); Bluefin Tuna contest (game-fishing)

Sep: Blooming Tasmania (statewide, runs to May)

Dec: Great Aussie Yarn Contest, Sorell; Bushranger Festival, Sorell; Port Arthur Chopping Carnival

Activities: Inspecting colonial ruins, swimming, surfing, beach activities, browsing craft and antique shops, bushwalking, birdwatching, mountain biking, horseriding, rockclimbing and abseiling, sea-kayaking, diving, game-fishing, hang-gliding, scenic flights

Highlights: Tessellated Pavement wave platform; lookout over Pirates Bay; Port Arthur Historic Site; coastal walks; fresh local seafood

Tip: The entry pass to Port Arthur is valid for 2 days to allow visitors to join the after-dark ghost tour; to take advantage of this, arrange accommodation on the peninsula.

Kids' stuff: Tasmanian Devil Park, Tarana (visit mid-morning for feeding time and birds-of-prey flight display), entry fee, Ph: (03) 6250 3230; Bush Mill Steam Railway, fee, Ph: (03) 6250 2221

Further information: Visitor Centre, Port Arthur Historic Site, Port Arthur, Tas 7182, Ph: 1800 659 101, www.portarthur.org.au; Tasmanian Travel & Information Centre, cnr Davey and Elizabeth Sts, Hobart, Tas 7000, Ph: (03) 6230 8233, www.discovertasmania.com

Located less than 2hr from Hobart, the Tasman Peninsula is a place of rugged beauty and sombre human history. Towering sea cliffs and dramatic rock formations, including blowholes, caves, arches and tessellated pavement, edge much of the coastline, which is also home to sizable breeding colonies of Australian fur seals. In 1830, the peninsula was selected as an ideal place to isolate convicts who had re-offended; between 1833 and 1877 thousands were sent here and forced into hard labour, cutting timber and splitting stone.

The **Port Arthur** prison settlement was at that time regarded as a hell on earth; today, more than 30 stabilised ruins and restored buildings are open to the public, including the grim penitentiary, elegant church and 2 period-furnished houses; entry fee (includes guided tour and harbour cruise), Ph: 1800 659 101.

Seaplanes operate scenic flights over the peninsula from Port Arthur. Keen walkers can hike the dramatic Tasman Trail (6–8hr one way) along the cliff-line from **Fortescue Bay** north to **Waterfall Bay**, savouring the sweeping views.

In convict times, the narrow isthmus of **Eaglehawk Neck** was guarded by a line of chained, snarling dogs to prevent escape from the peninsula; it's now a holiday resort, with sandy beaches, a fishing fleet and game-fishing charter vessels.

To the north, **Maria Island**, reached via a 25min ferry crossing from **Louisville** to **Darlington**, was the site of another convict station established in 1825. Now a national park, it protects a number of endangered species that were introduced to boost their numbers; short walking tracks lead to scenic spots including the Fossil Cliffs and Painted Cliffs. The island has no vehicles and no shops.

Port Arthur Historic Site

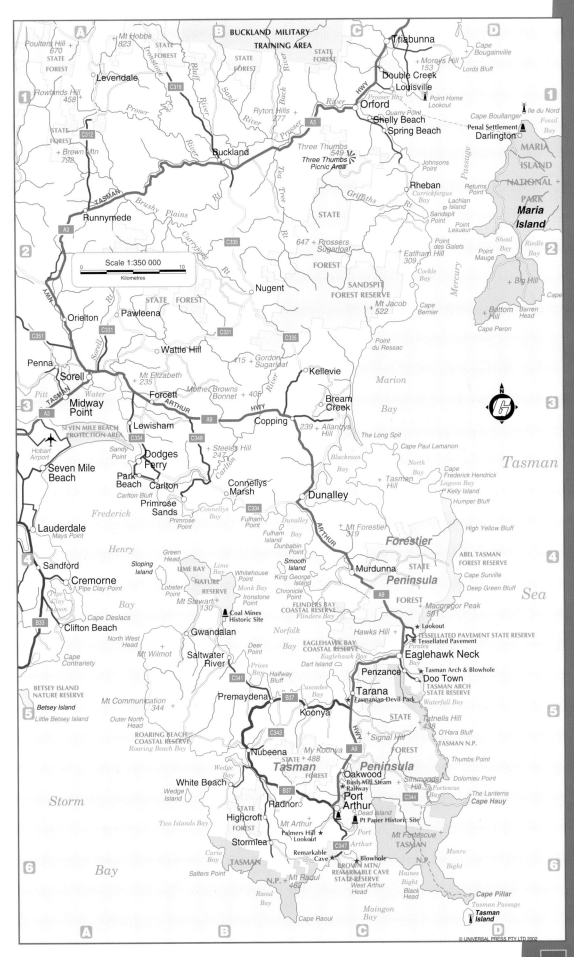

Index   Bold indicates map references